A WORLD ATLAS OF MILITARY HISTORY

1861-1945

A WORLD ATLAS

by ARTHUR BANKS

OF MILITARY HISTORY

1861-1945

SEELEY SERVICE & CO

London 1978

First published in Great Britain in 1978 by
Seeley, Service & Co Ltd,
196 Shaftesbury Avenue, London WC2H 8JL

Copyright © 1978 by Arthur Banks

ISBN 0 85422 140 9

Printed in Great Britain by
Hollen Street Press Ltd at Slough, Berkshire

CONTENTS

V The Inter-War Years

VI The Second World War

ACKNOWLEDGEMENTS

During the preparation of this atlas, I was aided by a number of friends and military organizations. I wish to express my gratitude and thanks to Mrs J Campbell, Mr R Holmes, Mr E Jennings, Mr A Palmer and Mr M Willis. In particular, the Imperial War Museum and the Royal United Services Institute for Defence Studies were generous in the facilities they placed at my disposal. I am also indebted to Messrs Heinemann Educational Ltd for allowing me to reproduce twelve maps which I originally drew for my *Military Atlas of the First World War*.

Arthur Banks

I
PHYSICAL FEATURES

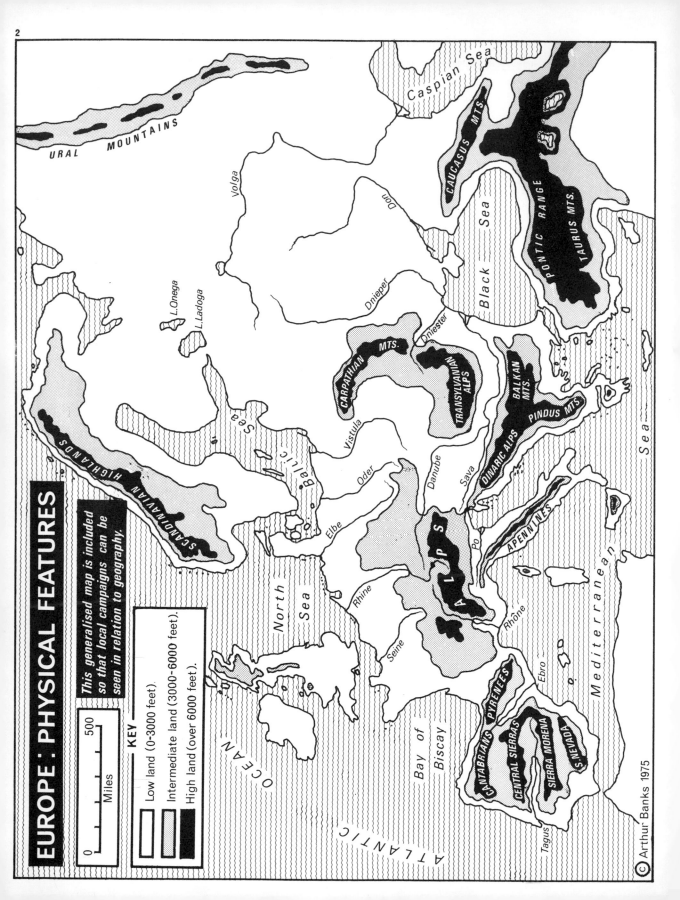

EUROPE: PHYSICAL FEATURES

This generalised map is included so that local campaigns can be seen in relation to geography.

KEY

☐ Low land (0-3000 feet).

▨ Intermediate land (3000-6000 feet).

■ High land (over 6000 feet).

500

Miles

0

URAL MOUNTAINS

Caspian Sea

Volga

Don

CAUCASUS MTS.

PONTIC RANGE

TAURUS MTS.

Black Sea

Dnieper

Dniester

L.Onega

L.Ladoga

CARPATHIAN MTS.

TRANSYLVANIAN ALPS

BALKAN MTS.

PINDUS MTS.

DINARIC ALPS

Vistula

Oder

Danube

Sava

SCANDINAVIAN HIGHLANDS

Baltic Sea

Elbe

ALPS

APENNINES

Po

Mediterranean Sea

North Sea

Rhine

Seine

Rhône

Bay of Biscay

PYRENEES

CANTABRIANS

CENTRAL SIERRAS

SIERRA MORENA

S.NEVADA

Ebro

Tagus

ATLANTIC OCEAN

© Arthur Banks 1975

ASIA: PHYSICAL FEATURES

1000
0
Miles

PACIFIC OCEAN

ARCTIC OCEAN

Indigirka
Lena
Amur
Liao Ho
Hwang Ho
Yangtze
Sikiang
SOUTH CHINA SEA

L. Baikal
Yenisei
L. Balkash
Ob
Irtysh
Tobol
URAL MTS.
ARAL SEA
CASPIAN SEA
Volga
Ural
Don
Dnieper
Dniester
BLACK SEA
MEDITERRANEAN SEA

KUNLUN MTS.
HIMALAYAS
MT. EVEREST
Hindu Kush
Ganges
Indus
Narbada
Godavari
Krishna
BAY OF BENGAL
Irrawaddy
Salween
Mekong
Red

Tigris
Euphrates
ARABIAN SEA
RED SEA

INDIAN OCEAN

EUROPE

AFRICA

KEY
Low land (0-3000 feet).
Intermediate land (3000-6000 feet).
High land (over 6000 feet).

This generalised map is included in order that local campaigns can be seen in relation to geography.

© Arthur Banks 1975

4

NORTH AMERICA: PHYSICAL FEATURES

U.S.S.R.

Beaufort

Sea

GREENLAND

Davis Strait

Yukon

Mackenzie

▷ Mt. McKinley

Gt. Bear Lake

Back

Gt. Slave Lake

ROCKY

Athabaska Lake

HUDSON

BAY

Saskatchewan

L. Winnipeg

PACIFIC

Columbia

Great Plains

Prairies

St. Lawrence

Snake

MOUNTAINS

Gt. Salt Lake

OCEAN

GREAT LAKES

Missouri

Ohio

Appalachian Mountains

ATLANTIC

OCEAN

Arkansas

Tennessee

Rio Grande

Red

Mississippi

Gulf of Mexico

Mt. Popocatepetl ▲

CUBA

JAMAICA

Caribbean Sea

KEY

Low land (0-3000 feet).

Intermediate land (3000-6000 feet).

High land (over 6000 feet).

This generalised map is included so that local campaigns can be seen in relation to the surrounding geography.

SOUTH AMERICA

PACIFIC

OCEAN

0   500
Miles

© Arthur Banks 1975

SOUTH AMERICA : PHYSICAL FEATURES

Caribbean

Sea

ATLANTIC

OCEAN

LLANOS

Orinoco

GUIANA

HIGHLANDS

Branco

Negro

S

E

Japura

Putumayo

Amazon

▲ CHIMBORAZO

L

Jurva

Purus

Madeira

Tapajoz

Araguaia

Tocantins

V

A

S

C

A

T

I

N

G

A

S

Sao
Francisco

A

N

PACIFIC

OCEAN

▲ SAJAMA

D

CHACO

E

Pilcomayo

Paraguay

Parana

▲ OJOS DEL
SALADO

S

Parana

Uruguay

Parana

G
R
A
N

F
A
M
P
A
S

▲ ACONCAGUA

ATLANTIC

OCEAN

**This generalised map is
included so that individual
campaigns can be seen in broad
relation to local geography.**

0   500

Miles

KEY

Low land (0-3000 feet).

Intermediate land (3000-6000 feet).

High land (over 6000 feet).

▲ Important heights.

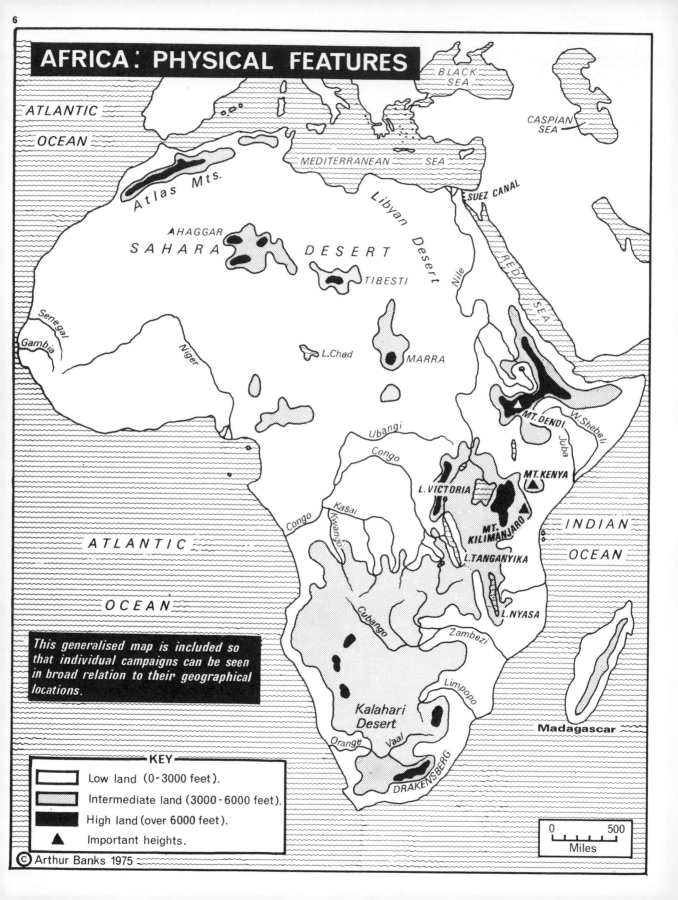

AFRICA: PHYSICAL FEATURES

ATLANTIC

OCEAN

BLACK SEA

CASPIAN SEA

MEDITERRANEAN SEA

SUEZ CANAL

Atlas Mts.

Libyan Desert

Nile

RED SEA

AHAGGAR

SAHARA   DESERT

TIBESTI

Senegal

Gambia

Niger

L.Chad

MARRA

W.Shebeli

MT. DENDI

Juba

Ubangi

Congo

MT. KENYA

L.VICTORIA

INDIAN

Congo

Kasai

Kwango

MT. KILIMANJARO

L.TANGANYIKA

OCEAN

ATLANTIC

OCEAN

L. NYASA

Cubango

Zambezi

Limpopo

This generalised map is included so that individual campaigns can be seen in broad relation to their geographical locations.

Kalahari Desert

Madagascar

Orange

Vaal

DRAKENSBERG

KEY

☐ Low land (0-3000 feet).

▨ Intermediate land (3000-6000 feet).

■ High land (over 6000 feet).

▲ Important heights.

© Arthur Banks 1975

0   500
Miles

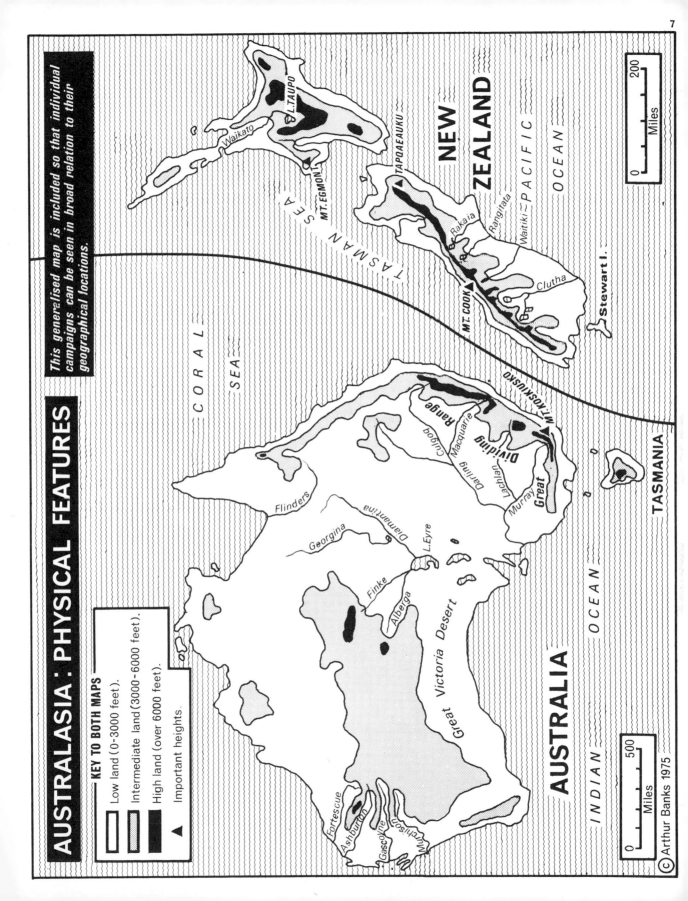

AUSTRALASIA: PHYSICAL FEATURES

This generalised map is included so that individual campaigns can be seen in broad relation to their geographical locations.

KEY TO BOTH MAPS

- Low land (0–3000 feet).
- Intermediate land (3000–6000 feet).
- High land (over 6000 feet).
- ▲ Important heights.

© Arthur Banks 1975

500 Miles 0

200 Miles 0

AUSTRALIA

INDIAN OCEAN

CORAL SEA

Great Victoria Desert

Fortescue
Ashburton
Gascoyne
Murchison

Finke
Alberga
Georgina
Diamantina
L.Eyre
Flinders

Cooper
Darling
Macquarie
Lachlan
Murray

Great Dividing Range

MT.KOSKIUSKO

TASMANIA

TASMAN SEA

Waikato
L.TAUPO
MT. EGMONT

NEW ZEALAND

PACIFIC OCEAN

TAPQAEAUKU
Rakaia
Rangitata
Waitiki
MT. COOK ▲
Clutha
Stewart I.

II
THE AMERICAN CIVIL WAR

EVE OF THE AMERICAN CIVIL WAR 1861

The political issues concerned not merely slavery, but also the doctrine of States' rights. The Northern States were mainly manufacturing and mining, whereas the Southern States were almost wholly agricultural (especially in the growth of cotton).

Mason & Dixon Line

12 April 1861, bombardment of fort marks opening of Civil War

THE TWO PRESIDENTS
1. *JEFFERSON DAVIS elected President of the Confederate States on 18 February 1861.*
2. *ABRAHAM LINCOLN inaugurated as President of the United States on 4 March 1861.*

CANADA

ATLANTIC OCEAN

MAINE
MASS.
N.H.
VT.
NEW YORK
R.I.
CONN.
PENNSYL-VANIA
Washington D.C.
DELAWARE
MARYLAND
Richmond
VIRGINIA
N. CAROLINA
S. CAROLINA
Ft. Sumter
GEORGIA
FLORIDA
MICHIGAN
OHIO
INDIANA
KENTUCKY
TENNESSEE
ALABAMA
WISCONSIN
ILLINOIS
MISSISSIPPI
IOWA
MISSOURI
ARKANSAS
LOUISIANA
MINNESOTA

Gulf of Mexico

DAKOTA TERRITORY
NEBRASKA TERRITORY
KANSAS
Unorganised Territory
COLORADO TERRITORY
NEW MEXICO TERRITORY
TEXAS
WASHINGTON TERRITORY
UTAH TERRITORY
NEVADA TERRITORY
OREGON
CALIFORNIA

MEXICO

PACIFIC OCEAN

KEY

	Free States.
	Free Territories.
	Slave States.
	Slave Territories.
▬	Boundary between the United and Confederate States.

300
Miles
0

© Arthur Banks 1975

THE OPPOSING FORCES IN THE AMERICAN CIVIL WAR 1861-1865

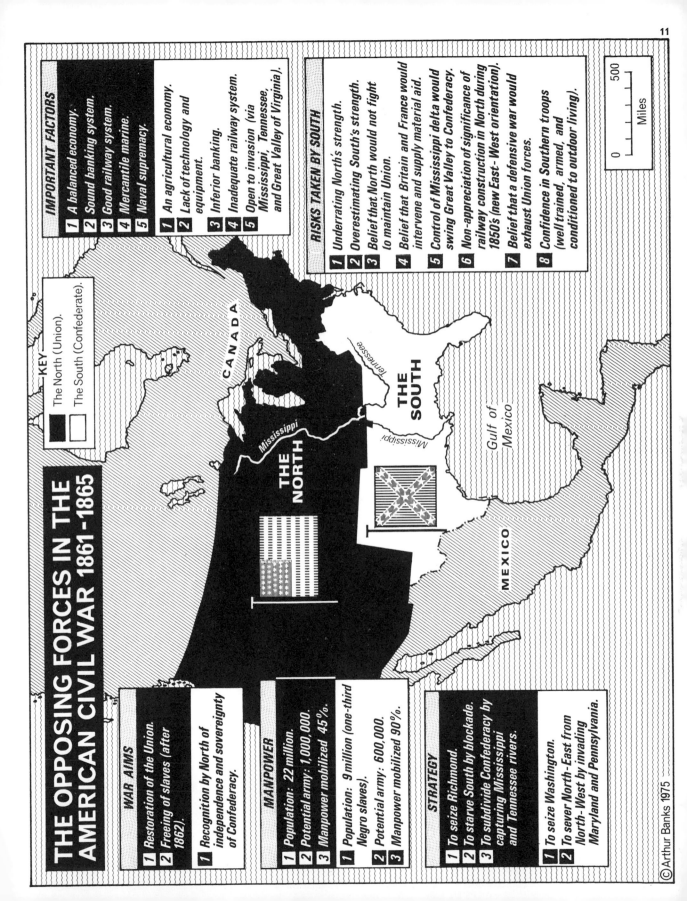

KEY

■ The North (Union).

□ The South (Confederate).

IMPORTANT FACTORS

1 A balanced economy.
2 Sound banking system.
3 Good railway system.
4 Mercantile marine.
5 Naval supremacy.

1 An agricultural economy.
2 Lack of technology and equipment.
3 Inferior banking.
4 Inadequate railway system.
5 Open to invasion (via Mississippi, Tennessee, and Great Valley of Virginia).

RISKS TAKEN BY SOUTH

1 Underrating North's strength.
2 Overestimating South's strength.
3 Belief that North would not fight to maintain Union.
4 Belief that Britain and France would intervene and supply material aid.
5 Control of Mississippi delta would swing Great Valley to Confederacy.
6 Non-appreciation of significance of railway construction in North during 1850's (new East-West orientation).
7 Belief that a defensive war would exhaust Union forces.
8 Confidence in Southern troops (well trained, armed, and conditioned to outdoor living).

WAR AIMS

1 Restoration of the Union.
2 Freeing of slaves (after 1862).

1 Recognition by North of independence and sovereignty of Confederacy.

MANPOWER

1 Population: 22 million.
2 Potential army: 1,000,000.
3 Manpower mobilized 45%.

1 Population: 9 million (one-third Negro slaves).
2 Potential army: 600,000.
3 Manpower mobilized 90%.

STRATEGY

1 To seize Richmond.
2 To starve South by blockade.
3 To subdivide Confederacy by capturing Mississippi and Tennessee rivers.

1 To seize Washington.
2 To sever North-East from North-West by invading Maryland and Pennsylvania.

CANADA

THE NORTH

Mississippi

THE SOUTH

Tennessee

Mississippi

Gulf of Mexico

MEXICO

0   500
Miles

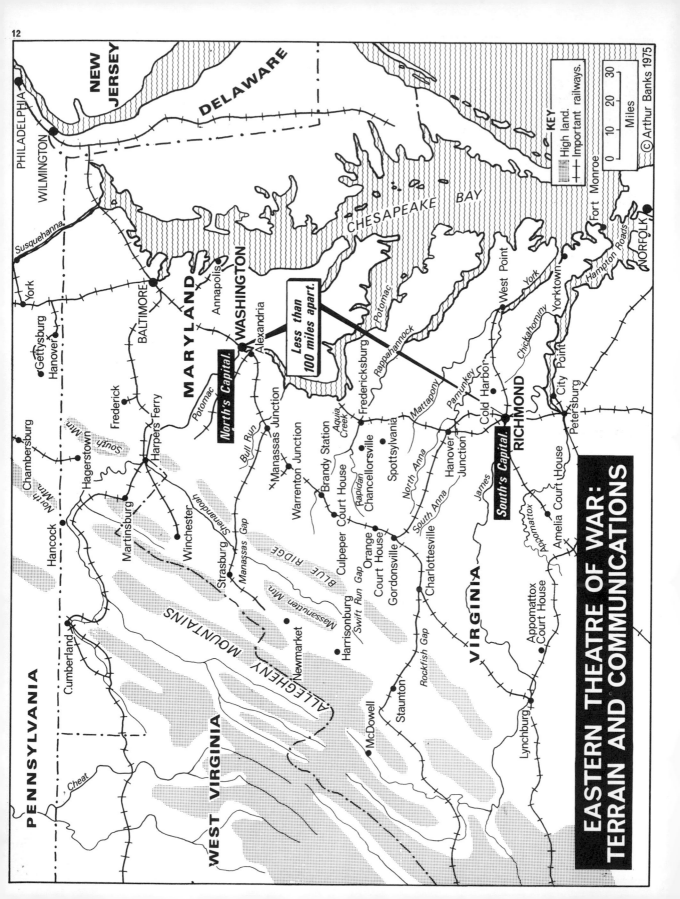

EASTERN THEATRE OF WAR: TERRAIN AND COMMUNICATIONS

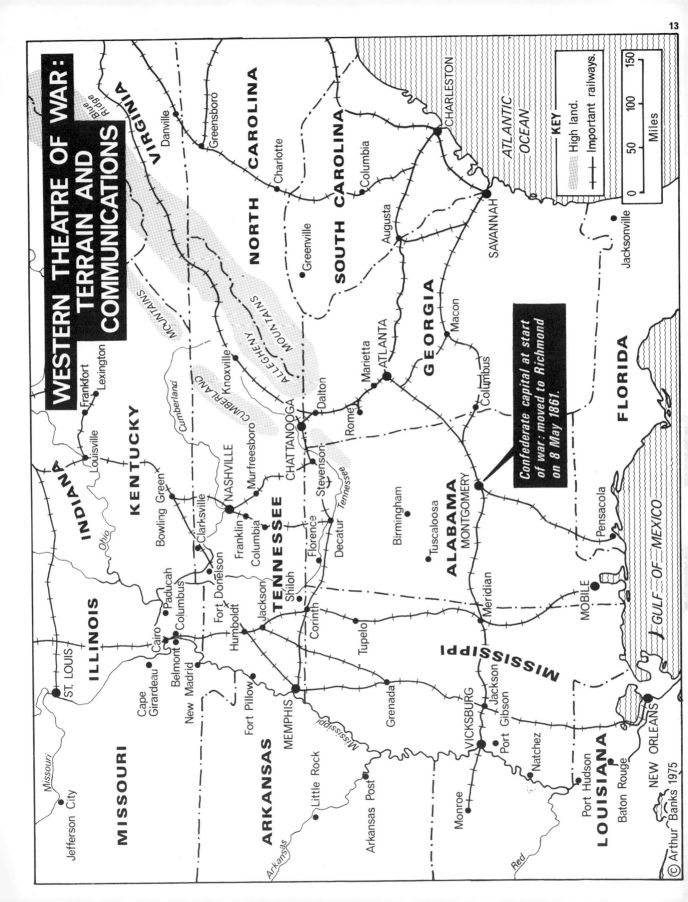

13

WESTERN THEATRE OF WAR:
TERRAIN AND
COMMUNICATIONS

KEY

High land.

Important railways.

Miles
0   50   100   150

Confederate capital at start
of war: moved to Richmond
on 8 May 1861.

© Arthur Banks 1975

MILITARY ORGANIZATION

Both sides commenced with similar organizations but changes occurred as the war progressed. Neither side started with army corps, but, in March 1862, the Union (on Lincoln's initiative) formed several of these. Strengths of units varied considerably: commanders were given maximum and minimum figures to work to most of the time.

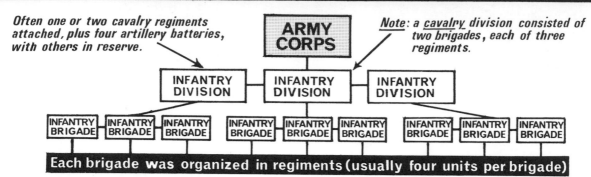

Often one or two cavalry regiments attached, plus four artillery batteries, with others in reserve.

ARMY CORPS

Note: a cavalry division consisted of two brigades, each of three regiments.

INFANTRY DIVISION — INFANTRY DIVISION — INFANTRY DIVISION

INFANTRY BRIGADE · INFANTRY BRIGADE · INFANTRY BRIGADE · INFANTRY BRIGADE · INFANTRY BRIGADE · INFANTRY BRIGADE · INFANTRY BRIGADE · INFANTRY BRIGADE · INFANTRY BRIGADE

Each brigade was organized in regiments (usually four units per brigade)

UNION INFANTRY REGIMENT

REGIMENTAL HEADQUARTERS

OFFICERS:
- COLONEL
- LIEUTENANT-COLONEL
- MAJOR
- ADJUTANT
- QUARTERMASTER
- SURGEON-MAJOR
- ASSISTANT SURGEONS (2)
- CHAPLAIN

ENLISTED PERSONNEL:
- SERGEANT-MAJOR
- QUARTERMASTER-SERGEANT
- COMMISSARY-SERGEANT
- PRINCIPAL MUSICIANS (2)
- HOSPITAL STEWARD

The regiment was the basic tactical unit of the United States army both in peace and war, and was similar to the British battalion. Its field strength averaged about 900 officers and men. In theory, Union and Confederate regiments were organized on similar lines but, in practice, there were many variations on the Conferate side: for example, the 55th. Alabama had battalions.

AVERAGE REGIMENTAL STRENGTHS AT BATTLE OF CHANCELLORSVILLE WERE:
UNION _____ 433 ⎫ Officers & men per regt.
CONFEDERATE _ 409 ⎭

AVERAGE COMPANY STRENGTH AT BATTLE OF GETTYSBURG WAS 32 OFFICERS AND MEN.

COMPANIES (10)

Note: except heavy artillery regiments retained as infantry which had 12.

A · B · C · D · E · F · G · H · I · K

Note: 'J' omitted

COMPANY		
Maximum strength: 101		Minimum strength : 83
CAPTAIN	SERGEANTS (4)	PRIVATES (64-82)
FIRST LIEUTENANT	CORPORALS (8)	
SECOND LIEUTENANT	MUSICIANS (2)	
FIRST SERGEANT	WAGGONER	

Usually six squadrons, each of two companies.

CAVALRY REGIMENT

THIS HAD <u>12</u> COMPANIES AND THESE WENT FROM 'A' TO 'M' (WITH 'J' OMITTED). 725 all ranks.

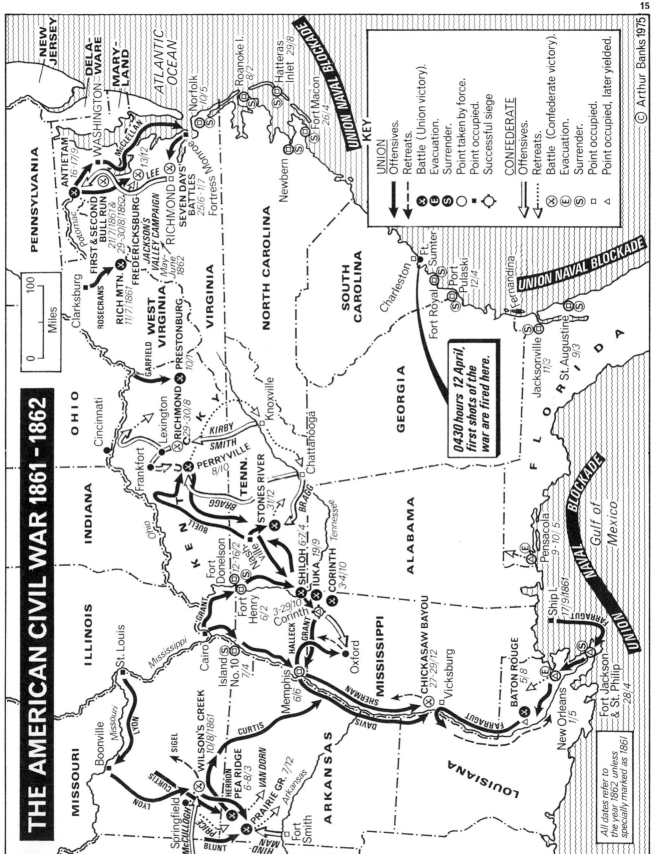

THE AMERICAN CIVIL WAR 1861–1862

© Arthur Banks 1975

KEY

UNION
Offensives.
Retreats.
Battle (Union victory).
Evacuation.
Surrender.
Point taken by force.
Point occupied.
Successful siege

CONFEDERATE
Offensives.
Retreats.
Battle (Confederate victory).
Evacuation.
Surrender.
Point occupied.
Point occupied, later yielded.

UNION NAVAL BLOCKADE

0430 hours 12 April, first shots of the war are fired here.

All dates refer to the year 1862 unless specially marked as 1861.

NEW JERSEY
DELAWARE
MARYLAND
ATLANTIC OCEAN
PENNSYLVANIA
WASHINGTON
ANTIETAM 16-17/9
McCLELLAN
LEE 13/12
FIRST & SECOND BULL RUN 21/7/1861 & 29-30/8/1862
FREDERICKSBURG 13/12
JACKSON'S VALLEY CAMPAIGN May-June 1862
RICHMOND
SEVEN DAYS' BATTLES 25/6-1/7
Fortress Monroe
Norfolk 10/5
Roanoke I. 8/2
Hatteras Inlet 29/8
Fort Macon 26/4
Newbern
Clarksburg
ROSECRANS
RICH MTN. 11/7/1861
WEST VIRGINIA
VIRGINIA
NORTH CAROLINA
GARFIELD
PRESTONBURG 10/1
OHIO
Cincinnati
Frankfort
Lexington
RICHMOND 29-30/8
KIRBY SMITH
KENTUCKY
Knoxville
Chattanooga
SOUTH CAROLINA
Charleston
Fort Royal
GEORGIA
Ft. Sumter
Port Pulaski 12/4
Fernandina
UNION NAVAL BLOCKADE
Jacksonville 11/3
St. Augustine 9/3
FLORIDA
INDIANA
ILLINOIS
St. Louis
Boonville
Missouri
LYON
PERRYVILLE 8/10
BRAGG
BUELL
STONES RIVER 31/12
TENN.
Nashville
Fort Donelson 12-16/2
Fort Henry 6/2
GRANT
SHILOH 6-7/4
IUKA 19/9
CORINTH 3-4/10
Corinth 3-29/10
HALLECK
GRANT
Oxford
Memphis 6/6
Island No. 10 7/4
Cairo
Mississippi
MISSISSIPPI
SHERMAN
DAVIS
CHICKASAW BAYOU 27-29/12
Vicksburg
ALABAMA
Pensacola 9-10/5
Ship I. 17/9/1861
Gulf of Mexico
UNION NAVAL BLOCKADE
BATON ROUGE 5/8
FARRAGUT
New Orleans 1/5
Fort Jackson & St. Philip 28/4
LOUISIANA
ARKANSAS
Fort Smith
CURTIS
VAN DORN
PEA RIDGE 6-8/3
PRAIRIE GR. 7/12
HERRON
BLUNT
HINDMAN
PRICE
McCULLOCH
WILSON'S CREEK 10/8/1861
Springfield
SIGEL
Arkansas
MISSOURI
0 Miles 100

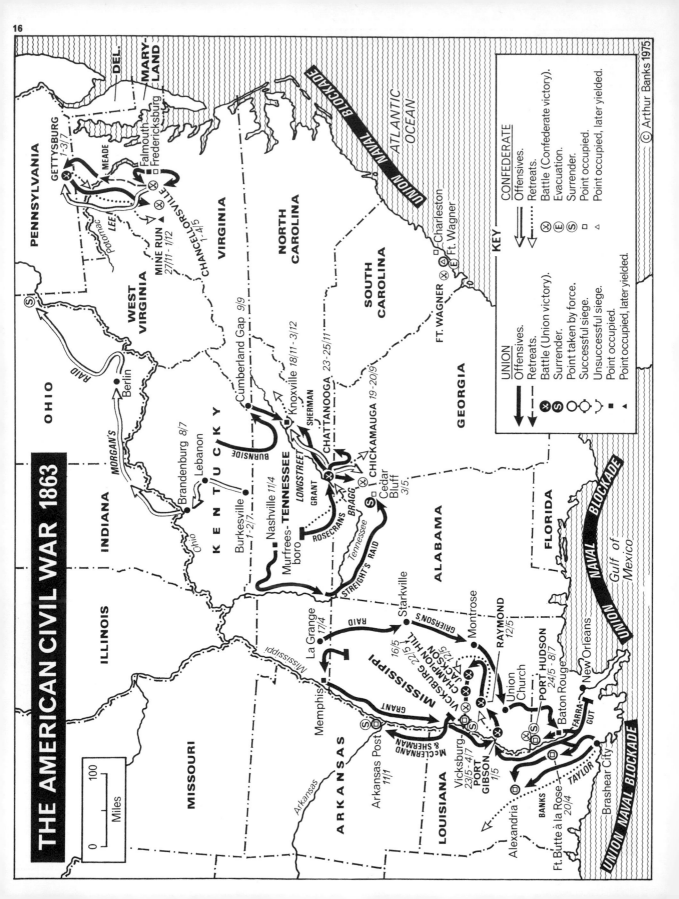

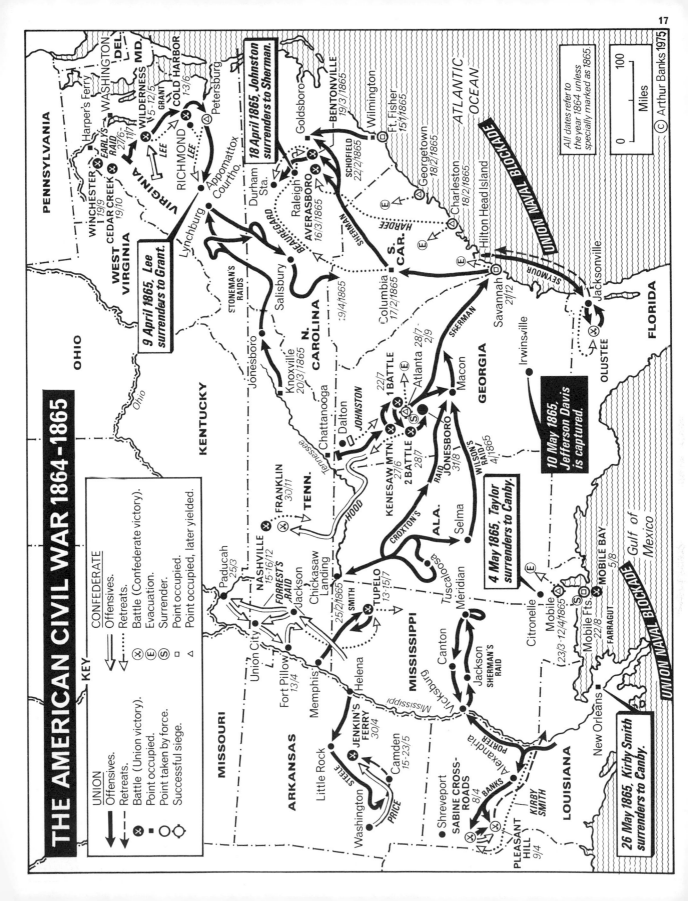

THE BATTLES OF ULYSSES S. GRANT

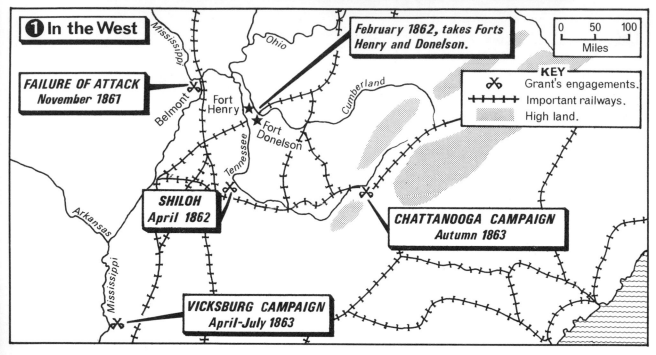

1 In the West

February 1862, takes Forts Henry and Donelson.

FAILURE OF ATTACK
November 1861

KEY
- ✂ Grant's engagements.
- ┼┼┼ Important railways.
- ▒ High land.

0   50   100
Miles

Mississippi
Ohio
Cumberland
Belmont
Fort Henry
Fort Donelson
Tennessee
Arkansas
Mississippi

SHILOH
April 1862

CHATTANOOGA CAMPAIGN
Autumn 1863

VICKSBURG CAMPAIGN
April-July 1863

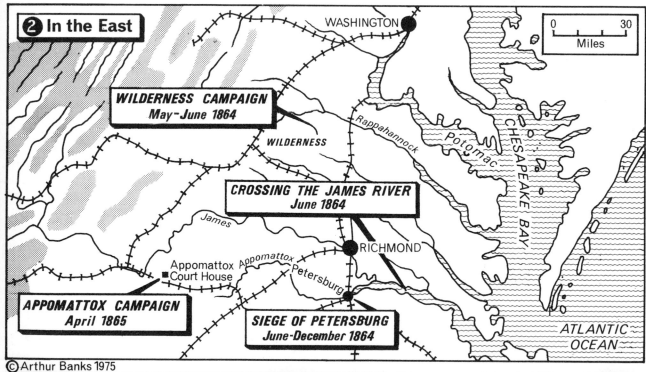

2 In the East

0   30
Miles

WASHINGTON

WILDERNESS CAMPAIGN
May-June 1864

WILDERNESS

Rappahannock
Potomac
CHESAPEAKE BAY

CROSSING THE JAMES RIVER
June 1864

James

RICHMOND

Appomattox Court House
Appomattox
Petersburg

APPOMATTOX CAMPAIGN
April 1865

SIEGE OF PETERSBURG
June-December 1864

ATLANTIC OCEAN

© Arthur Banks 1975

Ulysses Simpson Grant (1822–1885) served as an infantry officer in the Mexican War but resigned from the army in 1854 following a period of heavy drinking. He volunteered for service in the Union army in 1861, and was speedily given command of an infantry regiment. Rapidly promoted brigadier-general, he became lieutenant-general in March 1864 and general-in-chief three days later. In 1868 he was elected president and served twice.

THE BATTLES OF WILLIAM T. SHERMAN

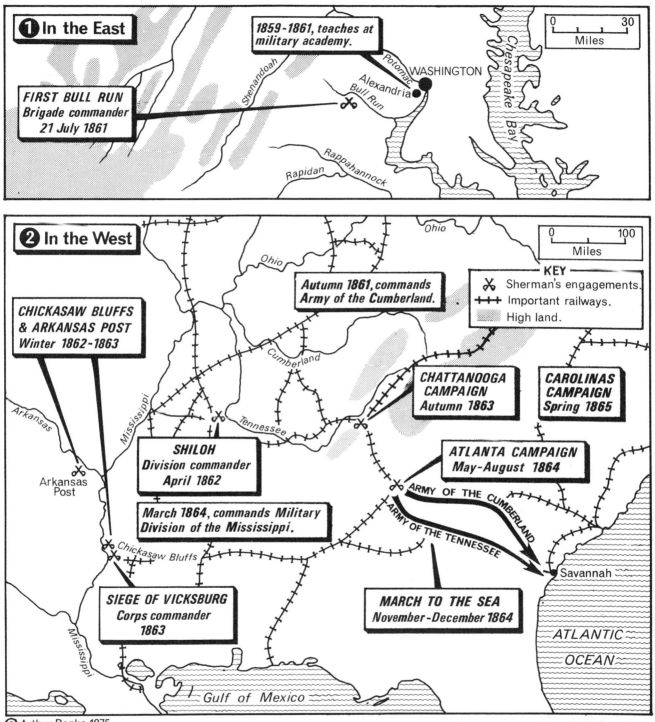

1 In the East

1859-1861, teaches at military academy.

FIRST BULL RUN
Brigade commander
21 July 1861

WASHINGTON

Alexandria
Bull Run

Potomac

Shenandoah

Rapidan

Rappahannock

Chesapeake Bay

0   30
Miles

2 In the West

0   100
Miles

— KEY —
✂ Sherman's engagements.
┼┼┼ Important railways.
▒ High land.

Ohio

Ohio

Autumn 1861, commands Army of the Cumberland.

CHICKASAW BLUFFS & ARKANSAS POST
Winter 1862-1863

Cumberland

CHATTANOOGA CAMPAIGN
Autumn 1863

CAROLINAS CAMPAIGN
Spring 1865

Arkansas

Tennessee

SHILOH
Division commander
April 1862

Mississippi

Arkansas Post

ATLANTA CAMPAIGN
May-August 1864

ARMY OF THE CUMBERLAND

March 1864, commands Military Division of the Mississippi.

ARMY OF THE TENNESSEE

Chickasaw Bluffs

SIEGE OF VICKSBURG
Corps commander
1863

Savannah

MARCH TO THE SEA
November-December 1864

Mississippi

Gulf of Mexico

ATLANTIC OCEAN

© Arthur Banks 1975

William Tecumseh Sherman (1820-1891) resigned from the army in 1853 and, after working as a banker and practising law, became superintendent of a military academy in 1859. In 1861 he volunteered for Federal service and was promoted to brigadier-general in August, major-general in May 1862, lieutenant-general in July 1866, and, as a full general, succeeded Grant as commander-in-chief in 1869. He held this post until 1883.

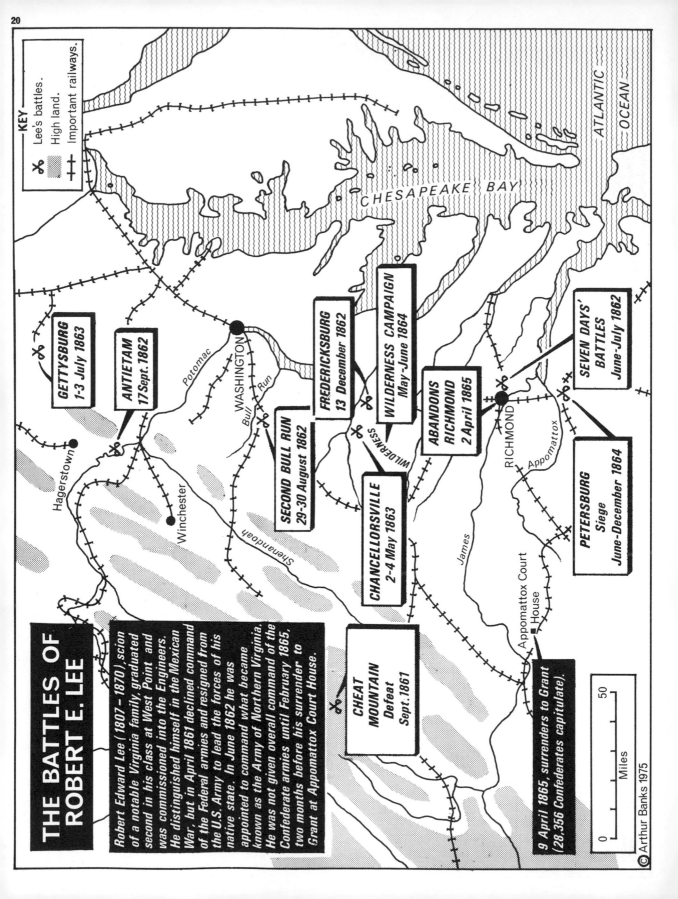

KEY
Lee's battles.
High land.
Important railways.

THE BATTLES OF ROBERT E. LEE

Robert Edward Lee (1807–1870), scion of a notable Virginia family, graduated second in his class at West Point and was commissioned into the Engineers. He distinguished himself in the Mexican War, but in April 1861 declined command of the Federal armies and resigned from the U.S. Army to lead the forces of his native state. In June 1862 he was appointed to command what became known as the Army of Northern Virginia. He was not given overall command of the Confederate armies until February 1865, two months before his surrender to Grant at Appomattox Court House.

CHESAPEAKE BAY

ATLANTIC OCEAN

GETTYSBURG
1-3 July 1863

ANTIETAM
17 Sept. 1862

FREDERICKSBURG
13 December 1862

WILDERNESS CAMPAIGN
May–June 1864

SEVEN DAYS' BATTLES
June–July 1862

ABANDONS RICHMOND
2 April 1865

SECOND BULL RUN
29-30 August 1862

CHANCELLORSVILLE
2-4 May 1863

PETERSBURG
Siege
June–December 1864

CHEAT MOUNTAIN
Defeat
Sept. 1861

9 April 1865, surrenders to Grant
(28,356 Confederates capitulate).

Hagerstown

Winchester

WASHINGTON

Potomac

Bull Run

Shenandoah

WILDERNESS

RICHMOND

James

Appomattox

Appomattox Court House

0   50
Miles

© Arthur Banks 1975

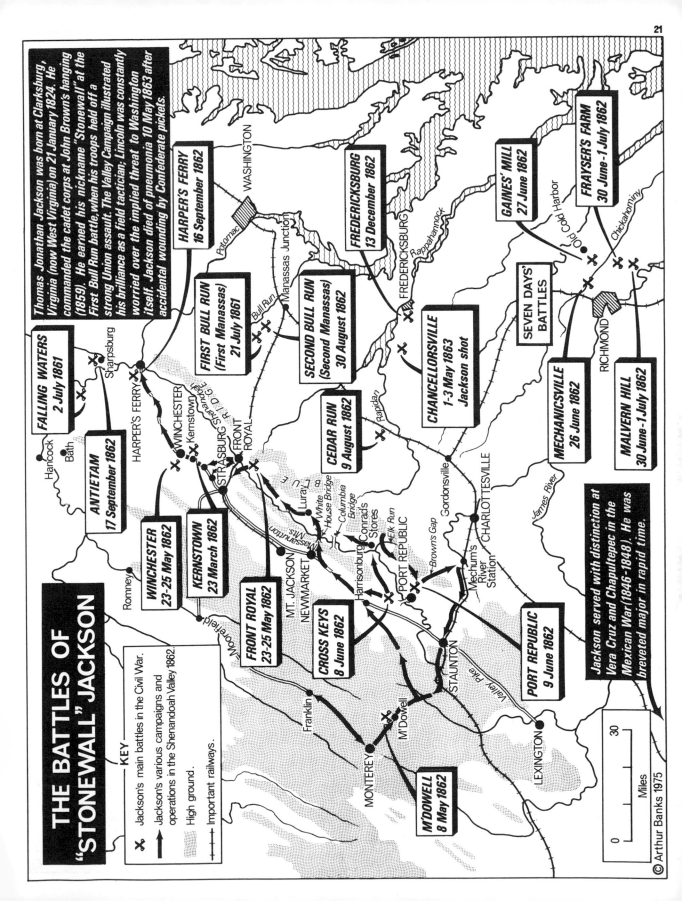

THE BATTLES OF "STONEWALL" JACKSON

Thomas Jonathan Jackson was born at Clarksburg, Virginia (now West Virginia) on 21 January 1824. He commanded the cadet corps at John Brown's hanging (1859). He earned his nickname "Stonewall" at the First Bull Run battle, when his troops held off a strong Union assault. The Valley Campaign illustrated his brilliance as a field tactician. Lincoln was constantly worried over the implied threat to Washington itself. Jackson died of pneumonia 10 May 1863 after accidental wounding by Confederate pickets.

Jackson served with distinction at Vera Cruz and Chapultepec in the Mexican War (1846-1848). He was breveted major in rapid time.

KEY
— Jackson's main battles in the Civil War.
→ Jackson's various campaigns and operations in the Shenandoah Valley 1862.
High ground.
+++ Important railways.

HARPER'S FERRY
16 September 1862

FALLING WATERS
2 July 1861

ANTIETAM
17 September 1862

WINCHESTER
23-25 May 1862

KERNSTOWN
23 March 1862

FRONT ROYAL
23-25 May 1862

CROSS KEYS
8 June 1862

McDOWELL
8 May 1862

PORT REPUBLIC
9 June 1862

FIRST BULL RUN
(First Manassas)
21 July 1861

SECOND BULL RUN
(Second Manassas)
30 August 1862

CEDAR RUN
9 August 1862

FREDERICKSBURG
13 December 1862

CHANCELLORSVILLE
1-3 May 1863
Jackson shot

MECHANICSVILLE
26 June 1862

SEVEN DAYS' BATTLES

GAINES' MILL
27 June 1862

FRAYSER'S FARM
30 June-1 July 1862

MALVERN HILL
30 June-1 July 1862

WASHINGTON

Manassas Junction

Bull Run

HARPER'S FERRY

Sharpsburg

Hancock
Bath

Romney

Moorefield

Franklin

MONTEREY

McDowell

LEXINGTON

STAUNTON

Valley Pike

WINCHESTER
Kernstown
STRASBURG
FRONT ROYAL
Luray
White House Bridge
Columbia Bridge
Conrad's Stores
Elk Run
MT. JACKSON
NEWMARKET
Harrisonburg
PORT REPUBLIC
Brown's Gap
Mechum's River Station
CHARLOTTESVILLE
Gordonsville

B L U E   R I D G E

M A S S A N U T T E N   M T S

S H E N A N D O A H   R I D G E

Potomac
Shenandoah
Rappahannock
Rapidan
James River
Chickahominy
Old Cold Harbor

FREDERICKSBURG

RICHMOND

Miles
0   30

© Arthur Banks 1975

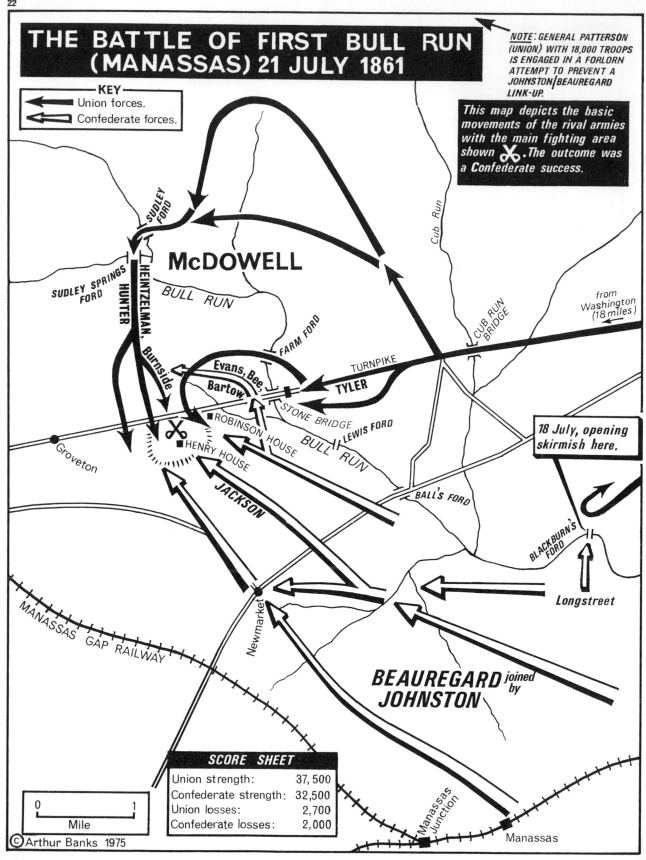

THE BATTLE OF FIRST BULL RUN (MANASSAS) 21 JULY 1861

KEY
Union forces.
Confederate forces.

NOTE: GENERAL PATTERSON (UNION) WITH 18,000 TROOPS IS ENGAGED IN A FORLORN ATTEMPT TO PREVENT A JOHNSTON/BEAUREGARD LINK-UP.

This map depicts the basic movements of the rival armies with the main fighting area shown ✂. The outcome was a **Confederate** success.

SUDLEY FORD

McDOWELL

SUDLEY SPRINGS FORD

HUNTER

HEINTZELMAN,

Burnside

BULL RUN

FARM FORD

Evans, Bee, Bartow

STONE BRIDGE

TYLER

TURNPIKE

Cub Run

CUB RUN BRIDGE

from Washington (18 miles)

ROBINSON HOUSE

LEWIS FORD

BULL RUN

Groveton

HENRY HOUSE

JACKSON

BALL'S FORD

18 July, opening skirmish here.

BLACKBURN'S FORD

Longstreet

Newmarket

MANASSAS GAP RAILWAY

BEAUREGARD JOINED by JOHNSTON

0   1
Mile

© Arthur Banks 1975

SCORE SHEET	
Union strength:	37,500
Confederate strength:	32,500
Union losses:	2,700
Confederate losses:	2,000

Manassas Junction

Manassas

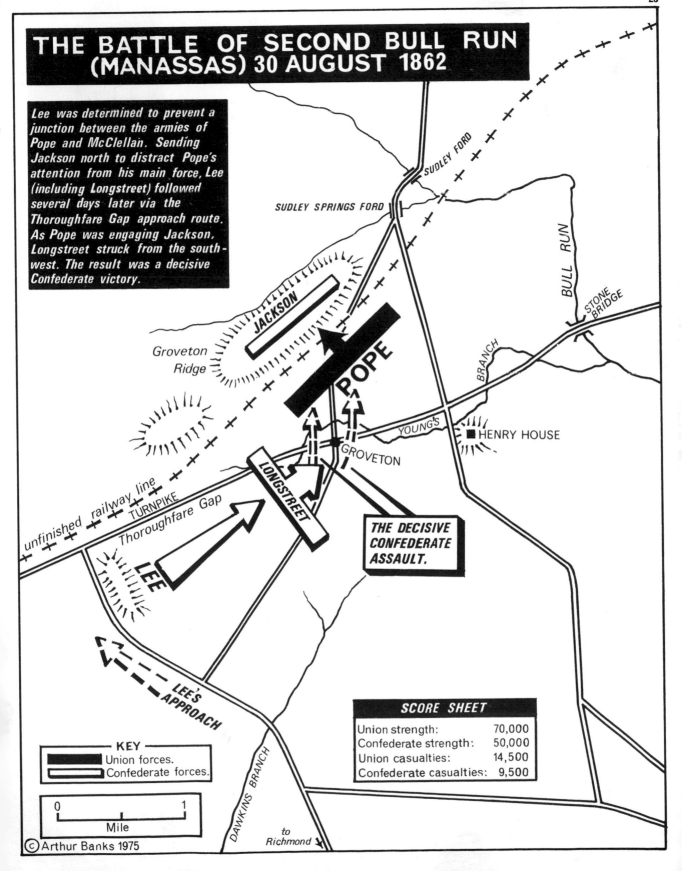

THE BATTLE OF SECOND BULL RUN (MANASSAS) 30 AUGUST 1862

Lee was determined to prevent a junction between the armies of Pope and McClellan. Sending Jackson north to distract Pope's attention from his main force, Lee (including Longstreet) followed several days later via the Thoroughfare Gap approach route. As Pope was engaging Jackson, Longstreet struck from the south-west. The result was a decisive Confederate victory.

SUDLEY FORD

SUDLEY SPRINGS FORD

BULL RUN

STONE BRIDGE

JACKSON

Groveton Ridge

POPE

BRANCH

YOUNG'S

HENRY HOUSE

GROVETON

LONGSTREET

THE DECISIVE CONFEDERATE ASSAULT.

unfinished railway line

TURNPIKE

Thoroughfare Gap

LEE

LEE'S APPROACH

DAWKINS BRANCH

to Richmond

KEY
Union forces.
Confederate forces.

0   1
Mile

© Arthur Banks 1975

SCORE SHEET
Union strength:	70,000
Confederate strength:	50,000
Union casualties:	14,500
Confederate casualties:	9,500

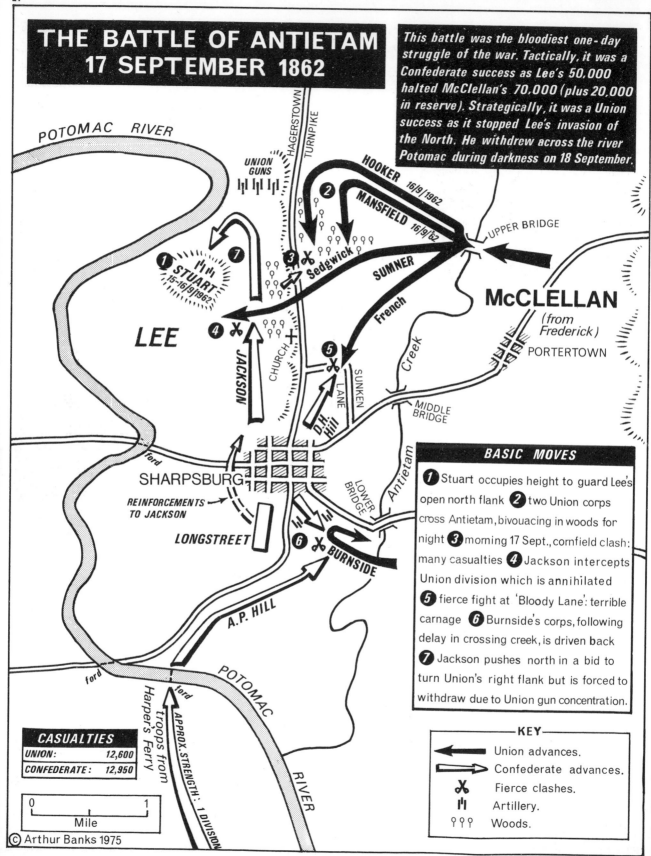

THE BATTLE OF ANTIETAM 17 SEPTEMBER 1862

This battle was the bloodiest one-day struggle of the war. Tactically, it was a Confederate success as Lee's 50,000 halted McClellan's 70,000 (plus 20,000 in reserve). Strategically, it was a Union success as it stopped Lee's invasion of the North. He withdrew across the river Potomac during darkness on 18 September.

POTOMAC RIVER

HAGERSTOWN TURNPIKE

UNION GUNS

HOOKER 16/9/1962

2

MANSFIELD 16/9/'62

UPPER BRIDGE

3 Sedgwick

SUMNER

French

1 STUART 15-16/9/1862

7

LEE

4

JACKSON

CHURCH

5

LANE

Sunken

McCLELLAN
(from Frederick)
PORTERTOWN

Creek

MIDDLE BRIDGE

D.H. Hill

SHARPSBURG

REINFORCEMENTS TO JACKSON

LONGSTREET

A.P. HILL

Antietam

LOWER BRIDGE

6 BURNSIDE

ford

POTOMAC

ford

RIVER

ford

troops from Harper's Ferry

APPROX. STRENGTH: 1 DIVISION

BASIC MOVES

1 Stuart occupies height to guard Lee's open north flank **2** two Union corps cross Antietam, bivouacing in woods for night **3** morning 17 Sept., cornfield clash: many casualties **4** Jackson intercepts Union division which is annihilated **5** fierce fight at 'Bloody Lane': terrible carnage **6** Burnside's corps, following delay in crossing creek, is driven back **7** Jackson pushes north in a bid to turn Union's right flank but is forced to withdraw due to Union gun concentration.

CASUALTIES

UNION:	12,600
CONFEDERATE:	12,950

0 ———— 1
Mile

© Arthur Banks 1975

KEY

← Union advances.

⇐ Confederate advances.

✂ Fierce clashes.

�𝗂𝗅𝗂 Artillery.

♀♀♀ Woods.

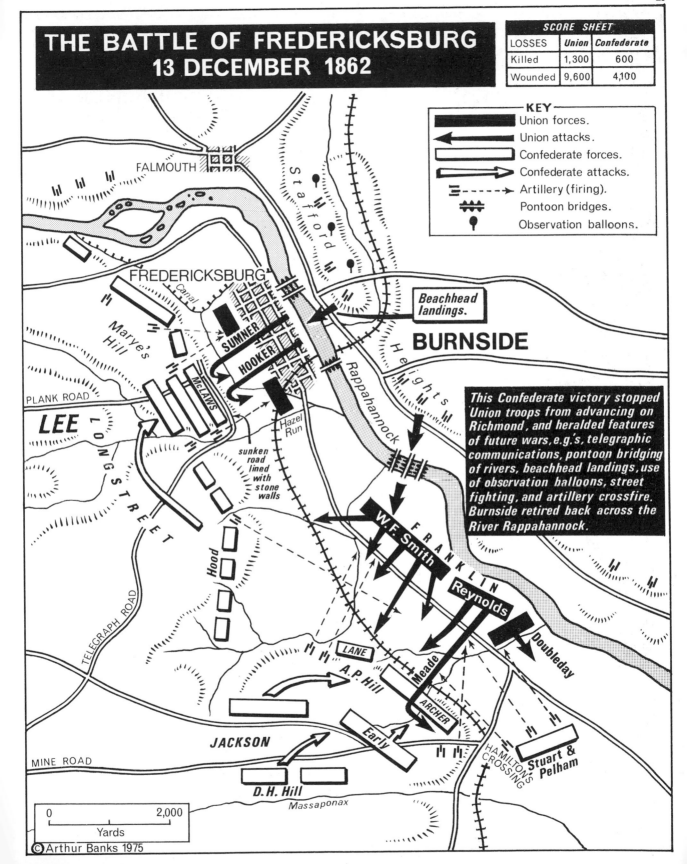

THE BATTLE OF FREDERICKSBURG 13 DECEMBER 1862

SCORE SHEET

LOSSES	Union	Confederate
Killed	1,300	600
Wounded	9,600	4,100

KEY
- Union forces.
- Union attacks.
- Confederate forces.
- Confederate attacks.
- Artillery (firing).
- Pontoon bridges.
- Observation balloons.

FALMOUTH

Stafford

FREDERICKSBURG

Canal

Beachhead landings.

BURNSIDE

Marye's Hill

SUMNER

HOOKER

PLANK ROAD

McLAWS

Rappahannock

LEE

LONGSTREET

Hazel Run

Heights

This Confederate victory stopped Union troops from advancing on Richmond, and heralded features of future wars, e.g.'s, telegraphic communications, pontoon bridging of rivers, beachhead landings, use of observation balloons, street fighting, and artillery crossfire. Burnside retired back across the River Rappahannock.

sunken road lined with stone walls

Hood

W.F. Smith

FRANKLIN

Reynolds

Doubleday

TELEGRAPH ROAD

LANE

A.P. Hill

Meade

ARCHER

JACKSON

Early

Hamilton's Crossing

Stuart & Pelham

MINE ROAD

D.H. Hill

Massaponax

0   2,000
Yards

© Arthur Banks 1975

THE SIEGE
May–July 1863

VICKSBURG

Sherman

McPherson

Ord

McClernand *later*

Lauman

Herron

Sta. PEMBERTON

CONFEDERATE WORKS

GRANT

MISSISSIPPI

SWAMP

0   1
Mile

KEY

Grierson's cavalry raid, 17 April–2 May 1863

MEMPHIS

Grand Junction

Jackson

VICKSBURG

600 MILES

NEW ORLEANS

Monroe

Red

MISSISSIPPI

Natchez

Port Hudson

Baton Rouge

GULF OF MEXICO

THE VICKSBURG CAMPAIGN
NOVEMBER 1862–JULY 1863

The fall of Vicksburg was the turning point of the war (4 July 1863). On 9 July Port Hudson fell to Banks: thus, the Mississippi was under Union control entirely and the western states were isolated.

JOHNSTON

JACKSON

Pearl

Clinton

Raymond

14/5/63

16/5/63

12/5/63

Champion's Hill

Bolton

Bridgeport

4 July 1863, 31,600 Confederates surrender

Big Black River

Yazoo

Haynes' Bluff

Chickasaw Bluffs

Sherman

Big Black River

VICKSBURG

PEMBERTON

Warrenton

SWAMP

Miliiken's Bend

Duckport

New Carthage

Bayou Vidal

Hard Times

Mississippi

Porter's Gunboat Flotilla

Grand Gulf

Port Gibson

Bruinsburg

1/5/63

2/5/63

1/5/63

McClernand's XIII Corps

Sherman's XV Corps

McPherson's XVII Corps

GRANT

KEY

Grant's approach march to invest Vicksburg, 1863.

Clashes.

© Arthur Banks 1975

THE BATTLE OF CHANCELLORSVILLE 1–6 MAY 1863

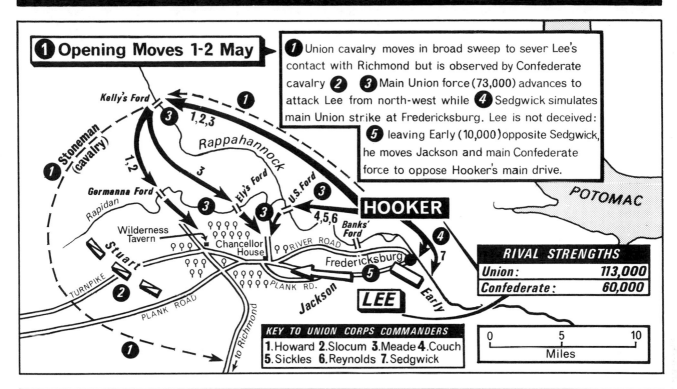

① Opening Moves 1-2 May

① Union cavalry moves in broad sweep to sever Lee's contact with Richmond but is observed by Confederate cavalry ② ③ Main Union force (73,000) advances to attack Lee from north-west while ④ Sedgwick simulates main Union strike at Fredericksburg. Lee is not deceived: ⑤ leaving Early (10,000) opposite Sedgwick, he moves Jackson and main Confederate force to oppose Hooker's main drive.

RIVAL STRENGTHS
Union:	113,000
Confederate:	60,000

KEY TO UNION CORPS COMMANDERS
1. Howard 2. Slocum 3. Meade 4. Couch
5. Sickles 6. Reynolds 7. Sedgwick

0   5   10
Miles

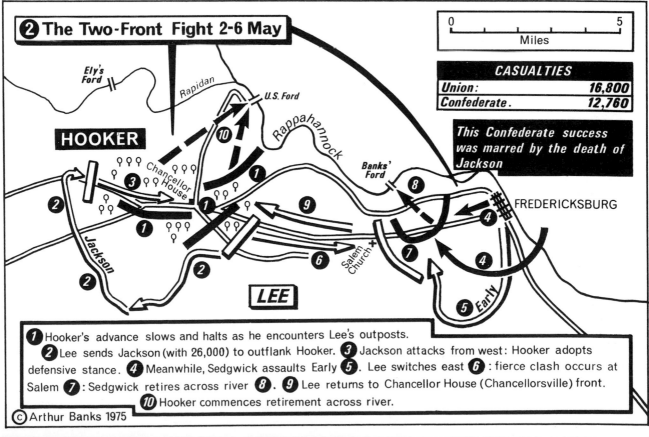

② The Two-Front Fight 2-6 May

0   5
Miles

CASUALTIES
Union:	16,800
Confederate.	12,760

This Confederate success was marred by the death of Jackson

① Hooker's advance slows and halts as he encounters Lee's outposts. ② Lee sends Jackson (with 26,000) to outflank Hooker. ③ Jackson attacks from west: Hooker adopts defensive stance. ④ Meanwhile, Sedgwick assaults Early ⑤. Lee switches east ⑥: fierce clash occurs at Salem ⑦: Sedgwick retires across river ⑧. ⑨ Lee returns to Chancellor House (Chancellorsville) front. ⑩ Hooker commences retirement across river.

© Arthur Banks 1975

THE BATTLE OF GETTYSBURG 1-3 JULY 1863

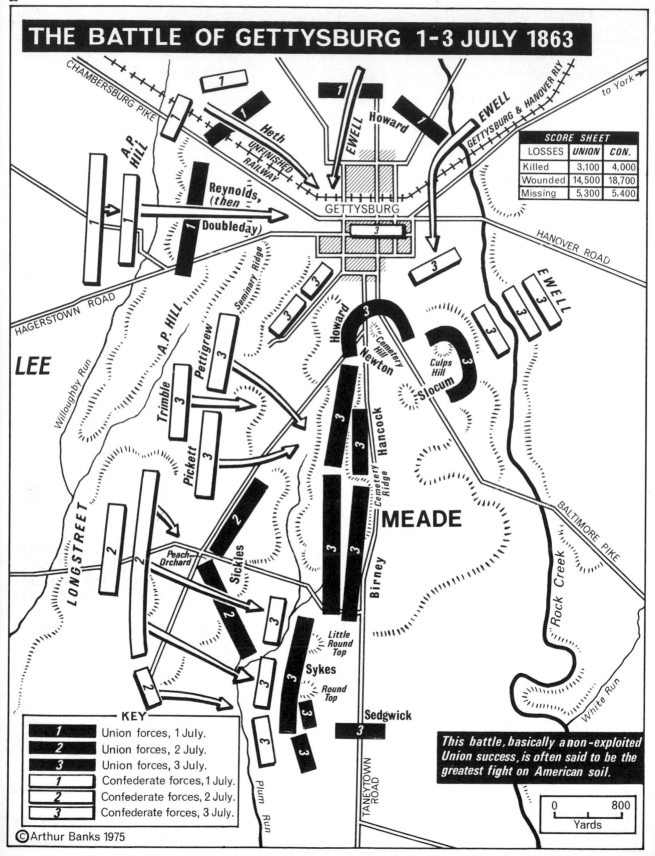

CHAMBERSBURG PIKE

to York

EWELL

GETTYSBURG & HANOVER RLY

EWELL

Howard

Heth

UNFINISHED RAILWAY

A.P. HILL

Reynolds (then Doubleday)

GETTYSBURG

HANOVER ROAD

SCORE SHEET		
LOSSES	UNION	CON.
Killed	3,100	4,000
Wounded	14,500	18,700
Missing	5,300	5,400

EWELL

HAGERSTOWN ROAD

LEE

Seminary Ridge

A.P. HILL

Pettigrew

Trimble

Pickett

Willoughby Run

Howard

Cemetery Hill

Newton

Culps Hill

Slocum

Hancock

Cemetery Ridge

MEADE

BALTIMORE PIKE

Rock Creek

LONGSTREET

Peach Orchard

Sickles

Birney

Little Round Top

Sykes

Round Top

White Run

Sedgwick

Plum Run

TANEYTOWN ROAD

KEY

1	Union forces, 1 July.
2	Union forces, 2 July.
3	Union forces, 3 July.
1	Confederate forces, 1 July.
2	Confederate forces, 2 July.
3	Confederate forces, 3 July.

© Arthur Banks 1975

This battle, basically a non-exploited Union success, is often said to be the greatest fight on American soil.

0   800

Yards

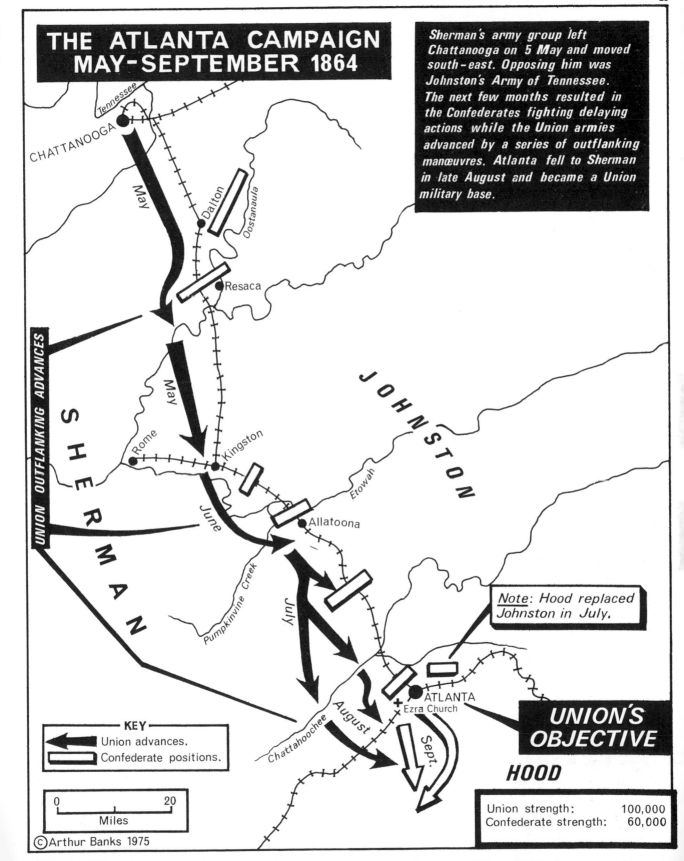

THE ATLANTA CAMPAIGN MAY–SEPTEMBER 1864

Sherman's army group left Chattanooga on 5 May and moved south-east. Opposing him was Johnston's Army of Tennessee. The next few months resulted in the Confederates fighting delaying actions while the Union armies advanced by a series of outflanking manœuvres. Atlanta fell to Sherman in late August and became a Union military base.

UNION OUTFLANKING ADVANCES

CHATTANOOGA

Tennessee

May

Dalton

Oostanaula

Resaca

S H E R M A N

May

Rome

Kingston

June

Etowah

Allatoona

Pumpkinvine Creek

July

J O H N S T O N

<u>Note</u>: *Hood replaced Johnston in July.*

ATLANTA
Ezra Church

Chattahoochee

August

Sept.

UNION'S OBJECTIVE

HOOD

KEY
Union advances.
Confederate positions.

0		20
	Miles	

© Arthur Banks 1975

Union strength:	100,000
Confederate strength:	60,000

LEE'S RETREAT FROM RICHMOND-PETERSBURG TO APPOMATTOX 31 MARCH - 9 APRIL 1865

Miles
0 5 10 15

to West Point

2 April, realising the significance of the fall of Petersburg, Lee abandons the Confederate capital which is sacked and burnt by its own inhabitants. Union forces are hailed as liberators.

4 April, Lincoln arrives by ship.

RICHMOND

Weitzel 3 April

GRANT

City Point

Ft. Stedman
PETERSBURG

2 April

2 April

2 April

Five Forks
1 April

PICKETT'S COUNTER-ATTACK 31 March

Dinwiddie Court House

These Union attacks prove to be decisive. Confederate lines are breached : Petersburg falls.

EWELL

LEE

GORDON
2-4 April

LONGSTREET
2-4 April

2-4 April

ANDERSON
2-4 April

Hatcher's Run

SHERIDAN

SOUTHSIDE RAILROAD

James

5 April, Lee arrives here to learn that Union forces have reached Jetersville ahead of him, thus severing the railway to the south. Lee detours to the north-west.

Appomattox

Amelia Court House

5-6 April

Jetersville

Burke's Station

Grant's aim is to control these railway lines to prevent Lee from joining with Johnston's forces to the south.

James

6 April, Union forces catch up with Confederate rearguard at Sailor's (or Sayler's) Creek. In fierce action, Union take 8,000 prisoners including Ewell, thus depleting Lee's force.

7 April

Burkesville

DANVILLE RAILROAD

9 April, recognizing the hopelessness of his situation, Lee surrenders to Grant. Terms are generous: Lee's men can return home on parole and officers retain their swords for prestige purposes. The war ended officially on 29 May.

James

7 April

7 April

Farmville

SHERIDAN

7 April

CAVALRY

Appomattox Court House

This Union advance seals fate of Lee's march-weary army.

to Lynchburg & mountainous terrain

KEY
- Confederate siege lines.
- Confederate retreats.
- Union siege lines.
- Union advances.
- Important railways.

© Arthur Banks 1975

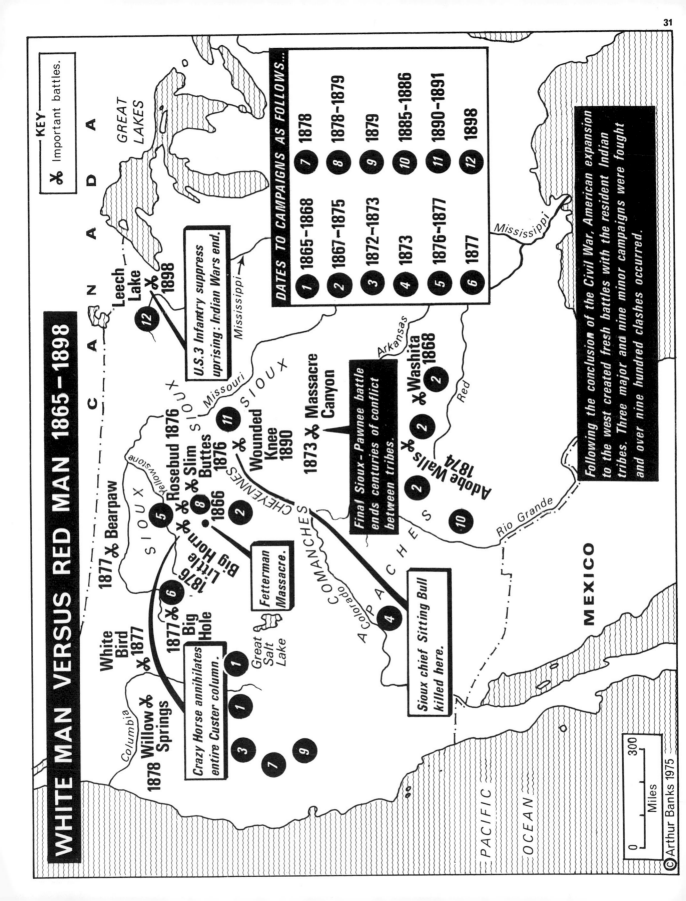

WHITE MAN VERSUS RED MAN 1865–1898

KEY
✘ Important battles.

GREAT LAKES

CANADA

DATES TO CAMPAIGNS AS FOLLOWS...

❶ 1865–1868		❼ 1878	
❷ 1867–1875		❽ 1878–1879	
❸ 1872–1873		❾ 1879	
❹ 1873		❿ 1885–1886	
❺ 1876–1877		⓫ 1890–1891	
❻ 1877		⓬ 1898	

Mississippi

Following the conclusion of the Civil War, American expansion to the west created fresh battles with the resident Indian tribes. Three major and nine minor campaigns were fought and over nine hundred clashes occurred.

Leech Lake ✘ 1898 ⓬

U.S.3 Infantry suppress uprising: Indian Wars end.

Missouri

Mississippi

SIOUX

SIOUX

Rosebud 1876 ✘ ❺
Slim Buttes 1876 ✘ ❽ 1866 ❷
Wounded Knee 1890 ✘ ⓫

Arkansas
Washita ✘ 1868 ❷
❷

Red

1873 ✘ Massacre Canyon

Final Sioux–Pawnee battle ends centuries of conflict between tribes.

CHEYENNES

Adobe Walls ✘ 1874 ❷

❿

Rio Grande

1877 ✘ Bearpaw

Yellowstone

SIOUX

Little Big Horn 1876 ✘ ❾

Fetterman Massacre.

COMANCHES

APACHES

Sioux chief Sitting Bull killed here. ❹

Colorado

MEXICO

White Bird ✘ 1877

1878 Willow ✘ Springs

Columbia

Big Hole 1877 ✘

Crazy Horse annihilates entire Custer column.

❶
Great Salt Lake
❶
❸
❼
❾

PACIFIC OCEAN

0 ____ 300
Miles

© Arthur Banks 1975

III

STRIFE & ALIGNMENTS

STRIFE IN AFRICA 1860–1899

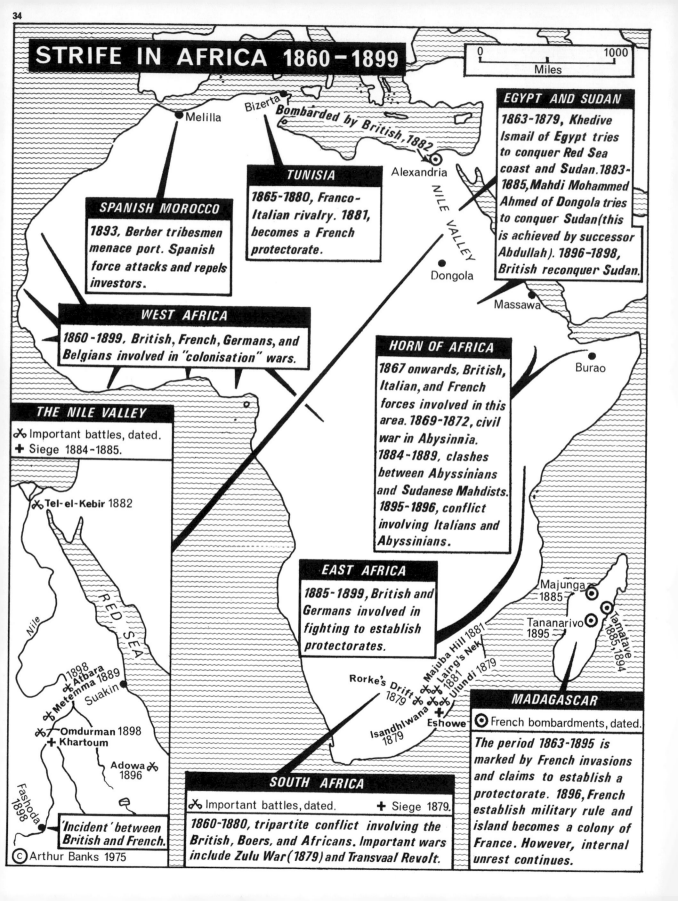

Miles
0   1000

Melilla

Bizerta

Bombarded by British, 1882

Alexandria

NILE VALLEY

EGYPT AND SUDAN

1863-1879, Khedive Ismail of Egypt tries to conquer Red Sea coast and Sudan. 1883-1885, Mahdi Mohammed Ahmed of Dongola tries to conquer Sudan (this is achieved by successor Abdullah). 1896-1898, British reconquer Sudan.

Dongola

Massawa

TUNISIA

1865-1880, Franco-Italian rivalry. 1881, becomes a French protectorate.

SPANISH MOROCCO

1893, Berber tribesmen menace port. Spanish force attacks and repels investors.

WEST AFRICA

1860-1899, British, French, Germans, and Belgians involved in "colonisation" wars.

HORN OF AFRICA

1867 onwards, British, Italian, and French forces involved in this area. 1869-1872, civil war in Abysinnia. 1884-1889, clashes between Abyssinians and Sudanese Mahdists. 1895-1896, conflict involving Italians and Abyssinians.

Burao

THE NILE VALLEY

⚔ Important battles, dated.
✚ Siege 1884-1885.

⚔ **Tel-el-Kebir** 1882

RED SEA

Nile

1898
⚔ **Atbara**
Metemma 1889
Suakin

⚔ **Omdurman** 1898
✚ **Khartoum**

Adowa ⚔
1896

Fashoda
1898

'Incident' between British and French.

EAST AFRICA

1885-1899, British and Germans involved in fighting to establish protectorates.

Majunga
1885

Tananarivo
1895

Tamatave
1885, 1894

Majuba Hill 1881
Laing's Nek
1881   Ulundi 1879
Rorke's Drift
1879

Isandhlwana
1879

✚ Eshowe

MADAGASCAR

◉ French bombardments, dated.

The period 1863-1895 is marked by French invasions and claims to establish a protectorate. 1896, French establish military rule and island becomes a colony of France. However, internal unrest continues.

SOUTH AFRICA

⚔ Important battles, dated.   ✚ Siege 1879.

1860-1880, tripartite conflict involving the British, Boers, and Africans. Important wars include Zulu War (1879) and Transvaal Revolt.

STRIFE IN AFRICA 1899-1914

0 — 1000
Miles

This map shows areas of local conflict numbered in chronological sequence.

5

NORTHERN SAHARA
1900, French establish their authority in desert areas (e.g. oases).

Tripoli

WADAI
1909-11, conquered by French.

NORTHERN NIGERIA
1900-3, British conquer area.

Agadir

MAURETANIA
1908-9, conquered by French.

16

BAGIRMI
1900, French defeat R. Zobeir.

N.W. NIGERIA
1906, insurrection in Sokoto.

14   **6**   **17**

4

SOMALILAND
1899-1900, Mohammed ben Abdullah clashes with British, Italians, Ethiopians.

1

3   **9**

12

10

GOLD COAST
1900, uprising: British suppress Ushantis.

FRENCH CONGO
1905, uprising.

13

SOUTHERN NIGERIA
1904, insurrection.

CAMEROON
1904-5, Germans suppress insurrection.

ANGOLA
1907, uprising (inspired by Herero uprising in German S.W. Africa).

15

7

ANGOLA
1902, uprising suppressed by Portuguese.

8

GERMAN S.W. AFRICA
1903, Hottentot uprising.

11

GERMAN EAST AFRICA
1905, insurrection.

2

18

GERMAN S.W. AFRICA
1904-8, uprising (Herero tribe plus Hottentots).

SOUTH AFRICA
1914, Boer uprising.

SOUTH AFRICA
1899-1902, Boer War (see page   ).

© Arthur Banks 1975

STRIFE IN SOUTH AMERICA 1864-1895

Caribbean   Sea

PANAMA

VENEZUELA

COLOMBIA

GUIANA

ECUADOR

PACIFIC

OCEAN

B R A Z I L

PERU

Callao

Lima

Tacna

ATLANTIC

ECUADOR

OCEAN

1866, naval bombardments by Spanish warships.

N

Rio de Janeiro

PARAGUAY

Humaita

Uruguayana

La Serena

CHILE

Valparaiso

ARGENTINA

URUGUAY

1895, frontier dispute.

1880, fierce battles involving Chileans and Peruvians.

1895, naval unrest and agitation.

1867, Brazilians versus Paraguayans.

1891, rebellion against government.

1865, battle involving Paraguayans versus Brazilians, Uruguayans, and Argentinians.

KEY

✳ Naval bombardments.

⚔ Notable land battles.

Ⓝ Naval engagements.

0 _____ 800
Miles

© Arthur Banks 1975

The main events were wars involving: Paraguay versus Argentina, Brazil, and Uruguay (1864-1870): Spanish operations against Peru and Chile (1864-1866), and a fight involving Chile, Bolivia, and Peru (1879-1884).

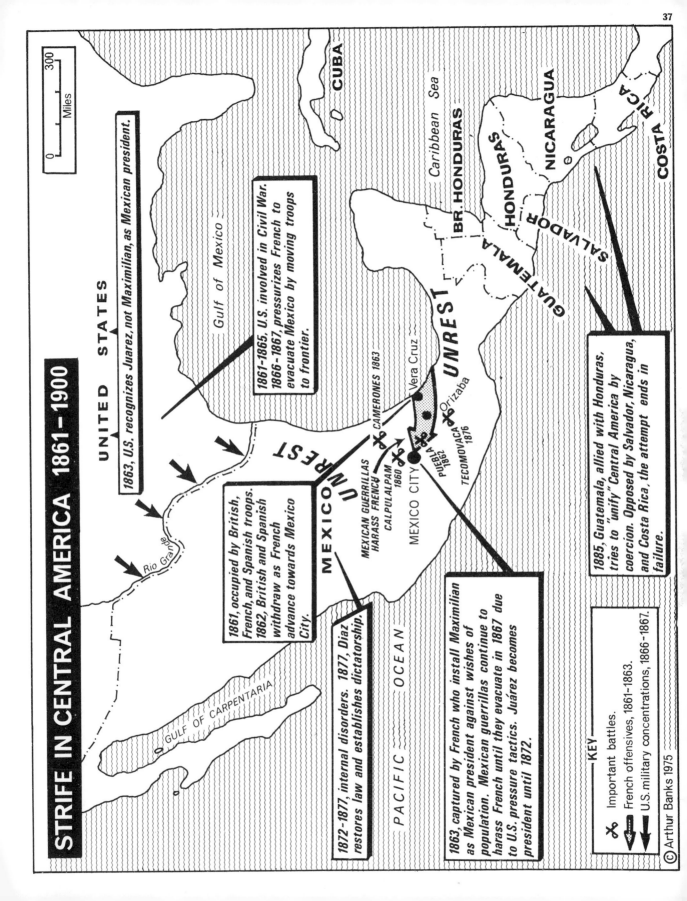

STRIFE IN CENTRAL AMERICA 1861–1900

300 Miles

UNITED STATES

CUBA

Caribbean Sea

Gulf of Mexico

1863, U.S. recognizes Juarez, not Maximilian, as Mexican president.

1861–1865, U.S. involved in Civil War. 1866–1867, pressurizes French to evacuate Mexico by moving troops to frontier.

BR. HONDURAS

HONDURAS

GUATEMALA

SALVADOR

NICARAGUA

COSTA RICA

Vera Cruz

CAMERONES 1863

Orizaba

TECOMOVACA 1876

PUEBLA 1862

MEXICAN GUERRILLAS HARASS FRENCH

CALPULALPAM 1860

MEXICO CITY

MEXICAN UNREST

Rio Grande

1861, occupied by British, French, and Spanish troops. 1862, British and Spanish withdraw as French advance towards Mexico City.

1872–1877, internal disorders. 1877, Diaz restores law and establishes dictatorship.

PACIFIC OCEAN

GULF OF CARPENTARIA

1863, captured by French who install Maximilian as Mexican president against wishes of population. Mexican guerrillas continue to harass French until they evacuate in 1867 due to U.S. pressure tactics. Juárez becomes president until 1872.

1885, Guatemala, allied with Honduras, tries to "unify" Central America by coercion. Opposed by Salvador, Nicaragua, and Costa Rica, the attempt ends in failure.

KEY

Important battles.

French offensives, 1861–1863.

U.S. military concentrations, 1866–1867.

© Arthur Banks 1975

THE UNIFICATION OF ITALY

KEY

⚔ Important battles.

━━━ Northern extent of Kingdom of Italy, 1866–1914.

••••• States joined with Kingdom of Italy.

1859, allied with France.

1860, Garibaldi and the 'Thousand' land here.

GARIBALDI

KINGDOM OF SARDINIA

KINGDOM OF THE TWO SICILIES

SAVOY

PIEDMONT

NICE

Genoa

LOMBARDY

MAGENTA 1859 ⚔

VENETIA

SOLFERINO 1859 ⚔

Po

PARMA

MODENA

LUCCA

PAPAL STATES

TUSCANY

ABRUZZI

ROME 1862 ⚔

PONTECORVO

BENEVENTO

VOLTURNO 1860 ⚔

CAMPANIA

APULIA

CALABRIA

ASPROMONTE 1862 ⚔

MILAZZO 1860 ⚔

SICILY

SICILIES

Marsala

SARDINIA

CORSICA

ADRIATIC SEA

MEDITERRANEAN SEA

0 — Miles — 300

In 1859, the Kingdom of Sardinia, supported by France, went to war to drive Austria out of Italy. Victories at Magenta and Solferino and Garibaldi's successes in the south encouraged revolutionary activities and these were followed by the collapse of most governments south of the River Po. In 1861, the Kingdom of Italy was proclaimed under Savoy, excluding Venetia and Rome: these were annexed to Italy in 1866 and 1870 respectively.

© Arthur Banks 1975

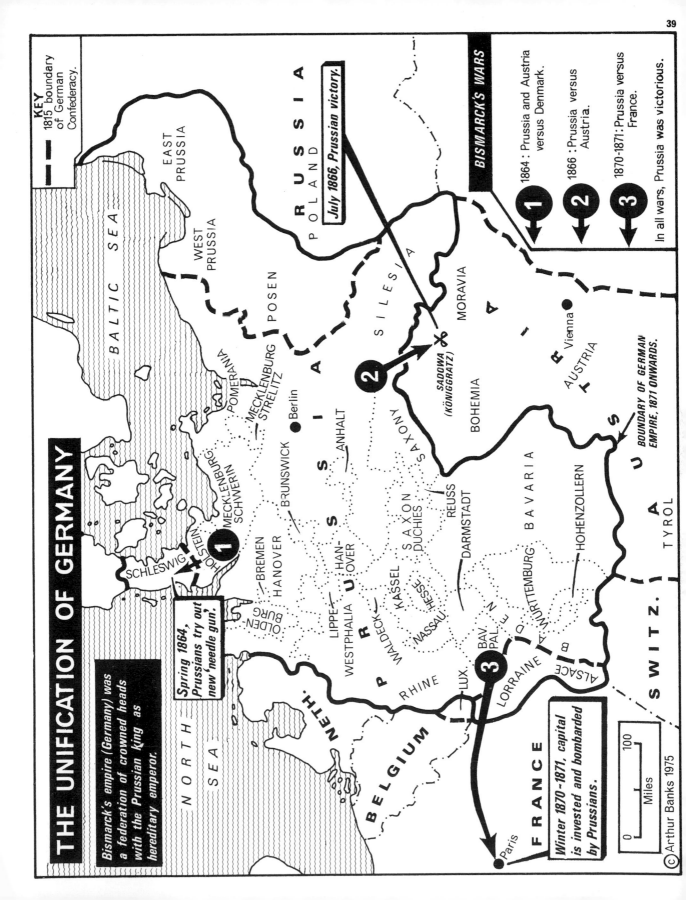

THE UNIFICATION OF GERMANY

KEY
1815 boundary of German Confederacy.

Bismarck's empire (Germany) was a federation of crowned heads with the Prussian king as hereditary emperor.

BISMARCK'S WARS

1 1864: Prussia and Austria versus Denmark.

2 1866: Prussia versus Austria.

3 1870-1871: Prussia versus France.

In all wars, Prussia was victorious.

July 1866, Prussian victory.

Spring 1864, Prussians try out new 'needle gun'.

Winter 1870-1871, capital is invested and bombarded by Prussians.

BOUNDARY OF GERMAN EMPIRE, 1871 ONWARDS.

RUSSIA

POLAND

EAST PRUSSIA

WEST PRUSSIA

POSEN

SILESIA

MORAVIA

BOHEMIA

Vienna

AUSTRIA

BALTIC SEA

POMERANIA

MECKLENBURG STRELITZ

MECKLENBURG SCHWERIN

Berlin

ANHALT

SADOWA (KÖNIGGRÄTZ)

SAXONY

SAXON DUCHIES

REUSS

BAVARIA

HOHENZOLLERN

TYROL

SWITZ.

NORTH SEA

SCHLESWIG

HOLSTEIN

BREMEN

HANOVER

OLDENBURG

BRUNSWICK

LIPPE

WESTPHALIA

HANOVER

KASSEL

HESSE

NASSAU

DARMSTADT

WÜRTTEMBURG

BAV. PAL.

ALSACE

LORRAINE

WALDECK

RHINE

LUX.

NETH.

BELGIUM

FRANCE

Paris

0 100
Miles

© Arthur Banks 1975

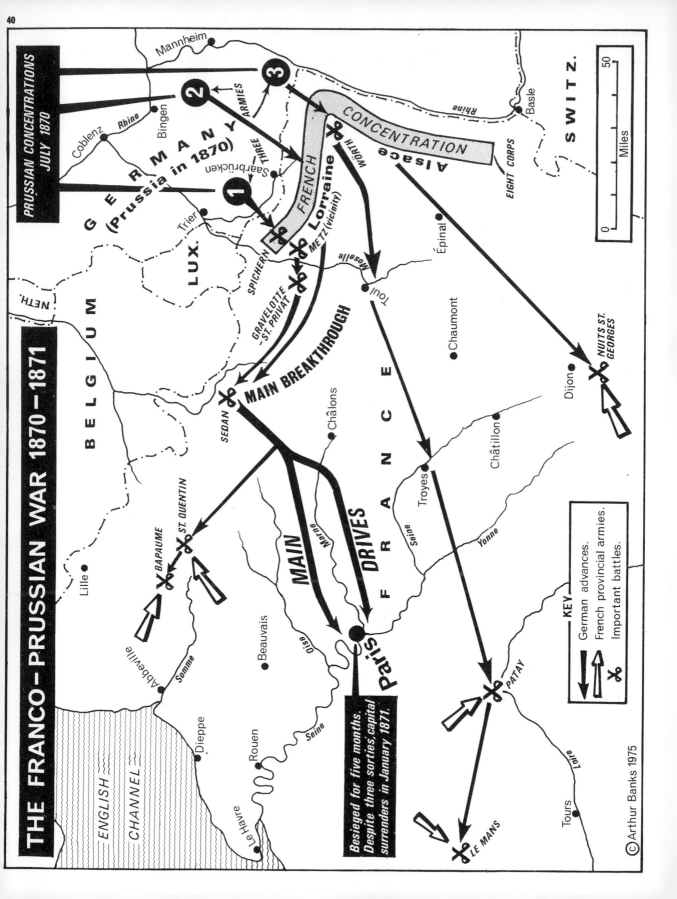

THE FRANCO-PRUSSIAN WAR 1870–1871

PRUSSIAN CONCENTRATIONS
JULY 1870

GERMANY
(Prussia in 1870)

Mannheim

Coblenz

Rhine

Bingen

Trier

LUX.

NETH.

BELGIUM

Lille

Abbeville

Somme

Dieppe

Le Havre

Rouen

Beauvais

Oise

Seine

ENGLISH CHANNEL

Saarbrucken

THREE

ARMIES

FRENCH

Lorraine

SPICHERN

METZ (vicinity)

GRAVELOTTE
– ST. PRIVAT

Moselle

WÖRTH

CONCENTRATION

Alsace

Rhine

Basle

SWITZ.

EIGHT CORPS

50

Miles

0

SEDAN

MAIN BREAKTHROUGH

Châlons

MAIN

Marne

DRIVES

F R A N C E

Toul

Épinal

Chaumont

Troyes

Seine

Yonne

Châtillon

Dijon

NUITS ST.
GEORGES

ST. QUENTIN

BAPAUME

Paris

Besieged for five months.
Despite three sorties, capital
surrenders in January 1871.

PATAY

LE MANS

Tours

Loire

KEY
German advances.
French provincial armies.
Important battles.

©Arthur Banks 1975

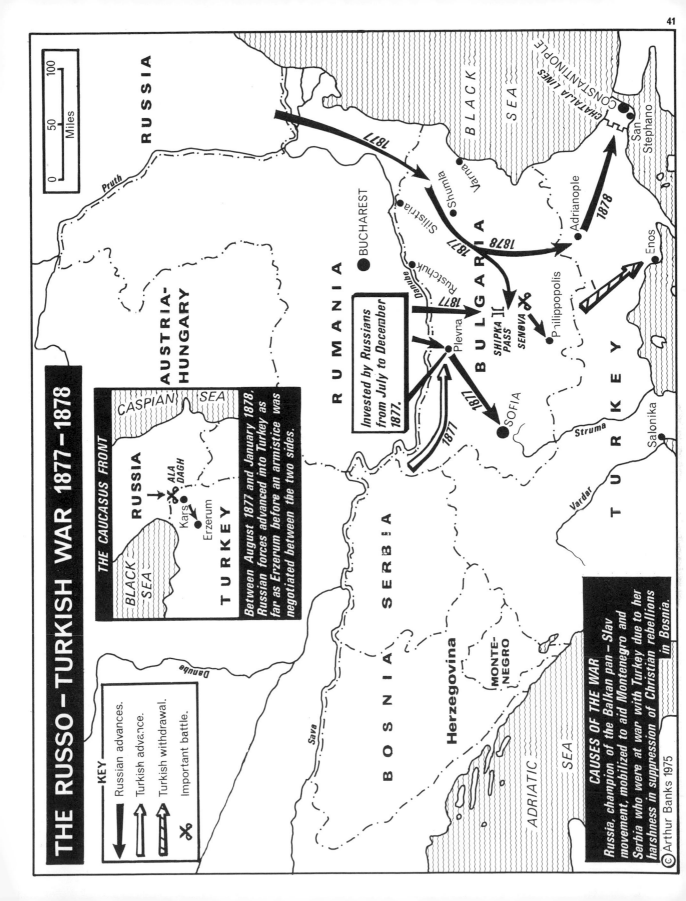

THE RUSSO-TURKISH WAR 1877-1878

KEY
- Russian advances.
- Turkish advance.
- Turkish withdrawal.
- Important battle.

THE CAUCASUS FRONT

Between August 1877 and January 1878, Russian forces advanced into Turkey as far as Erzerum before an armistice was negotiated between the two sides.

CASPIAN SEA

RUSSIA

ALA DAGH

Kars • Erzerum •

BLACK SEA

TURKEY

RUSSIA

AUSTRIA-HUNGARY

Pruth

Danube

Sava

BOSNIA

SERBIA

Herzegovina

MONTE-NEGRO

ADRIATIC SEA

RUMANIA

BUCHAREST

Danube

Silistria

Rustchuk

1877

Invested by Russians from July to December 1877.

Plevra

SOFIA

1877

BULGARIA

SHIPKA PASS

SENOVA

Phillippopilis

Struma

Vardar

BLACK SEA

Shumla

Varna

Adrianople

1878

1877

1878

1877

CHATALJA LINES

CONSTANTINOPLE

San Stephano

Enos

TURKEY

Salonika

1878

CAUSES OF THE WAR

Russia, champion of the Balkan pan-Slav movement, mobilized to aid Montenegro and Serbia who were at war with Turkey due to her harshness in suppression of Christian rebellions in Bosnia.

© Arthur Banks 1975

Miles
0 50 100

AUSTRIA–HUNGARY 1867–1918

KEY

— Frontier of Austria–Hungary 1918.

– – – Kingdom of Hungary.

R U S S I A

R O U M A N I A (Rumania)

BULGARIA

SERBIA

GERMANY

I T A L Y

SWITZ.

1878–1912, occupied by Austria.

Established with independent status in 1913.

Until 1878, part of Ottoman Empire: 1878–1908, under Austria: 1908, annexed to Austria.

Lemberg

Tarnopol

Czernowitz

GALICIA

Przemysl

Cracow

Teschen

SILESIA

Brünn

MORAVIA

Pilsen

Prague

Eger

BOHEMIA

Elbe

Kassa

Miskolcz

Debreczen

G A R Y

H U N

TRANSYLVANIA

Kolozsvar

Brasso

Maros

Temesvar

Orsova

Budapest

Szeged

Pecs

Danube

Vienna

Pozsony

LOWER AUSTRIA

Linz

UPPER AUSTRIA

Graz

STYRIA

CARINTHIA

CARNIOLA

Drava

Sava

SLAVONIA

CROATIA

Fiume

ISTRIA

Pola

Trieste

GRADISCA

GORIZIA

Salzburg

Innsbruck

VORARLBERG

TYROL

Trent

Po

DALMATIA

Spalato

Ragusa

BOSNIA

Sarajevo

HERZEGOVINA

MONTE-NEGRO

SANJAK OF NOVIBAZAR

ALBANIA

ADRIATIC SEA

Danube

0   300   Miles

© Arthur Banks 1975

THE WORLD FOLLOWING THE CONGRESS OF BERLIN 1878

KEY

- British territories.
- Russian territories.
- Turkish (Ottoman Empire) territories.
- United States' territories.
- French territories.
- Dutch territories.
- Danish territories.
- Spanish territories.
- Portuguese territories.

Note how Germany (growing in power in Europe) has no imperialist ambitions at this period.

ICELAND

GREENLAND

DENMARK
BRITAIN
FRANCE
SPAIN
PORTUGAL
HOL-LAND

Azores (P)
Madeira (P)
Canary Is. (S)
Gibraltar (B)

R U S S I A

TURKEY

PACIFIC OCEAN

Mariana Is. (S)
Caroline Is. (S)
PHILIPPINE IS. (S)
Hong Kong (B)
FR. INDO CHINA
BOR NEO
Andaman Is. (B)
CEYLON
INDIA
Laccadives (B)
Maldives (B)
DUTCH EAST INDIES

Fiji Is. (S)
New Caledonia (F)
Norfolk I. (B)
Chatham I. (B)
NEW ZEALAND
AUSTRALIA
Tasmania

Seychelles (B)
Mauritius (B)
Reunion (F)
MADAGASCAR
INDIAN OCEAN

Malta (B)
ALGERIA
EGYPT
SENEGAL
S. LEONE
GOLD COAST
ANGOLA
MOZAM-BIQUE
SOUTH AFRICA
Walvisch Bay (B)
Ascension (B)
St. Helena I. (B)
Tristan da Cunha (B)

ATLANTIC OCEAN

Bermuda (B)
Bahama Is. (B)
Porto Rico (S)
Cuba (S)
Jamaica (B)
Leeward Is. (B)
Windward Is. (B)
Trinidad (B)
BR. GUIANA
FR. GUIANA
BRAZIL
PERU
URUGUAY
ARGENTINA
CHILE
Falkland Is. (B)

CANADA
UNITED STATES
ALASKA
MEXICO
BRITISH HONDURAS
EQUADOR

PACIFIC OCEAN

Malden I. (B)
Marquesas Is. (F)
Paumotu Is. (F)
Society Is. (F)
Pitcairn I. (B)

0 — Miles — 2000

© Arthur Banks 1975

THE ZULU WAR 1879

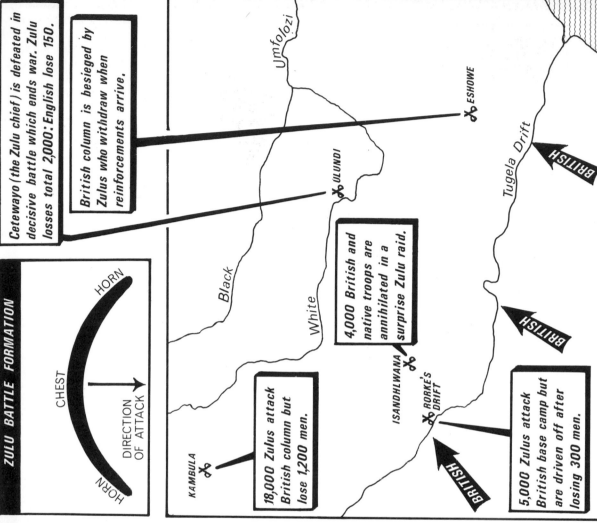

ZULU BATTLE FORMATION

HORN

CHEST

DIRECTION OF ATTACK

HORN

Cetewayo (the Zulu chief) is defeated in decisive battle which ends war. Zulu losses total 2,000: English lose 150.

British column is besieged by Zulus who withdraw when reinforcements arrive.

4,000 British and native troops are annihilated in a surprise Zulu raid.

18,000 Zulus attack British column but lose 1,200 men.

5,000 Zulus attack British base camp but are driven off after losing 300 men.

ESHOWE

ULUNDI

ISANDHLWANA

RORKE'S DRIFT

KAMBULA

BRITISH

Umfolozi

Black

White

Tugela Drift

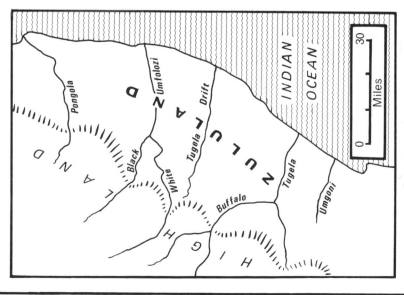

Pongola

Umfolozi

Black

White

Tugela Drift

Buffalo

Tugela

Umgoni

ZULULAND

HIGH

INDIAN OCEAN

Miles
0   30

MAIN EVENTS

1 22 JANUARY: Battle of Isandhlwana.
2 22/23 JANUARY: Battle of Rorke's Drift.
3 JANUARY-APRIL: Siege of Eshowe.
4 29 MARCH: Battle of Kambula.
5 4 JULY: Battle of Ulundi.

© Arthur Banks 1975

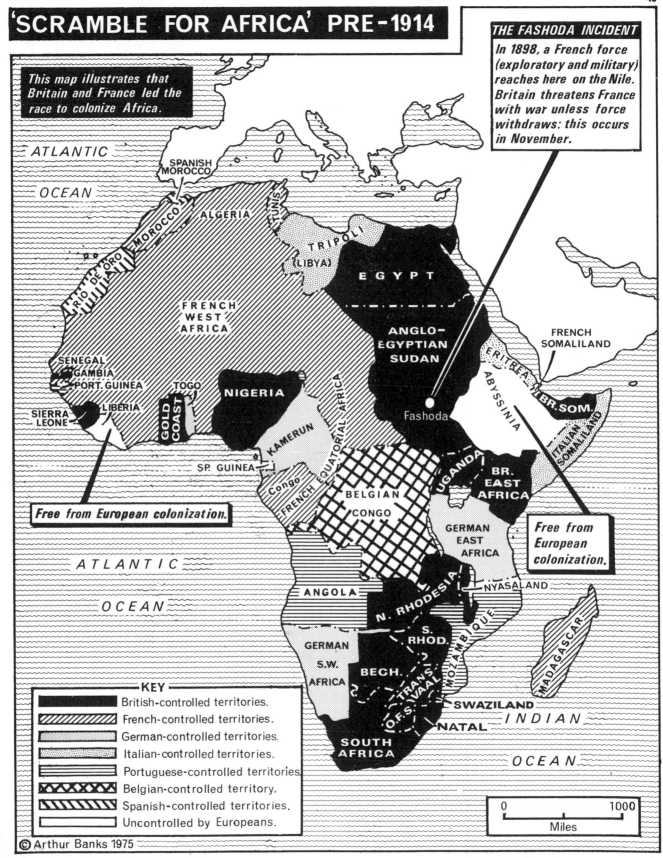

'SCRAMBLE FOR AFRICA' PRE-1914

THE FASHODA INCIDENT
In 1898, a French force (exploratory and military) reaches here on the Nile. Britain threatens France with war unless force withdraws: this occurs in November.

This map illustrates that Britain and France led the race to colonize Africa.

ATLANTIC
OCEAN

SPANISH MOROCCO

RIO DE ORO
MOROCCO
ALGERIA
TUNIS
TRIPOLI (LIBYA)
EGYPT
ANGLO-EGYPTIAN SUDAN

FRENCH WEST AFRICA

FRENCH SOMALILAND

ERITREA
BR. SOM.
ABYSSINIA

SENEGAL
GAMBIA
PORT. GUINEA
SIERRA LEONE
LIBERIA
TOGO
GOLD COAST
NIGERIA
SP. GUINEA
KAMERUN
Congo
FRENCH EQUATORIAL AFRICA

Fashoda

ITALIAN SOMALILAND

Free from European colonization.

BELGIAN CONGO

UGANDA
BR. EAST AFRICA

GERMAN EAST AFRICA

Free from European colonization.

ATLANTIC
OCEAN

ANGOLA

GERMAN S.W. AFRICA

BECH.

N. RHODESIA
NYASALAND
S. RHOD.

MOZAMBIQUE

MADAGASCAR

TRANS VAAL
O.F.S.
NATAL
SWAZILAND
SOUTH AFRICA

INDIAN
OCEAN

KEY
- British-controlled territories.
- French-controlled territories.
- German-controlled territories.
- Italian-controlled territories.
- Portuguese-controlled territories.
- Belgian-controlled territory.
- Spanish-controlled territories.
- Uncontrolled by Europeans.

© Arthur Banks 1975

0   1000
Miles

THE BATTLE OF TEL-EL-KEBIR 12–13 SEPTEMBER 1882

Following this British victory, the Egyptians were pursued to Cairo where they surrendered on 14 September.

BRITISH

Royal Marine Artillery

HQ

CAVALRY

1 BRIGADE

2 BRIGADE

ROYAL ARTILLERY BRIGADE

4 BRIGADE

3 BRIGADE

NAVAL BRIGADE

INDIAN CONTINGENT

D E S E R T

TRENCH

forward position

infantry   guns   infantry   guns   infantry

EGYPTIANS
(plus Sudanese)

TEL-EL-KEBIR VILLAGE

Railway

Sweetwater Canal

to Cairo

LOCATION MAP

Mediterranean Sea

Port Said
Ismailia
Suez Canal
Suez

TEL-EL-KEBIR

E G Y P T

Nile

CAIRO

Alexandria

0   100
Miles

0   3,000
Yards

SCORE SHEET

British engaged:	13,000
British casualties:	457
Egyptians engaged:	25,000
Egyptian casualties:	2,803

© Arthur Banks 1975

THE BATTLE OF OMDURMAN 2 SEPTEMBER 1898

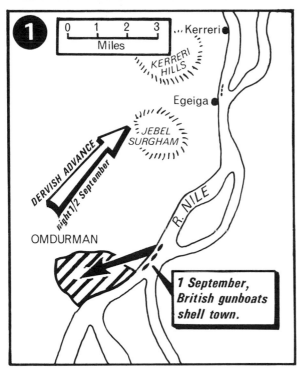

1

0 1 2 3
Miles

Kerreri

KERRERI HILLS

Egeiga

JEBEL SURGHAM

DERVISH ADVANCE
night 1/2 September

R. NILE

OMDURMAN

1 September, British gunboats shell town.

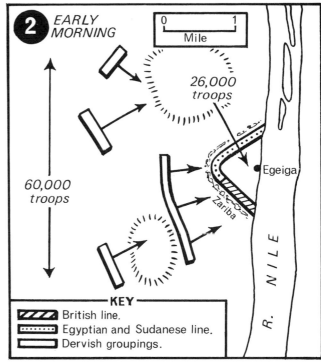

2 EARLY MORNING

0 1
Mile

26,000 troops

60,000 troops

Egeiga

Zariba

R. NILE

KEY
British line.
Egyptian and Sudanese line.
Dervish groupings.

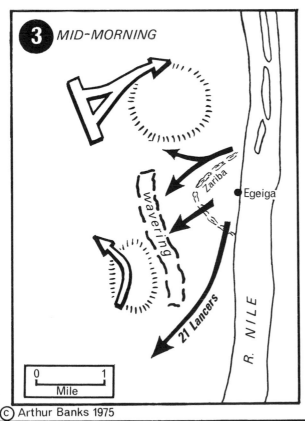

3 MID-MORNING

Zariba

Egeiga

wavering

21 Lancers

R. NILE

0 1
Mile

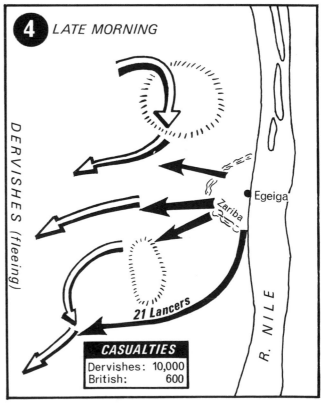

4 LATE MORNING

DERVISHES (fleeing)

Zariba

Egeiga

21 Lancers

R. NILE

CASUALTIES
Dervishes: 10,000
British: 600

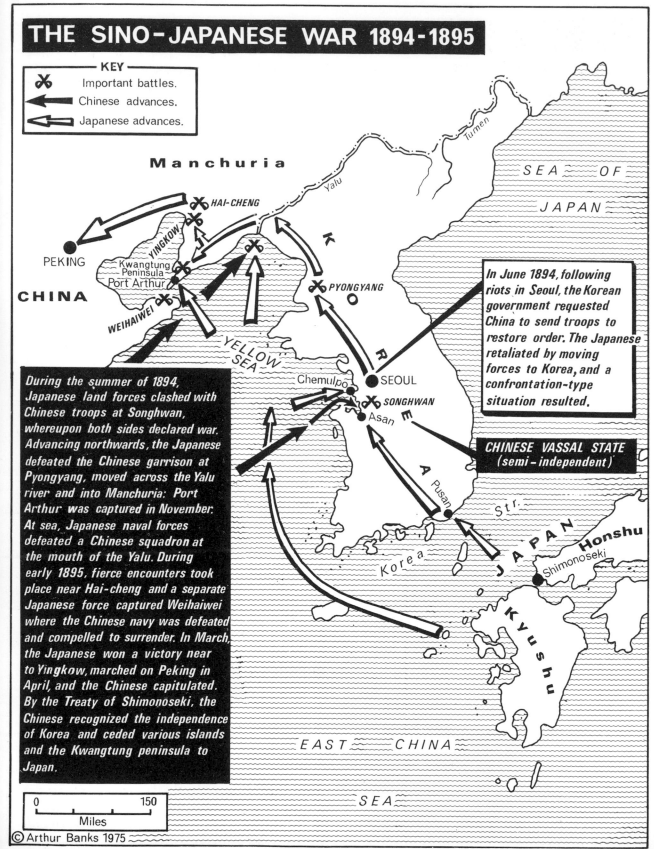

THE SINO-JAPANESE WAR 1894-1895

KEY
- ✂ Important battles.
- ⬅ Chinese advances.
- ⇐ Japanese advances.

Manchuria

SEA OF JAPAN

Turmen

Yalu

HAI-CHENG

YINGKOW

PEKING

Kwangtung Peninsula
Port Arthur

WEIHAIWEI

CHINA

PYONGYANG

K O R E A

In June 1894, following riots in Seoul, the Korean government requested China to send troops to restore order. The Japanese retaliated by moving forces to Korea, and a confrontation-type situation resulted.

YELLOW SEA

Chemulpo

SEOUL

SONGHWAN

Asan

CHINESE VASSAL STATE (semi-independent)

Pusan

Str.

JAPAN

Honshu

Shimonoseki

Korea

Kyushu

During the summer of 1894, Japanese land forces clashed with Chinese troops at Songhwan, whereupon both sides declared war. Advancing northwards, the Japanese defeated the Chinese garrison at Pyongyang, moved across the Yalu river and into Manchuria: Port Arthur was captured in November. At sea, Japanese naval forces defeated a Chinese squadron at the mouth of the Yalu. During early 1895, fierce encounters took place near Hai-cheng and a separate Japanese force captured Weihaiwei where the Chinese navy was defeated and compelled to surrender. In March, the Japanese won a victory near to Yingkow, marched on Peking in April, and the Chinese capitulated. By the Treaty of Shimonoseki, the Chinese recognized the independence of Korea and ceded various islands and the Kwangtung peninsula to Japan.

EAST CHINA

SEA

0   150
Miles

© Arthur Banks 1975

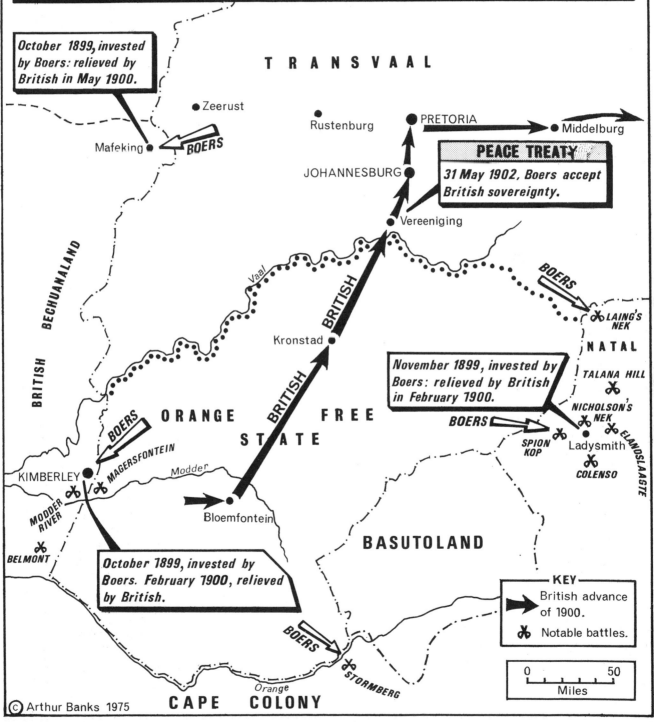

THE BOER (or SOUTH AFRICAN) WAR 1899-1902

The war was in two phases: the first (1899-1902) was an active open fight between Boers and British Empire troops which seemed to end with the victorious British advance of 1900. The second (1900-1902) was a guerrilla-style campaign by the Boers which caused the British to raid farms and homes and to force Boer women and children into concentration camps.

October 1899, invested by Boers: relieved by British in May 1900.

TRANSVAAL

Zeerust

Rustenburg

PRETORIA

Middelburg

Mafeking

BOERS

JOHANNESBURG

PEACE TREATY

31 May 1902, Boers accept British sovereignty.

Vereeniging

BECHUANALAND

BRITISH

Vaal

BOERS

LAING'S NEK

Kronstad

NATAL

November 1899, invested by Boers: relieved by British in February 1900.

TALANA HILL

BRITISH

NICHOLSON'S NEK

BOERS

BOERS

ORANGE

FREE

SPION KOP

Ladysmith

ELANDSLAAGTE

MAGERSFONTEIN

STATE

KIMBERLEY

Modder

COLENSO

MODDER RIVER

Bloemfontein

BASUTOLAND

BELMONT

October 1899, invested by Boers. February 1900, relieved by British.

KEY

British advance of 1900.

Notable battles.

BOERS

STORMBERG

0   50

Miles

Orange

© Arthur Banks 1975

CAPE COLONY

THE "BOXER" REBELLION 1900

THE TWO ALLIED ATTEMPTS TO RELIEVE PEKING

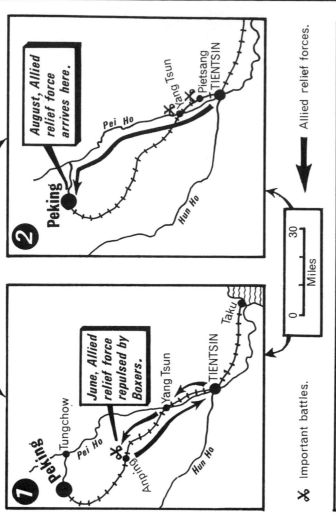

2 August, Allied relief force arrives here.

Peking · Pei Ho · Yang Tsun · Pietsang · TIENTSIN · Hun Ho

1 June, Allied relief force repulsed by Boxers.

Peking · Tungchow · Pei Ho · Anping · Yang Tsun · TIENTSIN · Taku · Hun Ho

0 — 30 Miles

→ Allied relief forces.

✄ Important battles.

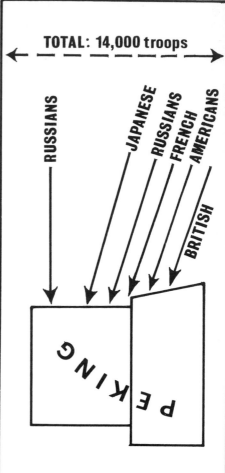

TOTAL: 14,000 troops

RUSSIANS · JAPANESE · RUSSIANS · FRENCH · AMERICANS · BRITISH

PEKING

PLAN OF PEKING

WALL · TARTAR CITY · Imperial City · Forbidden City · *Palace* · LEGATION AREA · *North Cathedral* · *South Cathedral* · BESIEGED DIPLOMATS AND FAMILIES · WALL · CHINESE CITY · WALL

For fifty-five days during the summer of 1900, some two thousand Europeans and Chinese Christians were besieged in Peking by a peasant army known as "Boxers" (Society of Righteous Harmonious Fists). Two attempts were made to relieve them by Allied (British, French, American, Russian, and Japanese) forces, the first (in June) being unsuccessful, the second (in August) succeeding.

51

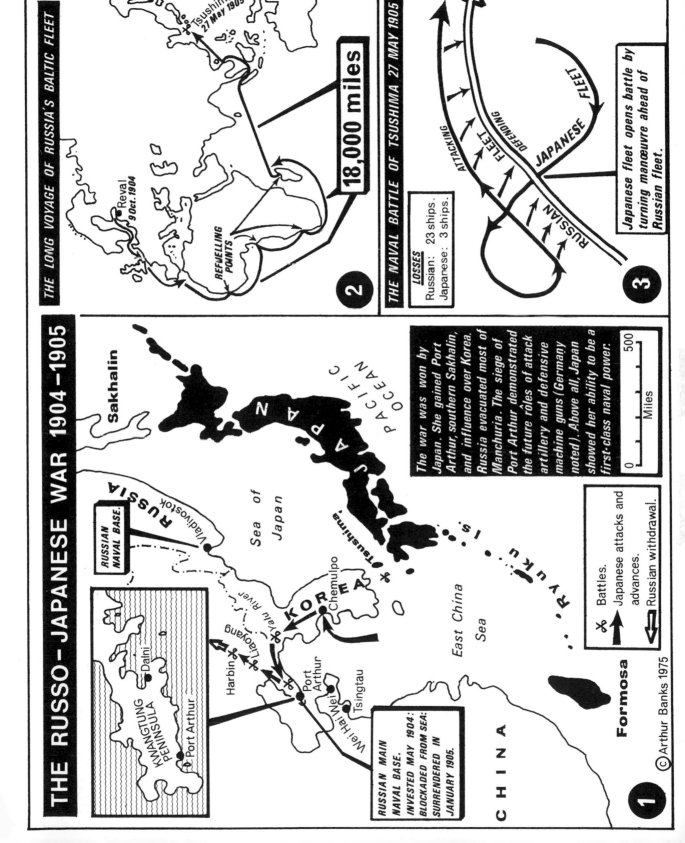

THE RUSSO-JAPANESE WAR 1904–1905

THE LONG VOYAGE OF RUSSIA'S BALTIC FLEET

Tsushima 27 May 1905

Reval 9 Oct. 1904

REFUELLING POINTS

18,000 miles

2

THE NAVAL BATTLE OF TSUSHIMA 27 MAY 1905

LOSSES
Russian: 23 ships.
Japanese: 3 ships.

ATTACKING

DEFENDING

JAPANESE FLEET

RUSSIAN FLEET

Japanese fleet opens battle by turning manoeuvre ahead of Russian fleet.

3

Sakhalin

J A P A N

P A C I F I C   O C E A N

Tsushima

RUSSIAN NAVAL BASE.

Vladivostok

Sea of Japan

Harbin

Liaoyang

Yalu River

KOREA

Chemulpo

Port Arthur

Wei Hai Wei

Tsingtau

East China Sea

RYUKYU IS.

Formosa

C H I N A

Dalni

KWANGTUNG PENINSULA

Port Arthur

RUSSIAN MAIN NAVAL BASE. INVESTED MAY 1904: BLOCKADED FROM SEA: SURRENDERED IN JANUARY 1905.

The war was won by Japan. She gained Port Arthur, southern Sakhalin, and influence over Korea. Russia evacuated most of Manchuria. The siege of Port Arthur demonstrated the future rôles of attack artillery and defensive machine guns (Germany noted). Above all, Japan showed her ability to be a first-class naval power.

0   500
Miles

✳ Battles.
➤ Japanese attacks and advances.
⇨ Russian withdrawal.

© Arthur Banks 1975

1

CHIEF ARMIES OF THE WORLD 1906

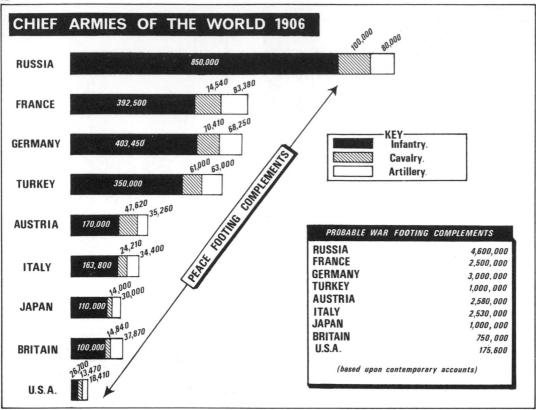

| RUSSIA | 850,000 | 100,000 | 80,000 |

PEACE FOOTING COMPLEMENTS

Country	Infantry	Cavalry	Artillery
RUSSIA	850,000	100,000	80,000
FRANCE	392,500	74,540	83,380
GERMANY	403,450	10,410	68,250
TURKEY	350,000	61,000	63,000
AUSTRIA	170,000	47,620	35,260
ITALY	163,800	24,210	34,400
JAPAN	110,000	14,000	30,000
BRITAIN	100,000	14,840	37,870
U.S.A.	26,700	13,470	18,410

KEY
- Infantry.
- Cavalry.
- Artillery.

PROBABLE WAR FOOTING COMPLEMENTS

RUSSIA	4,600,000
FRANCE	2,500,000
GERMANY	3,000,000
TURKEY	1,000,000
AUSTRIA	2,580,000
ITALY	2,530,000
JAPAN	1,000,000
BRITAIN	750,000
U.S.A.	175,600

(based upon contemporary accounts)

CHIEF NAVIES OF THE WORLD 1906

This was the year when the British 'Dreadnought' battleship was launched.

COUNTRY	BATTLESHIPS (first class)	BATTLESHIPS (other classes)	CRUISERS (first class)	CRUISERS (other classes)	DESTROYERS, SUBMARINES, M.T.B.'s	OFFICERS & MEN
BRITAIN	45	15	38	87	232	129,000
U.S.A.	15	11	7	14	47	37,000
FRANCE	11	19	10	37	271	29,500
GERMANY	18	13	6	24	103	33,500
RUSSIA	4	7	2	10	145	60,000
ITALY	4	9	3	17	61	26,800
JAPAN	10	4	9	17	72	36,000

<u>Note</u>: it was the axiom of British naval policy that her navy should roughly equal in strength the combined fleets of the next two largest naval powers.

THE ITALO-TURKISH WAR 1911-1912

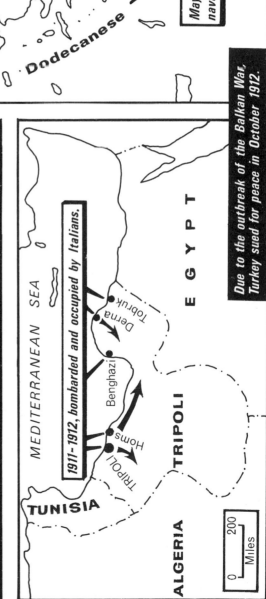

BLACK SEA

TURKEY

TURKEY

April 1912, Italian naval units attack straits which are closed by Turks.

Dardanelles

Rhodes

Dodecanese

May 1912, occupied by Italian naval forces.

SPAIN

ITALY

TURKEY

MEDITERRANEAN SEA

TRIPOLI

TUNISIA

ALGERIA

MOROCCO

FRENCH EMPIRE

MAIN CAUSE OF THE WAR. Italy wished to counterbalance the French empire in North Africa by conquering the Turkish colony of Tripoli (Libya).

MEDITERRANEAN SEA

EGYPT

1911-1912, bombarded and occupied by Italians.

Derna
Tobruk

Benghazi

Homs

TRIPOLI

TRIPOLI

TUNISIA

ALGERIA

Due to the outbreak of the Balkan War, Turkey sued for peace in October 1912.

0   200
Miles

© Arthur Banks 1975

CRISES IN NORTH AFRICA AND THE BALKANS 1905-1912

0   300 Miles

RUSSIA

GERMANY

AUSTRIA-HUNGARY

SWITZ.

ITALY

FRANCE

BRITAIN

SPAIN

Black Sea

Constantinople

T U R K E Y
(**O T T O M A N E M P I R E**)

BULGARIA

REVOLT SPREADS

Salonika

GREECE

union

Crete

Rhodes

Herzegovina

Bosnia

Mediterranean Sea

Cyrenaica

TRIPOLI (LIBYA)

Tripolitania

F E Z Z A N

ATLANTIC OCEAN

M O R O C C O

Algeciras
Tangier
Fez
Agadir
Ouchy
Tunis (French)

closer links

After the Bosnian crisis, Russia saw Germany as her future main foe, not Austria.

2 *1908 YOUNG TURK REVOLT*

Young Turkey Party demands constitutional government; this is conceded by Sultan of Turkey. Bulgaria violates Treaty of Berlin 1878 (Article One) by proclaiming herself an independent kingdom. Greece-Crete union.

5 *1911-1912 TURCO-ITALIAN WAR*

Having lost Tunis to France in 1881, Italy views activity in Morocco with suspicion. Fearful of eventually losing Tripoli also, she declares war on Turkey (29 September 1911) and her troops occupy Tripoli's coastal zone (shaded on map). Turkey fears an attack by the Balkan League and concludes peace with Italy at Ouchy (15 October 1912). Italy virtually (not formally) annexes the whole area.

1912, Italy seizes the Dodecanese and Rhodes.

3 *1908 CRISIS IN BOSNIA*

Austria annexes Bosnia and Herzegovina (mainly Serb-populated). Germany supports Austria. Slavs look to Russia for support, but latter is still weak after Russo-Japanese war (1904-1905). Faced by the Austro-German combination, Russia backs out.

As a result of the crisis in Bosnia, Italy distrusted Austria, thus weakening the Triple Alliance.

The crises in Morocco caused France to draw closer to Britain.

1 *1905-1906 CRISIS IN MOROCCO*

31 March 1905, Kaiser Wilhelm II visits Tangier and claims equal rights for Germany in Morocco and the maintenance of the Moorish Empire; this is a challenge to the position of France in Morocco. Britain supports France. The Algeciras Conference of 1906 avoids a Franco-German clash.

Britain was worried over development of Agadir; future naval base for Germany?

4 *1911 CRISIS IN MOROCCO*

French army units occupy Fez to assist Sultan in maintaining control against rebels. Germany views this action as a breach of the 1906 Algeciras Treaty and despatches warship SMS "Panther" to Agadir to safeguard German interests. 5 November 1911, Germany recognizes French protectorate in return for territorial adjustments in her favour in West Africa.

Italian occupation of the interior hampered by both Arab and Turkish hostility.

© Arthur Banks 1973

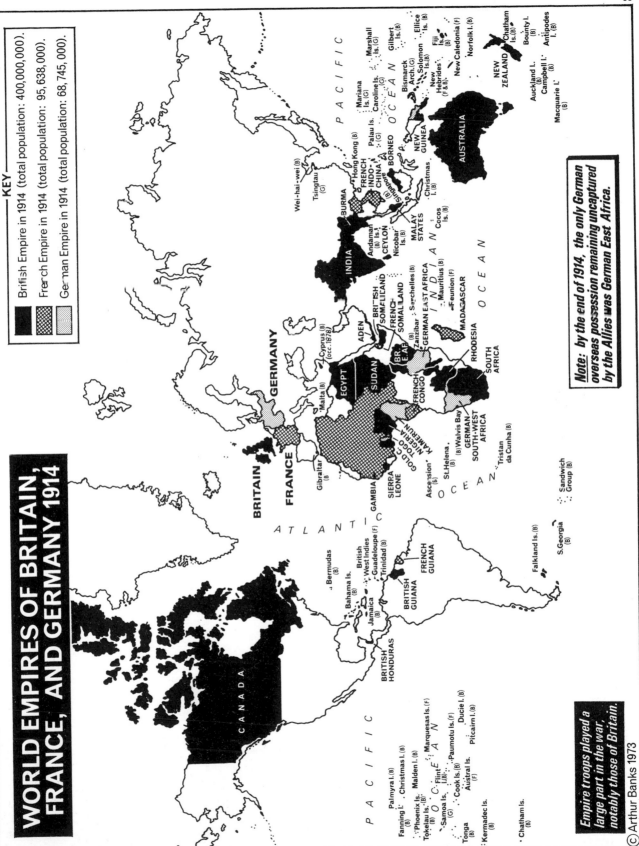

WORLD EMPIRES OF BRITAIN, FRANCE, AND GERMANY 1914

— KEY —

- British Empire in 1914 (total population: 400,000,000).
- French Empire in 1914 (total population: 95,638,000).
- German Empire in 1914 (total population: 68,745,000).

Note: by the end of 1914, the only German overseas possession remaining uncaptured by the Allies was German East Africa.

Empire troops played a large part in the war, notably those of Britain.

© Arthur Banks 1973

THE FIRST BALKAN WAR 1912-1913*

❶ The General Situation

Note: in two parts, viz.,
1. *18 Oct.- 3 Dec. 1912.*
2. *3 Feb.- 10 May 1913.*

Russia supports Serbia's demand for a port on the Adriatic coast.

Austria opposes Serbia's demand for a port on Adriatic coast

Rumania does not join Balkan allies but is keen to share in their gains.

Bulgaria is anxious to obtain territory to her south, most of which has been promised to her.

Greece occupies and wishes to retain Salonika, which is claimed by Bulgaria.

Montenegro declared war on Turkey on 8 October 1912, and the other three Christian states presented their ultimatums to Turkey on 18 October, whereupon Turkey replied by declaring war upon them. Britain and Germany restrained their allies temporarily to avoid a full-scale conflict enveloping Europe, but Turkey lost territory.

AUSTRIA-HUNGARY
RUMANIA
Belgrade
Bucharest
SERBIA
Black Sea
BULGARIA
Sofia
Scutari
Adriatic
ITALY
MONTE-NEGRO
Sea
Midia
Constantinople
OTTOMAN (TURKEY) EMPIRE
Adrianople
Salonika
Enos
Aegean Sea
GREECE
Athens
Dodecanese

KEY
░ Countries of the Balkan League.
▨ Territory lost by Turkey at Peace of London.

0 ——— 200
Miles

MAIN REASON FOR WAR: BALKAN STATES EAGER TO "LIBERATE" THEIR COMPATRIOTS STILL WITHIN TURKEY IN EUROPE.

❷ The Military Operations

RUMANIA

KEY
▷▷▷ Montenegrin advances.
▷▷▷ Serb advances.
▨▷ Greek advances.
⟩⟩⟩ Bulgar advances.
◀ Turkish counter-attacks.

BOSNIA
SERBIA
Drina *Lim* *Ibar*
Niš
Danube
Iskûr
BULGARIA
Sofia
Kustendil
Tunja Yambol
Black Sea
Burgas
Cetinje
FALLS 22/4/13
MONTE NEGRO
Scutari
Kumanovo
Skopje
Plovdiv
Kirk Kilisse
Armistice concluded.
Durazzo
Tirana
Vardar
Monastir
Maritsa
Adrianople
FALLS 25/3/13
Lule Burgas
Midia
Chatalja
OTTOMAN EMPIRE (TURKEY)
Aliakmon
Salonika
Dedeagach
Constantinople
Grevena
Enos
Gallipoli
FALLS 6/3/13
Janina
Larissa
GREECE
Preveza

The Serbs gained victories at Kumanovo (23 October) and Monastir (15 November). The Bulgarians gained victories at Kirk Kilisse (23 October) and Lule Burgas (30 October), but failed in their attack on the fortified lines of Chatalja (17-18 November). The Greeks moved into Macedonia occupying Salonika on 9 November.

0 ——— 50
Miles

© Arthur Banks 1973

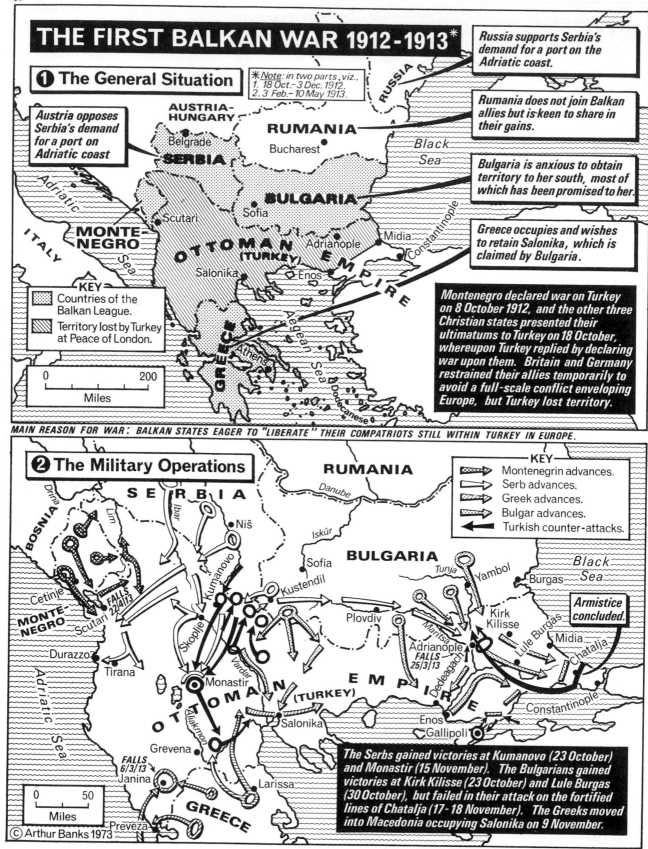

THE SECOND BALKAN WAR 1913 *

❶ The General Situation

✳ *Note: dates, viz., 30 June - 30 July.*

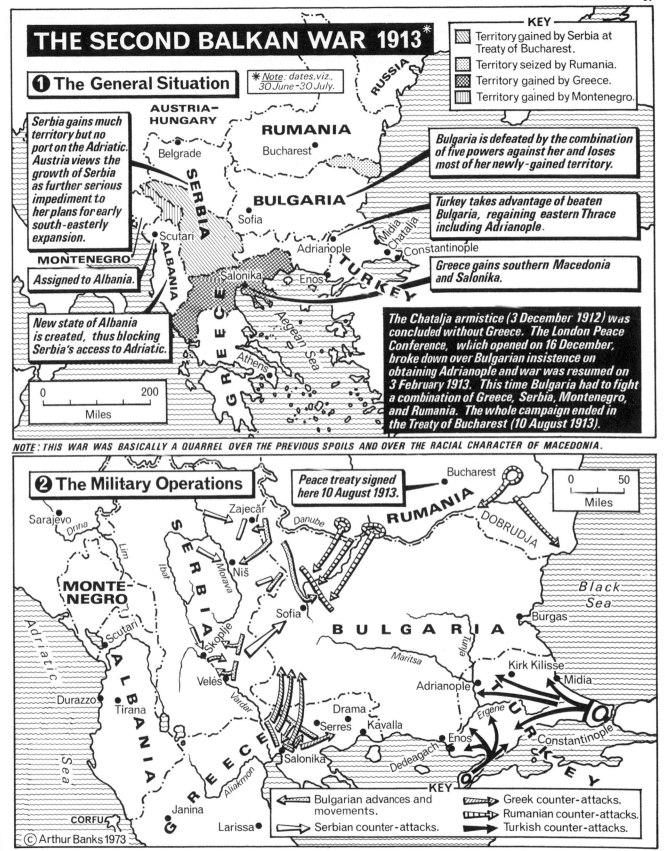

AUSTRIA-HUNGARY

RUSSIA

RUMANIA

Belgrade

Bucharest

Serbia gains much territory but no port on the Adriatic. Austria views the growth of Serbia as further serious impediment to her plans for early south-easterly expansion.

SERBIA

BULGARIA

Sofia

Scutari

MONTENEGRO

Assigned to Albania.

ALBANIA

Midia
Chatalja
Adrianople
Constantinople

TURKEY

Bulgaria is defeated by the combination of five powers against her and loses most of her newly-gained territory.

Turkey takes advantage of beaten Bulgaria, regaining eastern Thrace including Adrianople.

Greece gains southern Macedonia and Salonika.

Salonika

Enos

GREECE

New state of Albania is created, thus blocking Serbia's access to Adriatic.

Aegean Sea

Athens

The Chatalja armistice (3 December 1912) was concluded without Greece. The London Peace Conference, which opened on 16 December, broke down over Bulgarian insistence on obtaining Adrianople and war was resumed on 3 February 1913. This time Bulgaria had to fight a combination of Greece, Serbia, Montenegro, and Rumania. The whole campaign ended in the Treaty of Bucharest (10 August 1913).

0 ____ 200
Miles

NOTE: THIS WAR WAS BASICALLY A QUARREL OVER THE PREVIOUS SPOILS AND OVER THE RACIAL CHARACTER OF MACEDONIA.

❷ The Military Operations

Peace treaty signed here 10 August 1913.

0 ____ 50
Miles

Sarajevo

RUMANIA

Bucharest

DOBRUDJA

Drina

Lim

Zaječar

Danube

MONTE-NEGRO

SERBIA

Ibar

Morava

Niš

Scutari

Skoplje

Sofia

BULGARIA

Black Sea

Burgas

Veles

Vardar

Drama

Serres

Kavalla

Maritsa

Tunja

Adrianople

Kirk Kilisse

Midia

ALBANIA

Durazzo

Tirana

Ergene

Enos

Constantinople

TURKEY

GREECE

Salonika

Dedeagach

Aliakmon

Janina

Larissa

CORFU

© Arthur Banks 1973

THE GROWTH OF THE RUSSIAN EMPIRE IN EUROPE PRE - 1914

0 ___ 200
Miles

KOLA

Uleaborg

Archangel

FINLAND

N O V G O R O D

Helsingfors

St Petersburg

Vologda

Ustiug

Novgorod

Perm

Memel

Riga

Pskov

Tver

Nizhni Novgorod

Rzhev

Kazan

LITHUANIA

Vilna

Moscow

Ufa

Smolensk

Minsk

Niemen

Pripet

Warsaw

POLAND

VOLHYNIA

Orel

Samara

BULGARIANS OF KAZAN

Novgorod Severski

Voronezh

Kiev

UKRAINE

Saratov

Ural

Uralsk

Kharkov

T A R T A R S

GOLDEN

HORDE

A S T R A K H A N

Dniester

BESSARABIA

Odessa

Kherson

DON COSSACKS

Pruth

Dnieper

Don

Azov

Astrakhan

Volga

KRIM

Kuban

Sevastopol

Danube

Terek

Black Sea

Caspian Sea

Batum

Tiflis

Baku

Krasnovodsk

Kars

Aras

Atrek

KEY

- ■ Principality of Moscow 1462.
- Acquisitions 1462 - 1505.
- Acquisitions 1505 - 1584.
- Acquisitions 1584 - 1689.
- Acquisitions 1689 - 1762.
- Acquisitions 1762 - 1801.
- Acquisitions 1801 - 1914.

© Arthur Banks 1975

THE GROWTH OF BRITISH AND RUSSIAN INFLUENCE IN ASIA PRE–1914

KEY

- British possessions 1805.
- British acquisitions 1805–1858.
- British acquisitions 1858–1914.
- British dependent states in India 1914.
- Russian Empire 1725.
- Russian acquisitions 1725–1815.
- Russian acquisitions 1815–1855.
- Russian acquisitions 1855–1914.
- Important railways.
- Important canals.
- Treaty ports in China (opening dates).

Bering Sea

PACIFIC OCEAN

Sea of Okhotsk

JAPAN

Vladivostok
Newchwang 1858
Port Arthur
Weihaiwei 1898
Chefoo 1858
Peking
Tungchow 1858
Nanking 1861
Chinkiang 1861
Shanghai 1842
Ningpo 1842
Wenchow 1876
Foochow 1842
Swatow 1858
Hongkong
Wuhu 1876
Hankow 1876
Ichang 1876
Shashi 1895
Hangchow
Amoy 1842
Canton 1842
Pakhoi 1876
1895
1899

Verkhoyansk

MONGOLIA

SINKIANG

TIBET

CHINA

South China Sea

Singapore

RUSSIAN EMPIRE

Turukhansk

Omsk

TURKESTAN

Tashkent

AFGHANISTAN

Quetta

INDIA

Lahore
Delhi
Lucknow
Calcutta
Karachi
Madras
Colombo

Bay of Bengal

INDIAN OCEAN

St. Petersburg
Moscow
Warsaw
Kiev
Kars
Black Sea
Angora
Mediterranean Sea
Caspian Sea
Tehran
PERSIA
Baghdad
Kuwait
Arabian Sea

EUROPE

North Sea

Red Sea
Cairo
EGYPT
ANGLO EGYPTIAN-SUDAN
Aden

Miles
0   1000

© Arthur Banks 1975

THE MIDDLE EAST PRE – 1914

Russian Zone (1907 onwards).

British Zone (1907 onwards).

Neutral Zone (1907 onwards).

800

Miles

0

CHINA

INDIA

Bombay

TURKESTAN

Tashkent

Indus

Kabul

AFGHANISTAN

Herat

Samarkand

Merv

BALUCHISTAN

Karachi

Aral Sea

Meshed

Caspian Sea

P E R S I A

Muscat

OMAN

ARABIAN GULF

R U S S I A

Tehran

Isfahan

Persian Gulf

QATAR

Batum

Tigris

Euphrates

O T T O M A N   E M P I R E

N E J D

HADRAMAUT

Constantinople

Aleppo

Damascus

Jerusalem

HEJAZ

Medina

Jiddah

Mecca

ASSIR

Red Sea

YEMEN

Hodeida

Aden

FRENCH SOMALILAND

BRITISH SOMALI[LD]

ITALIAN SOMALILAND

ERITREA

Smyrna

Mediterranean Sea

Cairo

Nile

E G Y P T

ANGLO-EGYPTIAN SUDAN

ABYSSINIA

© Arthur Banks 1975

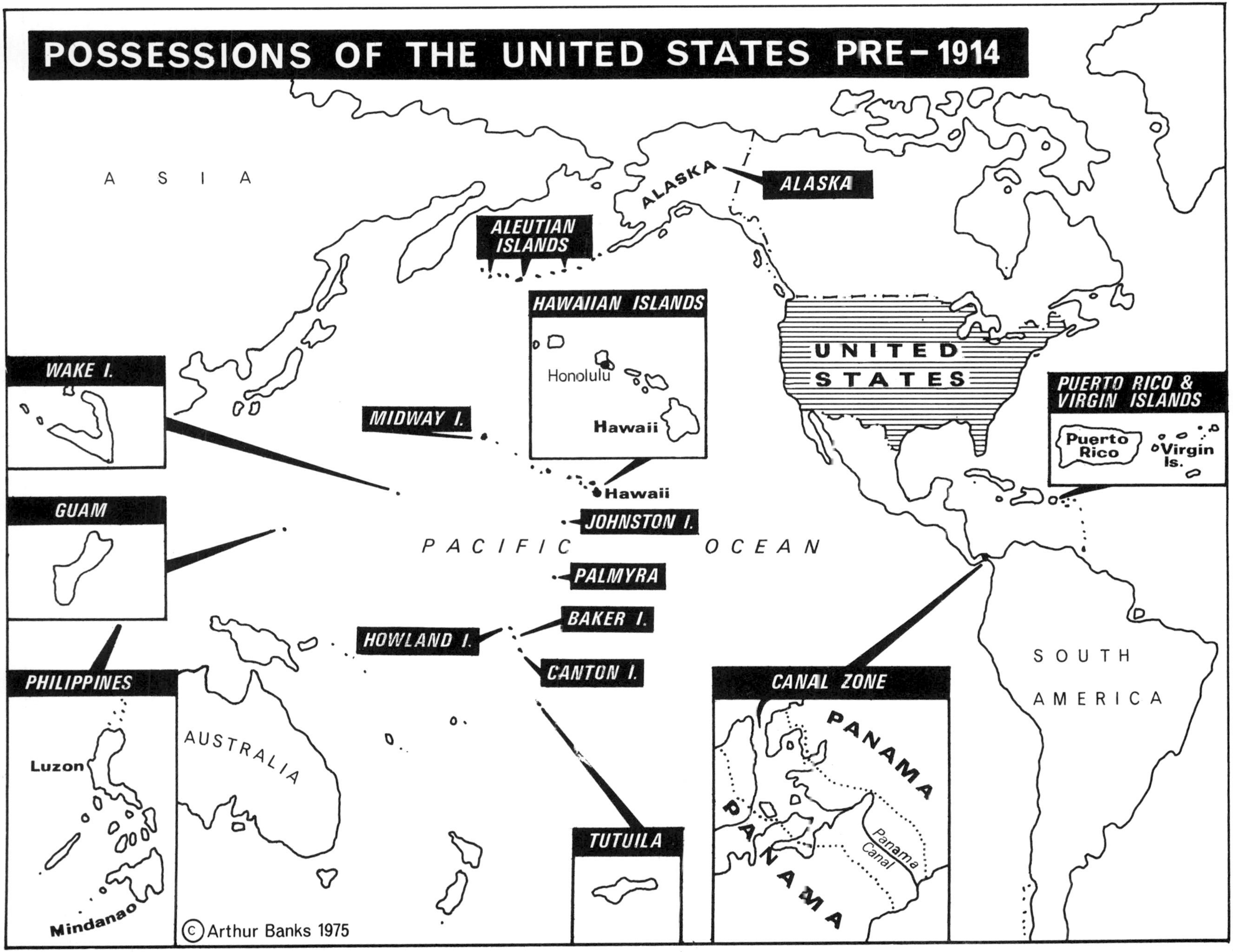

POSSESSIONS OF THE UNITED STATES PRE–1914

PUERTO RICO & VIRGIN ISLANDS

Virgin Is.

Puerto Rico

SOUTH AMERICA

ALASKA

ALASKA

UNITED STATES

PANAMA

Panama Canal

CANAL ZONE

PANAMA

PANAMA

HAWAIIAN ISLANDS

Honolulu

Hawaii

Hawaii

JOHNSTON I.

PALMYRA

BAKER I.

CANTON I.

TUTUILA

ALEUTIAN ISLANDS

PACIFIC OCEAN

MIDWAY I.

HOWLAND I.

WAKE I.

GUAM

PHILIPPINES

Luzon

Mindanao

AUSTRALIA

A S I A

© Arthur Banks 1975

IV
THE FIRST WORLD WAR

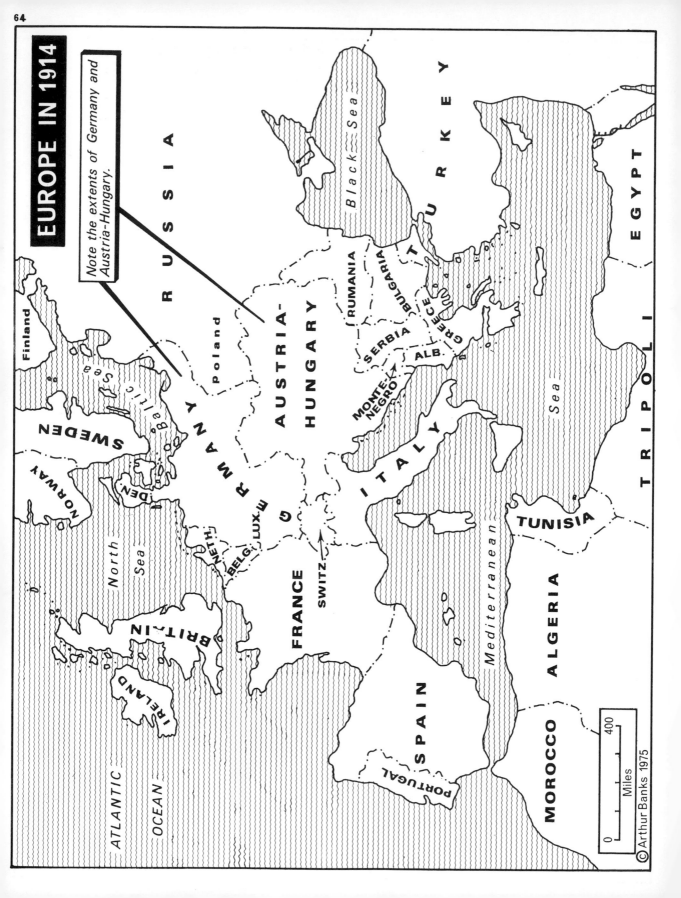

64

EUROPE IN 1914

Note the extents of Germany and Austria-Hungary.

ATLANTIC OCEAN

NORWAY

SWEDEN

Finland

Baltic Sea

RUSSIA

North Sea

DEN.

IRELAND

BRITAIN

NETH.

BELG.

LUX.

GERMANY

Poland

AUSTRIA-HUNGARY

RUMANIA

SERBIA

BULGARIA

MONTE-NEGRO

ALB.

GREECE

Black Sea

T U R K E Y

FRANCE

SWITZ.

ITALY

Sea

EGYPT

TRIPOLI

SPAIN

PORTUGAL

Mediterranean Sea

TUNISIA

ALGERIA

MOROCCO

0   400

Miles

© Arthur Banks 1975

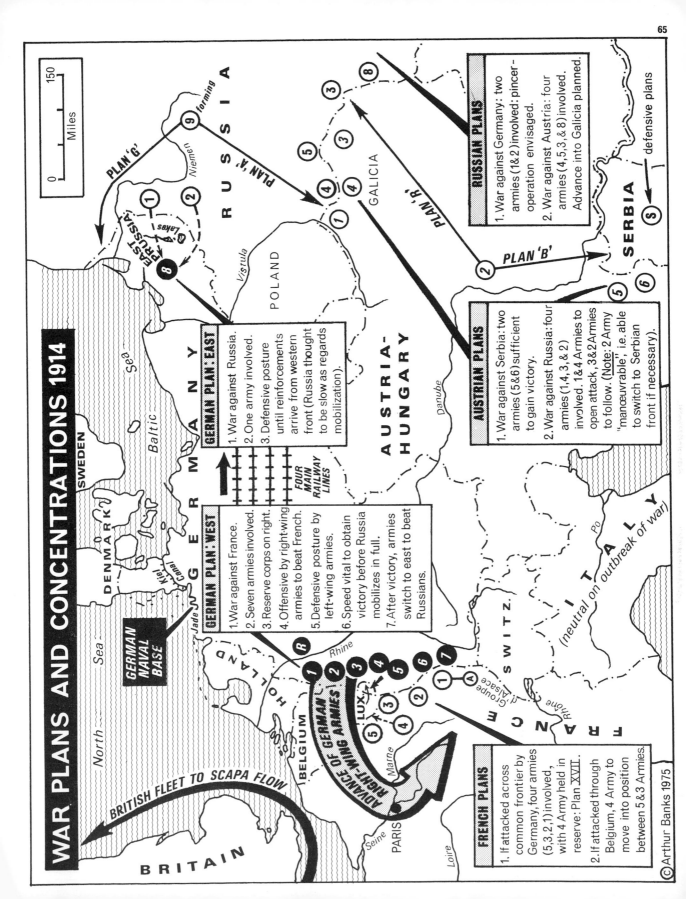

WAR PLANS AND CONCENTRATIONS 1914

PLAN 'G'

PLAN 'A'

PLAN 'R'

PLAN 'B'

SWEDEN

Baltic Sea

North Sea

DENMARK

Kiel Canal

Jade

GERMAN NAVAL BASE

G E R M A N Y

HOLLAND

BELGIUM

LUX.

ADVANCE OF GERMAN ARMIES

RIGHT-WING

F R A N C E

S W I T Z.

PARIS

Seine

Marne

Loire

Rhône

Groupe d'Alsace

Rhine

E.PRUSSIA

Lakes

R U S S I A

Niemen

forming

Vistula

POLAND

A U S T R I A - HUNGARY

Danube

GALICIA

SERBIA

I T A L Y

Po

(neutral on outbreak of war)

BRITAIN

BRITISH FLEET TO SCAPA FLOW

GERMAN PLAN: EAST
1. War against Russia.
2. One army involved.
3. Defensive posture until reinforcements arrive from western front (Russia thought to be slow as regards mobilization).

FOUR MAIN RAILWAY LINES

GERMAN PLAN: WEST
1. War against France.
2. Seven armies involved.
3. Reserve corps on right.
4. Offensive by right-wing armies to beat French.
5. Defensive posture by left-wing armies.
6. Speed vital to obtain victory before Russia mobilizes in full.
7. After victory, armies switch to east to beat Russians.

RUSSIAN PLANS
1. War against Germany: two armies (1&2) involved: pincer-operation envisaged.
2. War against Austria: four armies (4,5,3, & 8) involved. Advance into Galicia planned.

AUSTRIAN PLANS
1. War against Serbia: two armies (5&6) sufficient to gain victory.
2. War against Russia: four armies (1,4,3, & 2) involved. 1&4 Armies to open attack, 3&2 Armies to follow. (Note: 2 Army "manoeuvrable", i.e. able to switch to Serbian front if necessary).

FRENCH PLANS
1. If attacked across common frontier by Germany, four armies (5,3,2,1) involved, with 4 Army held in reserve: Plan XVII.
2. If attacked through Belgium, 4 Army to move into position between 5 & 3 Armies.

defensive plans

© Arthur Banks 1975

Scale: 0 — 150 Miles

THE WESTERN FRONT IN OUTLINE 1914–1918

The campaign was really one prolonged battle involving territorial gains and losses completely disproportionate to the casualties involved. The basic stages were: the initial German advance of 1914 which was halted at the Marne and Aisne battles: the resulting "race to the sea" (a series of outflanking moves): the fairly stabilized trench line being established: the Allied gains and fights at the Somme and Verdun: the German offensives in the spring of 1918: the Allied advance towards Germany that halted with the Armistice on 11 November 1918.

KEY

- **.........** Limit of German advance in September 1914.
- **▬ ▬ ▬** General front from end of 1914 to 30 June 1916 (prior to Somme battles).
- Allied gains in 1916 and 1917.
- German gains during 1918 offensives.
- **▬▬▬** Armistice line on 11 November 1918.
- **–·–·–** Frontiers in 1914.
- **●** Capital cities.
- **•** Other cities and towns.

NORTH SEA

Strait of Dover

GERMANY

LORRAINE

HOLLAND

BELGIUM

FRANCE

CHAMPAGNE

PICARDY

ARTOIS

Lunéville
Nancy
Metz
Moselle
Meuse
St. Mihiel
Verdun
Longwy
Sedan
Mézières
Liége
Namur
Charleroi
Louvain
BRUSSELS
Antwerp
Bruges
Ghent
Zeebrugge
Ostend
Dunkirk
Nieuport
Dixmude
Ypres
Messines
Calais
Boulogne
Dieppe
Rouen
PARIS
Meaux
Compiègne
Montdidier
Amiens
Albert
Péronne
Noyon
La Fère
St. Quentin
Le Cateau
Cambrai
Quéant
Douai
Valenciennes
Maubeuge
Landrecies
Mons
Tournai
Courtrai
Lille
Neuve Chapelle
La Bassée
Lens
Givenchy
Vimy
Arras
Drocourt
Soissons
Laon
Rheims
Épernay
Château-Thierry
St. Mihiel

CHEMIN DES DAMES
HINDENBURG'S LINE

Rivers: Meuse, Moselle, Marne, Aisne, Vesle, Oise, Sambre, Schelde, Lys, Somme, Ancre, Seine, Petit Morin, Grand Morin

Miles scale
0 ─ 30 Miles

© Arthur Banks 1973

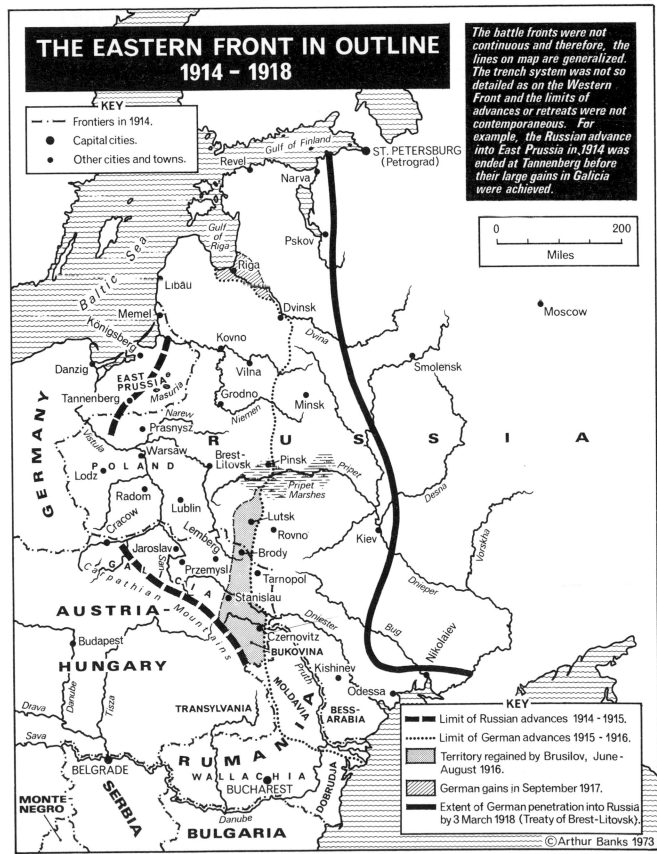

THE EASTERN FRONT IN OUTLINE 1914 – 1918

The battle fronts were not continuous and therefore, the lines on map are generalized. The trench system was not so detailed as on the Western Front and the limits of advances or retreats were not contemporaneous. For example, the Russian advance into East Prussia in 1914 was ended at Tannenberg before their large gains in Galicia were achieved.

KEY
—·—·— Frontiers in 1914.
● Capital cities.
• Other cities and towns.

0   200
Miles

KEY
▬ ▬ ▬ Limit of Russian advances 1914 - 1915.
·········· Limit of German advances 1915 - 1916.
▓ Territory regained by Brusilov, June - August 1916.
▨ German gains in September 1917.
▬▬▬ Extent of German penetration into Russia by 3 March 1918 (Treaty of Brest-Litovsk).

© Arthur Banks 1973

ST. PETERSBURG (Petrograd)
Revel
Narva
Pskov
Gulf of Finland
Gulf of Riga
Riga
Libau
Dvinsk
Memel
Königsberg
Kovno
Dvina
Moscow
Baltic Sea
Danzig
EAST PRUSSIA
Vilna
Smolensk
Tannenberg
Masuria
Grodno
Minsk
Narew
Niemen
Prasnysz
Vistula
Warsaw
Brest-Litovsk
Pinsk
Pripet
GERMANY
POLAND
Pripet Marshes
Lodz
Radom
Lublin
Lutsk
Desna
Cracow
Lemberg
Rovno
Kiev
Jaroslav
Brody
San
Przemysl
Tarnopol
Vorskha
GALICIA
Stanislau
Carpathian Mountains
Dniester
Dnieper
AUSTRIA-
Czernovitz
Bug
Budapest
BUKOVINA
Nikolaiev
HUNGARY
Kishinev
MOLDAVIA
Pruth
Odessa
Drava
Danube
Tisza
TRANSYLVANIA
BESS-ARABIA
Sava
RUMANIA
DOBRUDJA
BELGRADE
WALLACHIA
BUCHAREST
MONTE-NEGRO
SERBIA
Danube
BULGARIA
RUSSIA

OPENING MOVES INVOLVING GERMANY

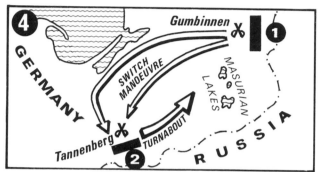

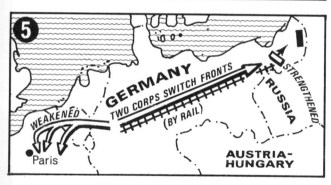

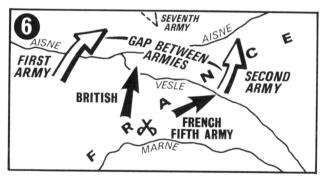

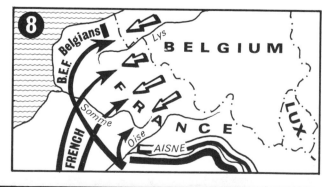

© Arthur Banks 1975

These sections depict basic military moves involving Germany in the first weeks of the European campaign and illustrate how events and situations on her western and eastern fronts affected and reacted upon each other. In brief, her overall effort was split and she rapidly became involved in an active two-front war situation, the very position for which her detailed pre-war plans had been designed to avoid. These moves are shown in more detail on following pages.

OPENING MOVES INVOLVING OTHER POWERS

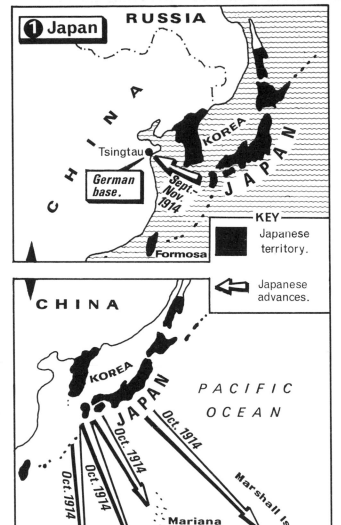

① Japan

RUSSIA

CHINA

KOREA

JAPAN

Tsingtau

German base.

Sept.-Nov. 1914

Formosa

KEY

Japanese territory.

Japanese advances.

CHINA

KOREA

JAPAN

PACIFIC OCEAN

Oct. 1914

Oct. 1914

Oct. 1914

Oct. 1914

Oct. 1914

Marshall Is.

Mariana Is.

Palau

Caroline Is.

German bases.

0   1000
Miles

② Austria-Hungary

RUSSIA

GERMANY

AUSTRIA-HUNGARY

Russians

SWITZ.

ITALY

MONTENEGRO

SERBIA

ALB.

RUMANIA

BULGARIA

GREECE

KEY
Austrian attacks.

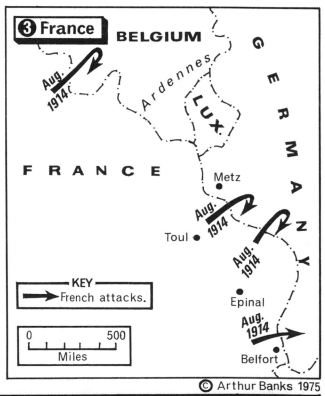

③ France

BELGIUM

GERMANY

Aug. 1914

Ardennes

LUX.

FRANCE

Metz

Aug. 1914

Toul

Aug. 1914

Epinal

Aug. 1914

Belfort

KEY
French attacks.

0   500
Miles

© Arthur Banks 1975

These sections depict basic moves involving Japan, Austria Hungary, and France during the opening months of the war. In the Far East, Japan attacked and captured the German mainland base at Tsingtau plus a number of German Pacific islands. In Europe, Austria-Hungary met with rebuffs in clashes with Russia and Serbia; France attempted operations against Germany, but these moves came to naught. Consequently, with Russia and Britain involved also, the conflict rapidly engulfed hundreds of millions of people.

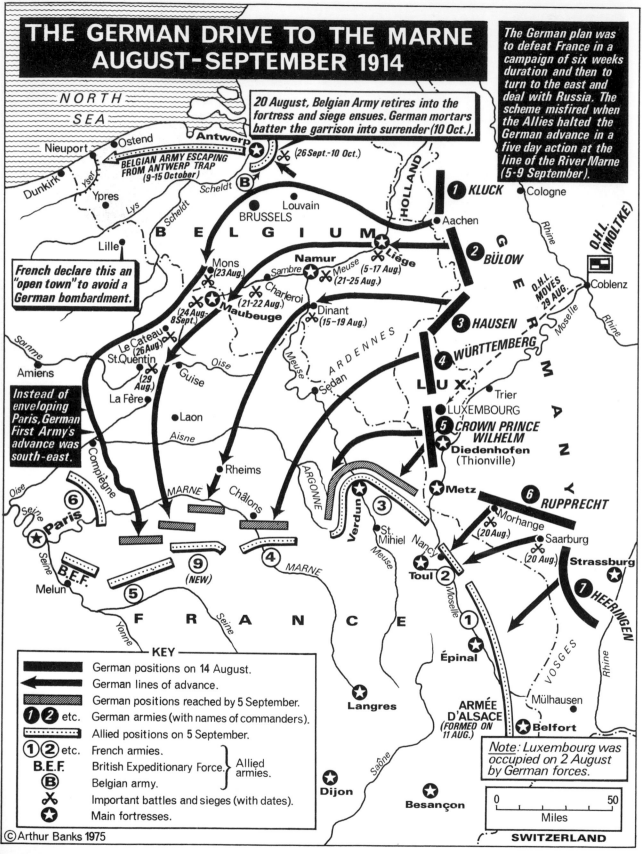

THE GERMAN DRIVE TO THE MARNE AUGUST-SEPTEMBER 1914

The German plan was to defeat France in a campaign of six weeks duration and then to turn to the east and deal with Russia. The scheme misfired when the Allies halted the German advance in a five day action at the line of the River Marne (5-9 September).

20 August, Belgian Army retires into the fortress and siege ensues. German mortars batter the garrison into surrender (10 Oct.).

BELGIAN ARMY ESCAPING FROM ANTWERP TRAP (9-15 October)

French declare this an "open town" to avoid a German bombardment.

Instead of enveloping Paris, German First Army's advance was south-east.

NORTH SEA

Nieuport
Ostend
Antwerp
(26 Sept.-10 Oct.)
Dunkirk
Ypres
Lille
BELGIUM
BRUSSELS
Louvain
HOLLAND
Aachen
Cologne
① KLUCK
② BÜLOW
O.H.L. (MOLTKE)
Coblenz
O.H.L. MOVES 29 AUG.
Liège (5-17 Aug.)
Namur (21-25 Aug.)
Mons (23 Aug.)
Charleroi (21-22 Aug.)
Dinant (15-19 Aug.)
③ HAUSEN
④ WÜRTTEMBERG
Maubeuge (24 Aug.-8 Sept.)
Le Cateau (26 Aug.)
St.Quentin (29 Aug.)
Guise
La Fère
Laon
Amiens
Compiègne
⑥
Paris
B.E.F.
Melun
⑤
⑨ (NEW)
④
MARNE
Rheims
Châlons
ARDENNES
Sedan
ARGONNE
③
Verdun
St. Mihiel
LUX
Trier
LUXEMBOURG
⑤ CROWN PRINCE WILHELM
Diedenhofen (Thionville)
Metz
⑥ RUPPRECHT
Morhange (20 Aug.)
Saarburg (20 Aug.)
Strassburg
Nancy
Toul ②
①
Épinal
⑦ HEERINGEN
VOSGES
Mülhausen
Langres
ARMÉE D'ALSACE (FORMED ON 11 AUG.)
Belfort
FRANCE
GERMANY
Rhine
Moselle
Meuse
Seine
Oise
Somme
Lys
Yser
Scheldt
Sambre
Aisne
Yonne
Saône

Note: Luxembourg was occupied on 2 August by German forces.

KEY

▬▬▬	German positions on 14 August.
◀▬▬	German lines of advance.
▨▨▨	German positions reached by 5 September.
①② etc.	German armies (with names of commanders).
•••••	Allied positions on 5 September.
①② etc.	French armies.
B.E.F.	British Expeditionary Force. } Allied armies.
Ⓑ	Belgian army.
✂	Important battles and sieges (with dates).
★	Main fortresses.

0 — 50 Miles

© Arthur Banks 1975

SWITZERLAND

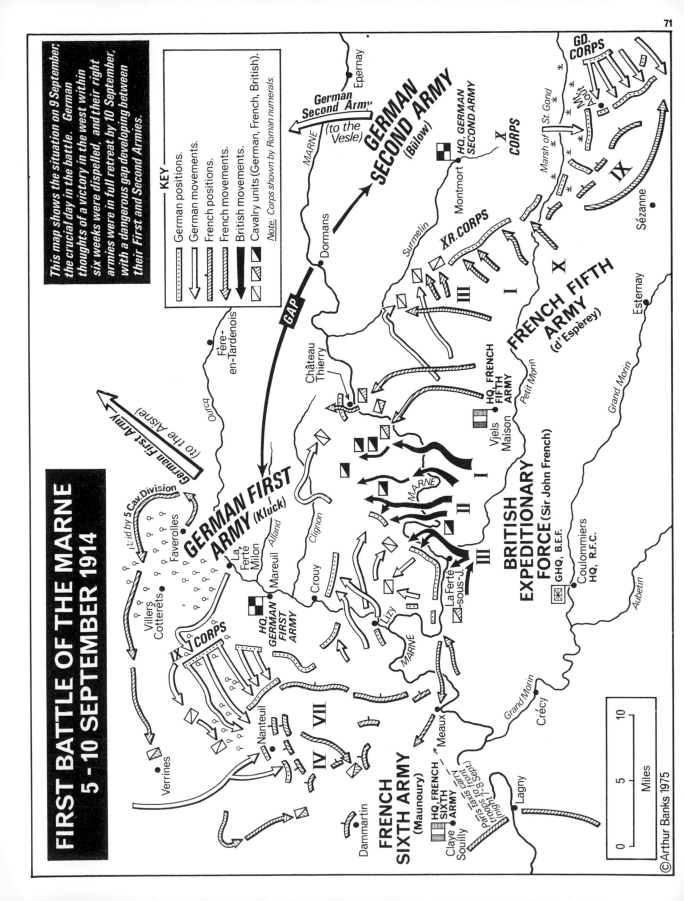

FIRST BATTLE OF THE MARNE 5 – 10 SEPTEMBER 1914

This map shows the situation on 9 September, the crucial day in the battle. German thoughts of a victory in the west within six weeks were dispelled, and their right armies were in full retreat by 10 September, with a dangerous gap developing between their First and Second Armies.

KEY

.... German positions.

⬇ German movements.

▨ French positions.

⬇ French movements.

⬇ British movements.

▨ Cavalry units (German, French, British).

Note: Corps shown by Roman numerals.

German Second Army (to the Vesle)

GERMAN SECOND ARMY (Bülow)

HQ, GERMAN SECOND ARMY

X CORPS

XR. CORPS

GD. CORPS

Marsh of St. Gond

IX

X

FRENCH FIFTH ARMY (d'Espèrey)

HQ FRENCH FIFTH ARMY

GAP

German First Army (to the Aisne)

GERMAN FIRST ARMY (Kluck)

h'd by 5 Cav. Division

HQ, GERMAN FIRST ARMY

IX CORPS

VII

IV

FRENCH SIXTH ARMY (Maunoury)

HQ, FRENCH SIXTH ARMY

Paris Taxis carry troops, 7–8 Sept. (night)

BRITISH EXPEDITIONARY FORCE (Sir John French)

GHQ, B.E.F.

HQ, R.F.C.

Epernay

MARNE

Dormans

Surmelin

Montmort

Sézanne

Esternay

Fère-en-Tardenois

Ourcq

Château Thierry

Vjels Maison

Petit Morin

Grand Morin

Grand Morin

Crécy

Aubetin

Coulommiers

La Ferté-sous-J.

Lizy

MARNE

Meaux

Lagny

Claye Souilly

Dammartin

Nanteuil

Verrines

Villers Cotterêts

Faverolles

La Ferté Milon

Mareuil

Crouy

Clignon

Alland

© Arthur Banks 1975

Miles

0   5   10

PRELUDE TO TRENCH WARFARE AUTUMN 1914

NETH.

GERMAN FOURTH ARMY

BELGIAN ARMY

0 ——— 20
Miles

NORTH SEA

Ostend

Bruges

Antwerp

Nieuport

Yser

Ghent

Schelde

BESELER 'GROUP'

Dixmude

Calais

Dunkirk

BELGIANS

de Mitry

Yser

Fr.Terr.

Roulers

Lys

Br. Cav.

Ypres

BRUSSELS

XXXX

B.E.F.

I

III

Messines

XIX

IV

St.Omer

Hazebrouck

II

XXXX

Lys

Armentières

I

II

BELGIUM

Escaut

XIII

VII

LILLE

Conneau

Béthune

La Bassée

XIV

XXXX

XXI

Lens

I Bav. R.

Mons

Charleroi

Sambre

d'Urbal

Vimy

IV

Scarpe

St.Pol

TENTH FRENCH ARMY

X

G

GERMAN SIXTH ARMY

Arras

F R A N C E

Maubeuge

Doullens

XI

XIV R

Somme

XXXX

II Bav.

B.E.F.

KEY

AMIENS

Chaulnes

XX

I Bav.

Oise

XXXX ———— Army boundaries.

Allied infantry corps.

Allied cavalry corps.

Allied moves.

German infantry corps.

German cavalry corps.

Canal.

Poix

XXI

XVIII

XXXX

FRENCH SECOND ARMY

XIV

IV

II

La Fère

Note how this army has plugged the gap between First and Second Armies.

GERMAN SEVENTH ARMY

Roye

IX R

IV

IV R

Laon

III

Craonne

Aisne

XIII

IX

GERMAN FIRST ARMY

Vailly

Compiègne

XXXX

Soissons

GERMAN SECOND ARMY

RHEIMS

I III II

FRENCH SIXTH ARMY

B. E. F.

Vesle

FRENCH FIFTH ARMY

XXXX

FRENCH FOURTH ARMY

5-15 October, British Expeditionary Force is transferred to Flanders thereby shortening its supply link from England (via the Channel ports).

© Arthur Banks 1975

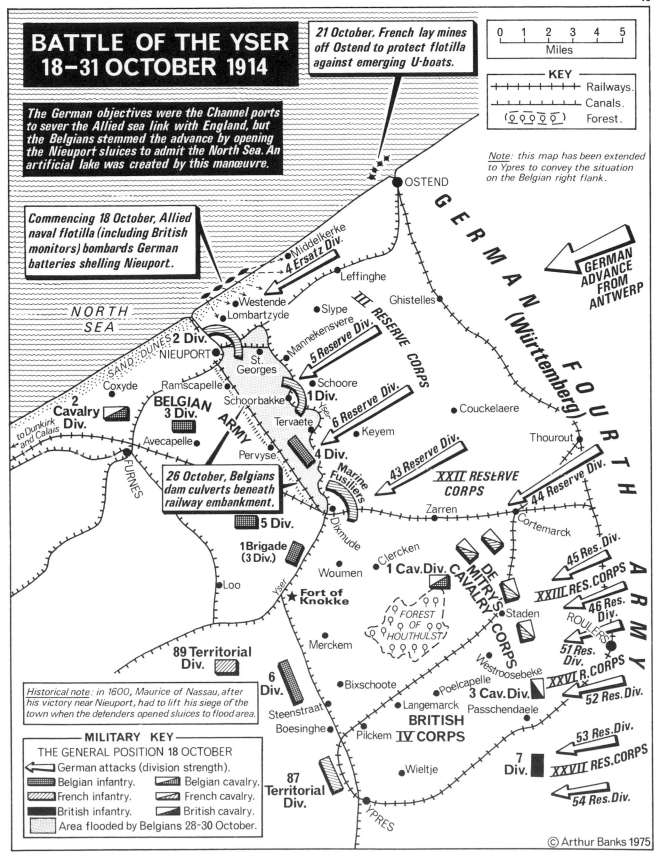

BATTLE OF THE YSER 18–31 OCTOBER 1914

21 October, French lay mines off Ostend to protect flotilla against emerging U-boats.

The German objectives were the Channel ports to sever the Allied sea link with England, but the Belgians stemmed the advance by opening the Nieuport sluices to admit the North Sea. An artificial lake was created by this manœuvre.

Commencing 18 October, Allied naval flotilla (including British monitors) bombards German batteries shelling Nieuport.

0 1 2 3 4 5
Miles

KEY
—†—†—†—†— Railways.
———————— Canals.
(꩜꩜꩜꩜꩜) Forest.

Note: this map has been extended to Ypres to convey the situation on the Belgian right flank.

OSTEND

GERMAN ADVANCE FROM ANTWERP

G E R M A N   F O U R T H   A R M Y (Württemberg)

Middelkerke
4 Ersatz Div.
Leffinghe
Ghistelles

NORTH SEA

Westende
Lombartzyde
Slype
Mannekensvere
III RESERVE CORPS
5 Reserve Div.

SAND DUNES
2 Div.
NIEUPORT
St. Georges
Schoore
6 Reserve Div.
Couckelaere

Coxyde
Ramscapelle
Schoorbakke
BELGIAN
3 Div.
1 Div.
Tervaete
Keyem
Thourout

2 Cavalry Div.
to Dunkirk and Calais
ARMY
Avecapelle
Pervyse
4 Div.

26 October, Belgians dam culverts beneath railway embankment.

Marine Fusiliers
43 Reserve Div.
XXII RESERVE CORPS
44 Reserve Div.
Zarren
Cortemarck

FURNES
5 Div.
Dixmude

1 Brigade (3 Div.)
Woumen
Clercken
1 Cav. Div.
DE MITRY'S CAVALRY CORPS
45 Res. Div.
XXIII RES. CORPS
46 Res. Div.
ROULERS

Loo
Yser
Fort of Knokke
FOREST OF HOUTHULST
Staden
51 Res. Div.

89 Territorial Div.
Merckem
Westroosebeke
XXVI R. CORPS
52 Res. Div.

Historical note: in 1600, Maurice of Nassau, after his victory near Nieuport, had to lift his siege of the town when the defenders opened sluices to flood area.

6 Div.
Steenstraat
Bixschoote
Poelcapelle
3 Cav. Div.
Passchendaele

MILITARY KEY
THE GENERAL POSITION 18 OCTOBER
← German attacks (division strength).
▦ Belgian infantry. ◩ Belgian cavalry.
▨ French infantry. ◪ French cavalry.
■ British infantry. ◨ British cavalry.
▒ Area flooded by Belgians 28–30 October.

Boesinghe
Pilckem
Langemarck
BRITISH IV CORPS
53 Res. Div.

87 Territorial Div.
Wieltje
7 Div.
XXVII RES. CORPS
54 Res. Div.

YPRES

© Arthur Banks 1975

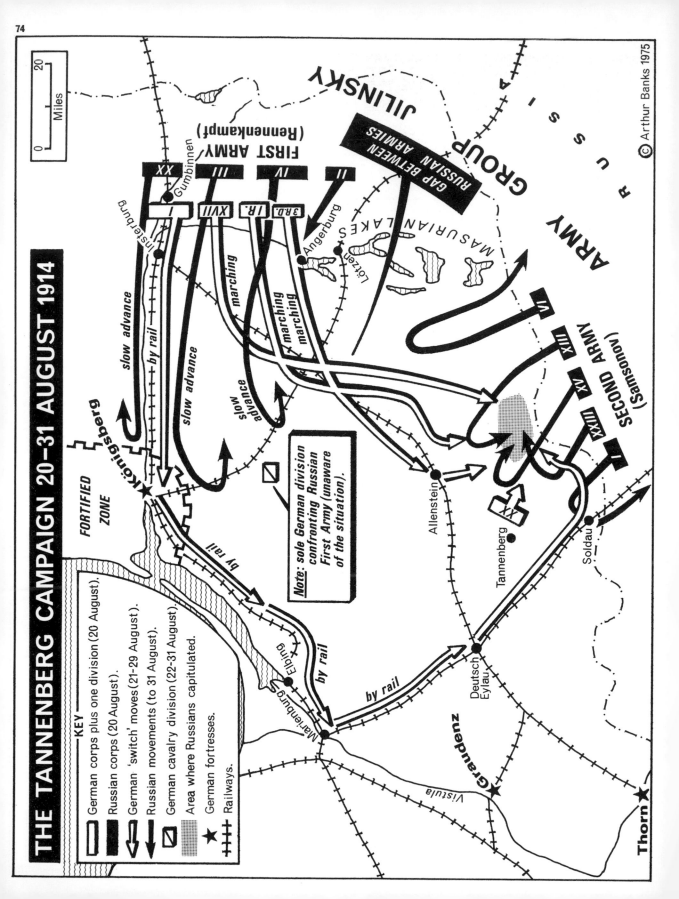

74

© Arthur Banks 1975

THE TANNENBERG CAMPAIGN 20–31 AUGUST 1914

KEY

- German corps plus one division (20 August).
- Russian corps (20 August).
- German 'switch' moves (21–29 August).
- Russian movements (to 31 August).
- German cavalry division (22–31 August).
- Area where Russians capitulated.
- ★ German fortresses.
- ┿┿┿ Railways.

20 Miles 0

FORTIFIED ZONE

Note: sole German division confronting Russian First Army (unaware of the situation).

Königsberg

Insterburg

Gumbinnen

Angerburg

Lötzen

MASURIAN LAKES

GAP BETWEEN RUSSIAN ARMIES

JILINSKY

ARMY GROUP

RUSSIA

FIRST ARMY (Rennenkampf)

XX III IV II

I XVII III. 3RD.

slow advance
slow advance
slow advance
slow advance
by rail
marching
marching
marching

Allenstein

XX

Tannenberg

Soldau

SECOND ARMY (Samsonov)

VI XIII XV XXIII I

Elbing

Marienburg

by rail

by rail

Deutsch Eylau

Graudenz

Vistula

Thorn

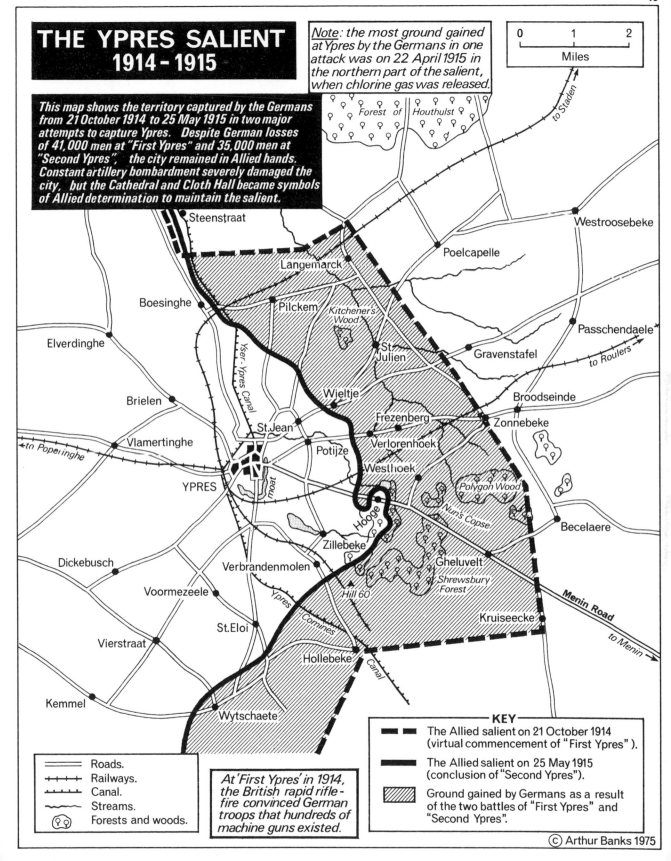

THE YPRES SALIENT 1914 - 1915

Note: the most ground gained at Ypres by the Germans in one attack was on 22 April 1915 in the northern part of the salient, when chlorine gas was released.

0   1   2
Miles

This map shows the territory captured by the Germans from 21 October 1914 to 25 May 1915 in two major attempts to capture Ypres. Despite German losses of 41,000 men at "First Ypres" and 35,000 men at "Second Ypres", the city remained in Allied hands. Constant artillery bombardment severely damaged the city, but the Cathedral and Cloth Hall became symbols of Allied determination to maintain the salient.

Forest of Houthulst

to Staden

Steenstraat

Westroosebeke

Poelcapelle

Langemarck

Boesinghe

Pilckem

Kitchener's Wood

Passchendaele

Elverdinghe

St. Julien

Gravenstafel

to Roulers

Yser-Ypres Canal

Wieltje

Brielen

Broodseinde

Frezenberg

St. Jean

Zonnebeke

Vlamertinghe

Verlorenhoek

to Poperinghe

Potijze

Westhoek

Polygon Wood

YPRES

moat

Nun's Copse

Becelaere

Hooge

Dickebusch

Zillebeke

Gheluvelt

Verbrandenmolen

Shrewsbury Forest

Menin Road

Voormezeele

Ypres

Hill 60

Kruiseecke

St. Eloi

Comines

to Menin

Vierstraat

Hollebeke

Canal

Kemmel

Wytschaete

KEY

– – – The Allied salient on 21 October 1914 (virtual commencement of "First Ypres").

——— The Allied salient on 25 May 1915 (conclusion of "Second Ypres").

▨ Ground gained by Germans as a result of the two battles of "First Ypres" and "Second Ypres".

Roads.
Railways.
Canal.
Streams.
Forests and woods.

At 'First Ypres' in 1914, the British rapid rifle-fire convinced German troops that hundreds of machine guns existed.

© Arthur Banks 1975

THE STATIC WESTERN FRONT 1915

0 ——— 40
Miles

Bruges

Antwerp

Düsseldorf

Ghent

Ypres

HOLLAND

Cologne

Rhine

BRUSSELS

Lille

N.Chapelle
Festubert
Loos

B E L G I U M

Liége

Bonn

Lens

Mons

Namur

G E R M A N Y

Douai

Arras

A R T O I S

Cambrai

Péronne

ARDENNES

St.Quentin

Hirson

LUXEMBOURG

Noyon

Mézières

Laon

Sedan

Compiègne

Soissons

Perthes

Verdun

Metz

© Arthur Banks 1973

Rheims

C H A M P A G N E

A R G O N N E

St. Mihiel

F   R   A   N   C   E

Châlons

LORRAINE

JOFFRE'S PLANS IN EARLY 1915

BRUSSELS

HOLL.

Cologne

Rhine

**THIS GERMAN
SALIENT EXISTED
(WITH VARIATIONS)
UNTIL SEPTEMBER
1918.**

Toul

Nancy

Lille   B E L G I U M

LUX.

G E R M A N Y

Douai

Hirson

trench

Noyon

Mézières

*Despite Allied efforts to achieve
a breakthrough, the basic shape
of the front line remained virtually
unaltered on small scale maps.
Note the important rail network
under German control.*

Épinal

F R A N C E

Rheims

warfare

Metz

St.Mihiel

0 ——— 60
Miles

Nancy

V O S G E S

A L S A C E

- KEY -
Front line in February.
Allied offensives.
German offensives.

- KEY -
Opening attacks.
Subsequent advances.

Belfort

THE MOBILE EASTERN FRONT 1915

0   50   100
Miles

BALTIC SEA

Libau *Fell on 8 May.*

Memel

Not captured by Germans.

Dvinsk ★   Dvina

Stormed by Germans 17-18 August.

Kovno

Königsberg

Danzig

EAST PRUSSIA

Vistula

Graudenz

MASURIAN LAKES

Niemen

Grodno

Germany's aim was to make the Eastern Front safe and passive so that she could switch her main assault to the Western Front (she did not hope to completely defeat Russia). Rather than instituting an "enveloping" operation, she decided to attempt a "breakthrough" attack between Gorlice and Tarnow. This commenced on 2 May 1915, in concert with the Austrians. This front contrasts sharply with the Western Front during 1915.

RUSSIA

Thorn

Narew

Vistula

Capitulated on 20 August.

Fell on 2 September.

Entered by Germans on 5 August.

Novo-Georgievsk

Warsaw ★

Bug

Brest-Litovsk

North of this position, the front line remained as shown (with minor variations) until the end of 1917.

POLAND

Vistula

Ivangorod

Surrendered on 26 August.

Pripet

South of this position, the front line remained as shown (with minor variations) until June 1916.

Fell on 5 August.

San

Evacuated by Russians on 22 June.

Vistula

Tarnow

Cracow

GALICIA

Lemberg ★

Przemysl

2 MAY 1915

GERMAN ELEVENTH ARMY

Gorlice

Fell on 3 June.

Dniester

CARPATHIAN MOUNTAINS

Tisza

Pruth

KEY

Opening assault by German and Austrian armies.
Advances by German and Austrian armies.
.... Front line, 2 May.
——— Front line, 1 June.
▬▬▬ Front line, 16 July.
▢▢▢ Front line, 15 August.
– – – Front line, 1 September.
▲▲▲ Front line, winter 1915.

© Arthur Banks 1973

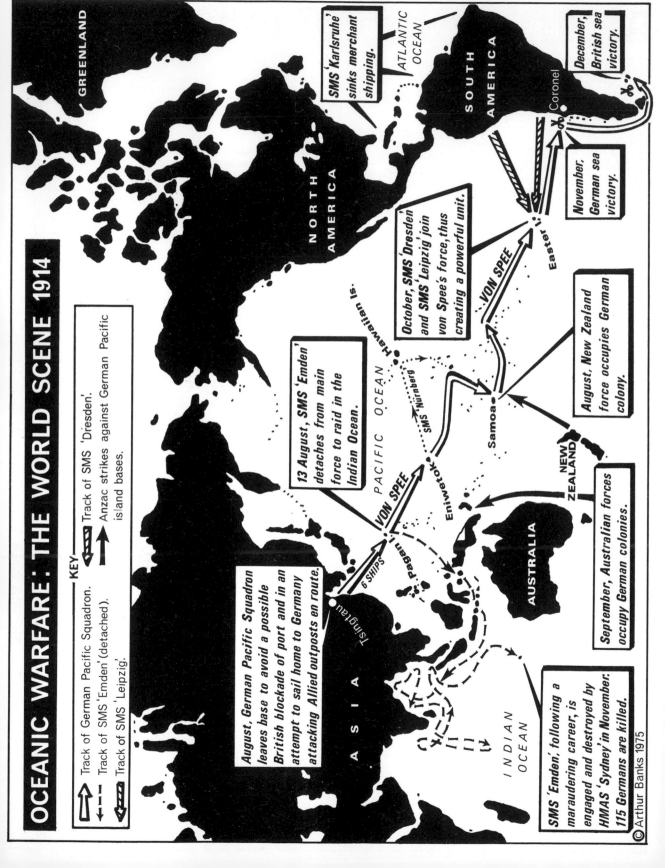

OCEANIC WARFARE: THE WORLD SCENE 1914

KEY
- ⟹ Track of German Pacific Squadron.
- ⇢ Track of SMS 'Dresden'.
- – – Track of SMS 'Emden' (detached).
- ◿ Track of SMS 'Leipzig'.
- ⟹ Anzac strikes against German Pacific island bases.

SMS 'Karlsruhe' sinks merchant shipping.

December, British sea victory.

November, German sea victory.

October, SMS 'Dresden' and SMS 'Leipzig' join von Spee's force, thus creating a powerful unit.

13 August, SMS 'Emden' detaches from main force to raid in the Indian Ocean.

August, New Zealand force occupies German colony.

August, German Pacific Squadron leaves base to avoid a possible British blockade of port and in an attempt to sail home to Germany attacking Allied outposts en route.

September, Australian forces occupy German colonies.

SMS 'Emden', following a marauding career, is engaged and destroyed by HMAS 'Sydney' in November. 115 Germans are killed.

GREENLAND

ATLANTIC OCEAN

NORTH AMERICA

SOUTH AMERICA

Coronel

Easter I.

VON SPEE

Hawaiian Is.

PACIFIC OCEAN

SMS 'Nürnberg'

Samoa

Eniwetok

VON SPEE

Pagan

6 SHIPS

Tsingtau

ASIA

INDIAN OCEAN

AUSTRALIA

NEW ZEALAND

© Arthur Banks 1975

FIRST BATTLE OF THE ATLANTIC 1915-1918

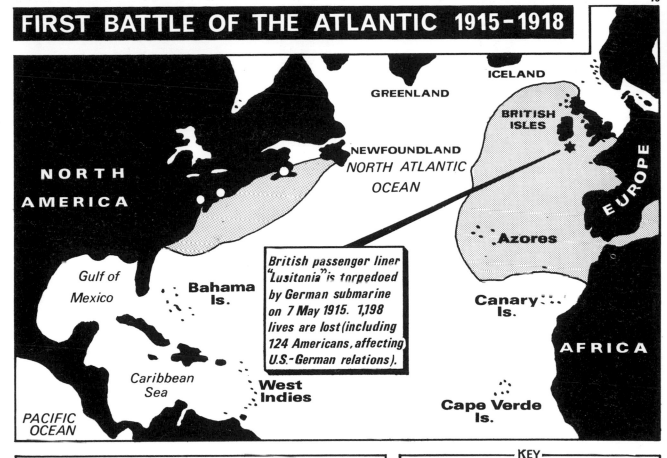

ICELAND

GREENLAND

BRITISH ISLES

NEWFOUNDLAND
NORTH ATLANTIC OCEAN

EUROPE

NORTH AMERICA

Azores

Gulf of Mexico

British passenger liner "Lusitania" is torpedoed by German submarine on 7 May 1915. 1,198 lives are lost (including 124 Americans, affecting U.S.-German relations).

Canary Is.

AFRICA

Bahama Is.

Caribbean Sea

West Indies

Cape Verde Is.

PACIFIC OCEAN

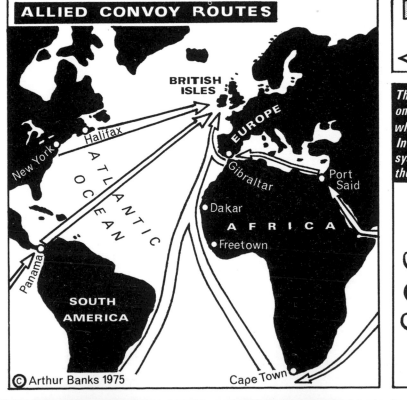

ALLIED CONVOY ROUTES

BRITISH ISLES

Halifax

New York

EUROPE

Gibraltar

Port Said

ATLANTIC OCEAN

Dakar

AFRICA

Freetown

Panama

SOUTH AMERICA

Cape Town

© Arthur Banks 1975

KEY

Areas where German U-boats sank large numbers of Allied and neutral merchant ships.

Allied convoy routes.

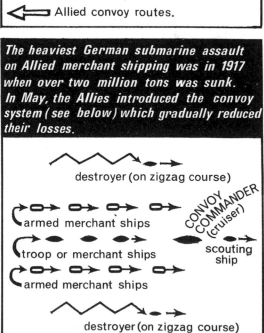

The heaviest German submarine assault on Allied merchant shipping was in 1917 when over two million tons was sunk. In May, the Allies introduced the convoy system (see below) which gradually reduced their losses.

destroyer (on zigzag course)

armed merchant ships

troop or merchant ships

armed merchant ships

CONVOY COMMANDER (cruiser)

scouting ship

destroyer (on zigzag course)

EUROPE: THE MIDDLE YEARS 1915–1917

① Land Events (1915)

The Eastern Front is very active: Germans advance up to 250 miles into Russia. The onset of winter halts their advance.

Serbia is overwhelmed as a result of a combined Austro-German-Bulgarian invasion.

Allies land on Gallipoli peninsula but operation ends in failure due to determined Turkish resistance.

The Western Front is basically unaltered. The main actions occur at Festubert, Aubers Ridge, Neuve Chapelle, Loos, Ypres, in Artois, and Champagne. Trench warfare sets in.

The Italian Front is the scene of offensives by both Italians and Austro-Hungarians. Small inroads into each other's territory results.

RUSSIA

TURKEY

Black Sea

RUMANIA

BULGARIA

GREECE

SERBIA

ALBANIA

MONTENEGRO

AUSTRIA-HUNGARY

GERMANY

ITALY

SWITZ.

FRANCE

NETH.

BEL.

DEN.

BRITAIN

North Sea

ATLANTIC OCEAN

Mediterranean Sea

SPAIN

PORTUGAL

0   500
Miles

© Arthur Banks 1975

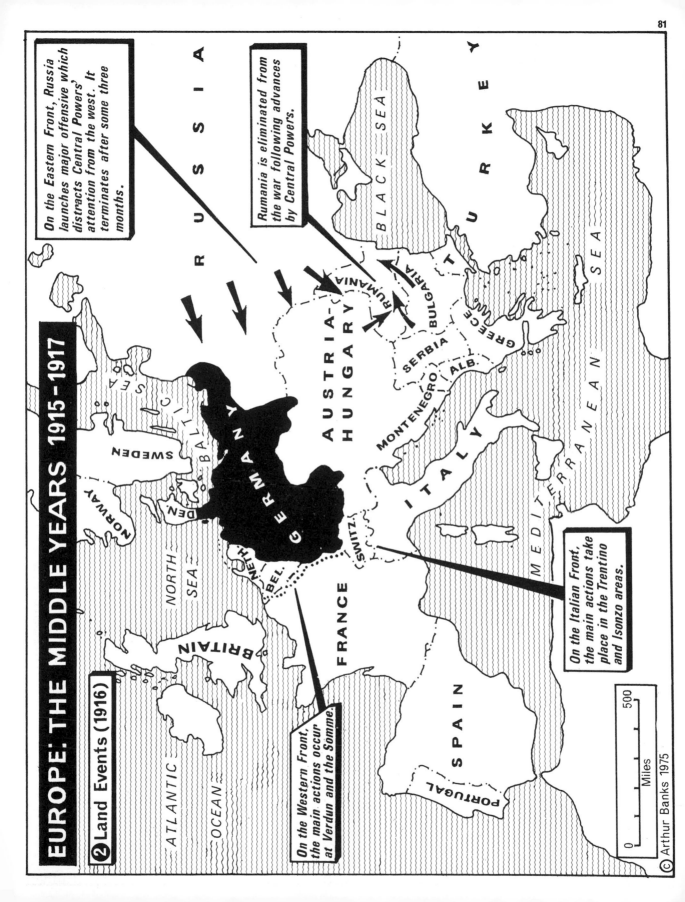

EUROPE: THE MIDDLE YEARS 1915–1917

② Land Events (1916)

On the Eastern Front, Russia launches major offensive which distracts Central Powers' attention from the west. It terminates after some three months.

Rumania is eliminated from the war following advances by Central Powers.

On the Italian Front, the main actions take place in the Trentino and Isonzo areas.

On the Western Front, the main actions occur at Verdun and the Somme.

© Arthur Banks 1975

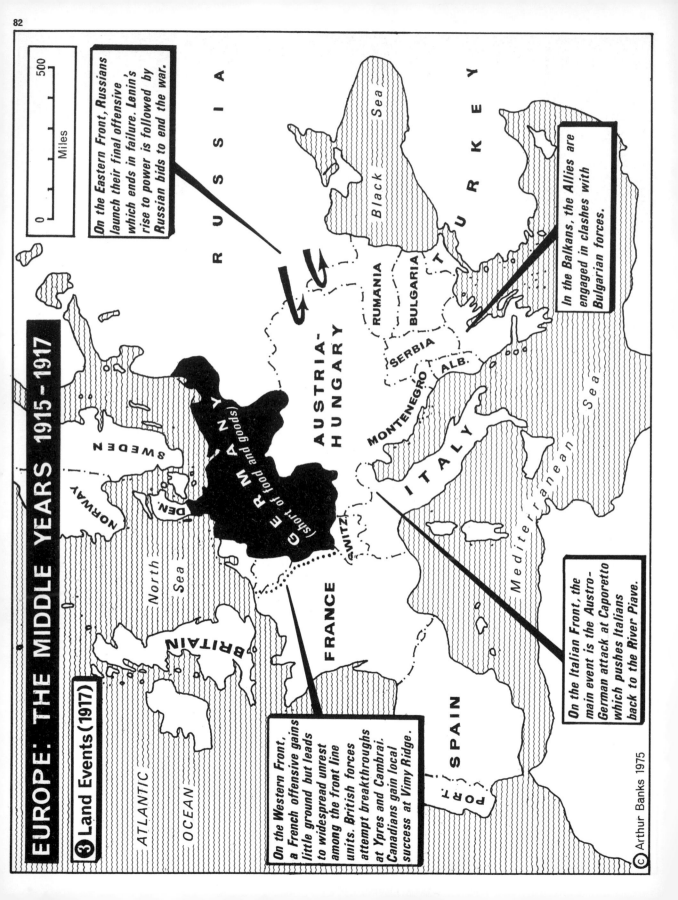

EUROPE: THE MIDDLE YEARS 1915-1917

③ Land Events (1917)

On the Eastern Front, Russians launch their final offensive which ends in failure. Lenin's rise to power is followed by Russian bids to end the war.

In the Balkans, the Allies are engaged in clashes with Bulgarian forces.

On the Italian Front, the main event is the Austro-German attack at Caporetto which pushes Italians back to the River Piave.

On the Western Front, a French offensive gains little ground but leads to widespread unrest among the front line units. British forces attempt breakthroughs at Ypres and Cambrai. Canadians gain local success at Vimy Ridge.

GERMANY (short of food and goods)

RUSSIA

SWEDEN

NORWAY

DEN.

BRITAIN

FRANCE

SWITZ.

AUSTRIA-HUNGARY

ITALY

SPAIN

PORT.

RUMANIA

BULGARIA

SERBIA

MONTENEGRO

ALB.

TURKEY

Black Sea

Mediterranean Sea

ATLANTIC OCEAN

North Sea

500 Miles 0

© Arthur Banks 1975

EUROPE: THE MIDDLE YEARS 1915–1917

④ Naval Events (1915–1917)

BLACK SEA

1915, Allied fleet fails to force passage.

1915, bombarded by Turco-German warships.

Odessa

DARDANELLES

SEA

BALTIC SEA

U-BOATS

U-BOATS

Adriatic Sea

1916, battle of Jutland.

1915, battle of Dogger Bank.

MEDITERRANEAN SEA

U-BOAT ROUTE

NORTH SEA

1917, destroyer clash.

Yarmouth
Lowestoft

U-BOAT ROUTE

1916, bombarded by German warships.

ATLANTIC OCEAN

500

Miles

0

© Arthur Banks 1975

THE DARDANELLES FIASCO IN 1915

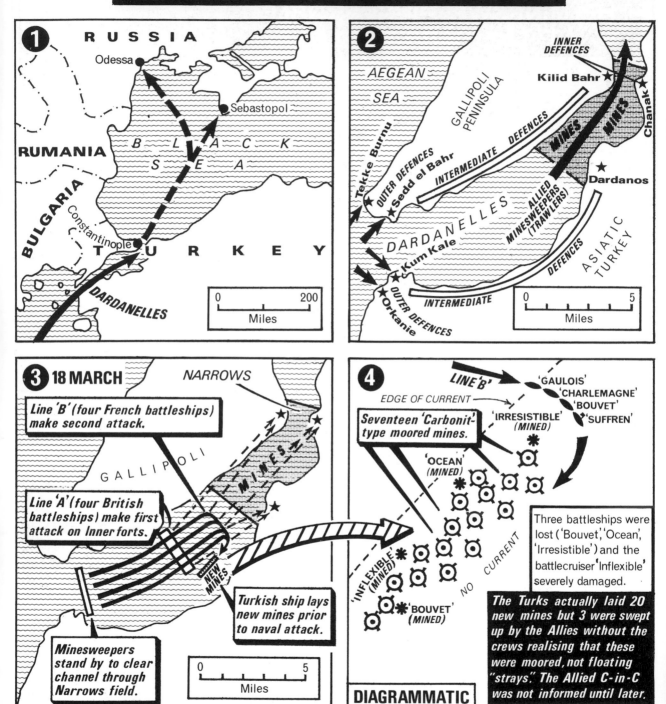

1 RUSSIA
Odessa
Sebastopol
RUMANIA
BLACK SEA
BULGARIA
Constantinople
TURKEY
DARDANELLES
0   200
Miles

2 AEGEAN SEA
GALLIPOLI PENINSULA
INNER DEFENCES
Kilid Bahr ★
Chanak ★
MINES
MINES
INTERMEDIATE DEFENCES
Tekke Burnu
OUTER DEFENCES
Sedd el Bahr ★
Dardanos ★
ALLIED MINESWEEPERS (TRAWLERS)
DARDANELLES
Kum Kale ★
INTERMEDIATE DEFENCES
ASIATIC TURKEY
OUTER DEFENCES
Orkanie ★
INTERMEDIATE
0   5
Miles

3 18 MARCH
NARROWS
Line 'B' (four French battleships) make second attack.
MINES
GALLIPOLI
Line 'A' (four British battleships) make first attack on Inner forts.
NEW MINES
Turkish ship lays new mines prior to naval attack.
Minesweepers stand by to clear channel through Narrows field.
0   5
Miles

4 LINE 'B'
'GAULOIS'
'CHARLEMAGNE'
'BOUVET'
'SUFFREN'
EDGE OF CURRENT
'IRRESISTIBLE' (MINED)
Seventeen 'Carbonit'-type moored mines.
'OCEAN' (MINED)
NO CURRENT
Three battleships were lost ('Bouvet','Ocean','Irresistible') and the battlecruiser'Inflexible' severely damaged.
'INFLEXIBLE' (MINED)
'BOUVET' (MINED)
The Turks actually laid 20 new mines but 3 were swept up by the Allies without the crews realising that these were moored, not floating "strays". The Allied C-in-C was not informed until later.
DIAGRAMMATIC

© Arthur Banks 1975

KEY TO SECTIONS

1 The Allied plan: fleet to steam through Dardanelles to threaten Constantinople and thence on to Russian ports.

2 Stages of plan:(a)destruction of outer defences (b)bombardment of other defences to cover minesweeping phase.

3 Allied fleet enters Dardanelles: bombardment proceeds: disaster overtakes plan when explosions rend warships.

4 Operation abandoned. Diagram illustrates cause of the mystery: group of mines laid at night unknown to Allies.

THE MINESWEEPING PROBLEM AT THE DARDANELLES

1

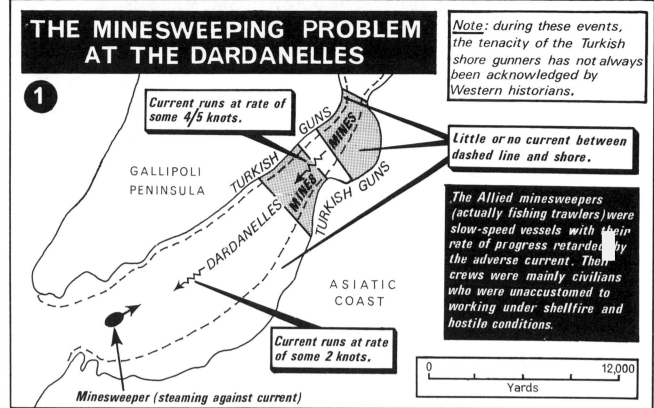

Note: during these events, the tenacity of the Turkish shore gunners has not always been acknowledged by Western historians.

Current runs at rate of some 4/5 knots.

GALLIPOLI PENINSULA

TURKISH GUNS

MINES

MINES

MINES

TURKISH GUNS

DARDANELLES

Little or no current between dashed line and shore.

The Allied minesweepers (actually fishing trawlers) were slow-speed vessels with their rate of progress retarded by the adverse current. Their crews were mainly civilians who were unaccustomed to working under shellfire and hostile conditions.

ASIATIC COAST

Current runs at rate of some 2 knots.

Minesweeper (steaming against current)

0 ————— 12,000
Yards

2

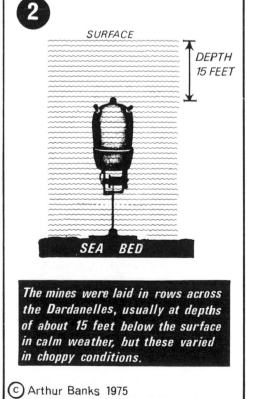

SURFACE

DEPTH 15 FEET

SEA BED

The mines were laid in rows across the Dardanelles, usually at depths of about 15 feet below the surface in calm weather, but these varied in choppy conditions.

© Arthur Banks 1975

3

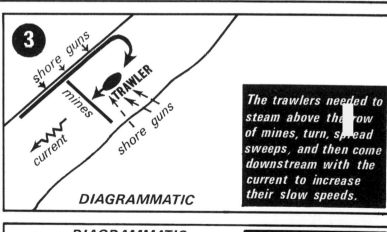

shore guns

TRAWLER

mines

current

shore guns

DIAGRAMMATIC

The trawlers needed to steam above the row of mines, turn, spread sweeps, and then come downstream with the current to increase their slow speeds.

DIAGRAMMATIC

4

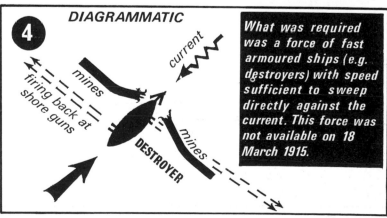

current

mines

firing back at shore guns

mines

DESTROYER

What was required was a force of fast armoured ships (e.g. destroyers) with speed sufficient to sweep directly against the current. This force was not available on 18 March 1915.

THE GALLIPOLI FIASCO IN 1915

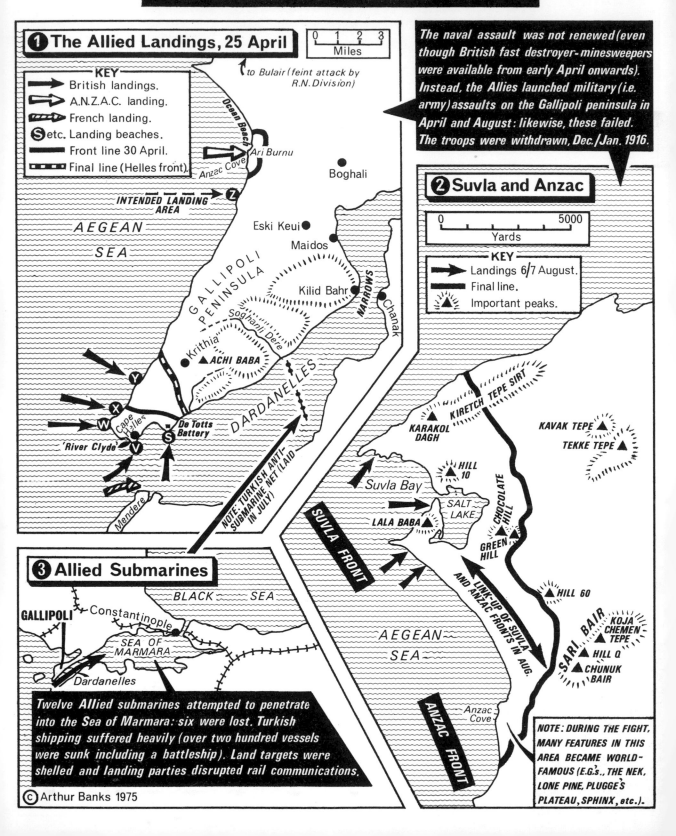

① The Allied Landings, 25 April

0 1 2 3
Miles

to Bulair (feint attack by R.N. Division)

KEY
- British landings.
- A.N.Z.A.C. landing.
- French landing.
- ⑤ etc. Landing beaches.
- Front line 30 April.
- Final line (Helles front).

Ocean Beach

Ari Burnu

Anzac Cove

Boghali

Ⓩ INTENDED LANDING AREA

AEGEAN SEA

Eski Keui

Maidos

Kilid Bahr

NARROWS

Chanak

GALLIPOLI PENINSULA

Soghanli Dere

Krithia

▲ ACHI BABA

DARDANELLES

Ⓨ

Ⓧ

Ⓦ Cape Helles

'River Clyde'

Ⓥ

Ⓢ De Totts Battery

Mendere

NOTE: TURKISH ANTI-SUBMARINE NET (LAID IN JULY)

The naval assault was not renewed (even though British fast destroyer-minesweepers were available from early April onwards). Instead, the Allies launched military (i.e. army) assaults on the Gallipoli peninsula in April and August: likewise, these failed. The troops were withdrawn, Dec./Jan. 1916.

② Suvla and Anzac

0 5000
Yards

KEY
- Landings 6/7 August.
- Final line.
- ▲ Important peaks.

KIRETCH TEPE SIRT

KARAKOL DAGH

KAVAK TEPE ▲

TEKKE TEPE ▲

▲ HILL 10

Suvla Bay

SALT LAKE

CHOCOLATE HILL

LALA BABA ▲

GREEN HILL

SUVLA FRONT

LINK-UP OF SUVLA AND ANZAC FRONTS IN AUG.

▲ HILL 60

AEGEAN SEA

SARI BAIR

KOJA CHEMEN TEPE ▲

▲ HILL Q

▲ CHUNUK BAIR

Anzac Cove

ANZAC FRONT

NOTE: DURING THE FIGHT, MANY FEATURES IN THIS AREA BECAME WORLD-FAMOUS (E.G's., THE NEK, LONE PINE, PLUGGE'S PLATEAU, SPHINX, etc.).

③ Allied Submarines

BLACK SEA

GALLIPOLI

Constantinople

SEA OF MARMARA

Dardanelles

Twelve Allied submarines attempted to penetrate into the Sea of Marmara: six were lost. Turkish shipping suffered heavily (over two hundred vessels were sunk including a battleship). Land targets were shelled and landing parties disrupted rail communications.

Ⓒ Arthur Banks 1975

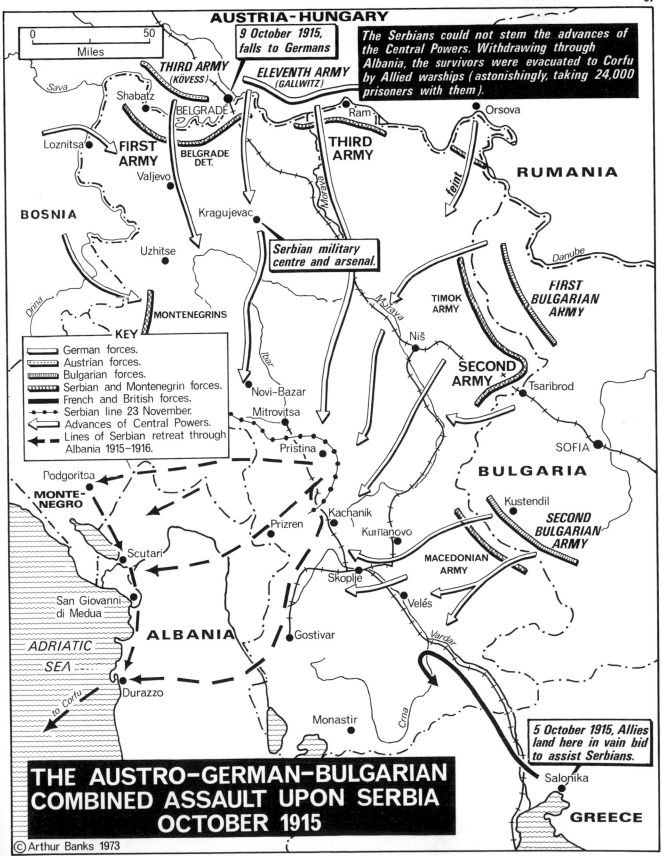

THE AUSTRO-GERMAN-BULGARIAN
COMBINED ASSAULT UPON SERBIA
OCTOBER 1915

© Arthur Banks 1973

THE CONFRONTATION OF THE BRITISH & GERMAN BATTLE FLEETS AT JUTLAND BANK ON 31 MAY 1916

❶ The Approach of the Rival Fleets

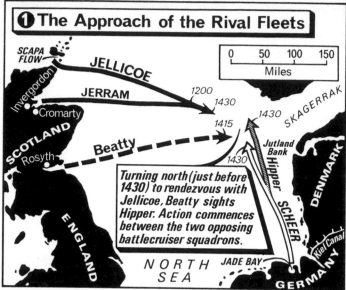

SCAPA FLOW

JELLICOE

JERRAM

Invergordon

Cromarty

SCOTLAND

Rosyth

Beatty

ENGLAND

NORTH SEA

JADE BAY

GERMANY

Kiel Canal

Jutland Bank

SKAGERRAK

DENMARK

Hipper

SCHEER

1200 · 1430 · 1415 · 1430 · 1430 · 1430

0 50 100 150 Miles

Turning north (just before 1430) to rendezvous with Jellicoe, Beatty sights Hipper. Action commences between the two opposing battlecruiser squadrons.

The Battle of Jutland ("Skagerrak" to Germans) was a direct confrontation between the British Grand Fleet and the German High Seas Fleet. Jellicoe possessed numerical and armament superiority and wished to fight in the northern North Sea, away from U-boats and minefields. Scheer wished to avoid a head-on clash and had perfected a "turn-away" manoeuvre for this event.

❸ Jellicoe versus Scheer

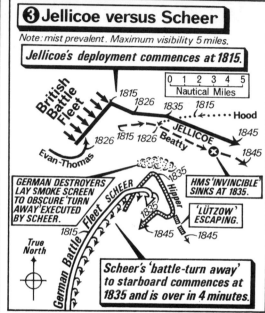

Note: mist prevalent. Maximum visibility 5 miles.

Jellicoe's deployment commences at 1815.

British Battle Fleet

0 1 2 3 4 5 Nautical Miles

1815 · 1826 · 1835 · 1815 · 1845 · 1845 · 1826 · 1815 · 1826 · 1835

Hood

JELLICOE

Beatty

Evan-Thomas

GERMAN DESTROYERS LAY SMOKE SCREEN TO OBSCURE 'TURN AWAY' EXECUTED BY SCHEER

HMS 'INVINCIBLE' SINKS AT 1835.

'LÜTZOW' ESCAPING.

German Battle Fleet SCHEER

Hipper

True North

Scheer's 'battle-turn away' to starboard commences at 1835 and is over in 4 minutes.

❷ Beatty versus Hipper

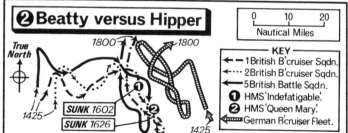

True North

1800 · 1800 · 1425 · 1425

SUNK 1602
SUNK 1626

KEY
- 1 British B'cruiser Sqdn.
- 2 British B'cruiser Sqdn.
- 5 British Battle Sqdn.
- ❶ HMS 'Indefatigable'.
- ❷ HMS 'Queen Mary'.
- German B'cruiser Fleet.

HMS "IRON DUKE" — JELLICOE'S FLAGSHIP

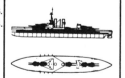

Main armament:	Ten 13·5-in. guns.
Secondary arm.:	Twelve 6-in. guns.
Laid down:	1912.
Completed:	1914.
Length:	620 feet.
Displacement:	25,000 tons.
Maximum speed:	23 knots.

SMS "FRIEDRICH DER GROSSE" — SCHEER'S FLAGSHIP

Main armament:	Ten 12-inch guns.
Secondary arm.:	Fourteen 6-in. gs.
Laid down:	1909.
Completed:	1912.
Length:	564 feet.
Displacement:	24,700 tons.
Maximum speed:	23 knots.

HMS "LION" — BEATTY'S FLAGSHIP

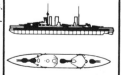

Main armament:	Eight 13·5-in. guns.
Secondary arm.:	Sixteen 4-in. guns.
Laid down:	1909.
Completed:	1912.
Length:	675 feet.
Displacement:	26,350 tons.
Maximum speed:	29 knots.

SMS "LÜTZOW" — HIPPER'S FLAGSHIP (until disabled)

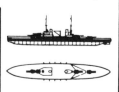

Main armament:	Eight 12-in. guns.
Secondary arm.:	Twelve 6-in. guns.
Laid down:	1912.
Completed:	1915.
Length:	590 feet.
Displacement:	28,000 tons.
Maximum speed:	29 knots.

❹ The Second Clash of the Fleets

Steering west following his 'battle turn' (1835-1839), Scheer was moving away from his Jade base. Under cover of the mist, he turned for home only to meet Jellicoe for the second time, whereupon he executed a further 'turn away.' A running chase now commenced.

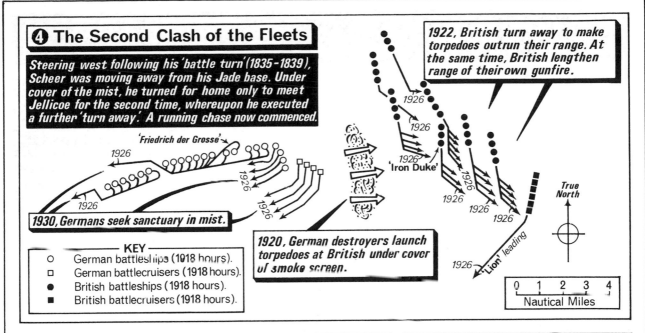

1922, British turn away to make torpedoes outrun their range. At the same time, British lengthen range of their own gunfire.

'Friedrich der Grosse'

1926

1926

1926

1926

1926

1930, Germans seek sanctuary in mist.

1920, German destroyers launch torpedoes at British under cover of smoke screen.

1926

'Iron Duke'

1926

1926

1926

1926

'Lion' leading

True North

KEY

○	German battleships (1918 hours).
□	German battlecruisers (1918 hours).
●	British battleships (1918 hours).
■	British battlecruisers (1918 hours).

0 1 2 3 4
Nautical Miles

❺ The Night Chase: Scheer's Escape

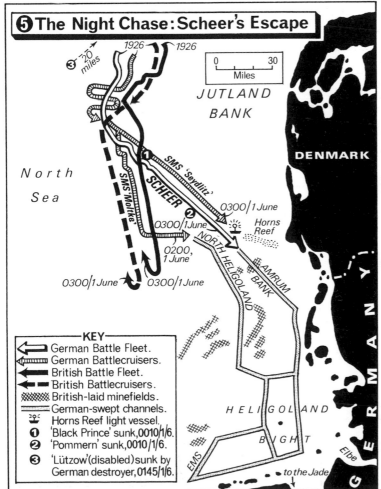

1926   *1926*

③ ~20 miles

0   30
Miles

JUTLAND BANK

DENMARK

North Sea

SMS 'Seydlitz'

① SCHEER

SMS 'Moltke'

0300/1 June

0300/1 June

0200/1 June

NORTH HELGOLAND BANK

Horns Reef

0300/1 June   0300/1 June

AMRUM BANK

HELIGOLAND BIGHT

EMS   Elbe

GERMANY

to the Jade

KEY

⬅	German Battle Fleet.
⬅	German Battlecruisers.
⬅	British Battle Fleet.
⬅	British Battlecruisers.
▨	British-laid minefields.
▤	German-swept channels.
♆	Horns Reef light vessel.
❶	'Black Prince' sunk, 0010/1/6.
❷	'Pommern' sunk, 0010/1/6.
❸	'Lützow' (disabled) sunk by German destroyer, 0145/1/6.

Despite British efforts to intercept the Germans on their homeward dash, the bulk of the High Seas Fleet made the Jade, battered but intact. Based upon ships lost and casualties, the encounter was a German success, but the North Sea strategical aspect remained as hitherto so far as the surface (not U-boat) war was concerned.

BRITISH DETAILS

Ships involved:	**151**
Sailors involved:	**60,000**
Battleships lost:	**0**
Battlecruisers lost:	**3**
Cruisers lost:	**3**
Destroyers lost:	**8**
Casualties:	**6,097**

GERMAN DETAILS

Ships involved:	**99**
Sailors involved:	**36,000**
Battleships lost:	**1**
Battlecruisers lost:	**1**
Cruisers lost:	**4**
Destroyers lost:	**5**
Casualties:	**2,551**

© Arthur Banks 1975

90

THE VERDUN BATTLE 1916

Geographical note: the River Meuse split the front into two sections, thus allowing Germans to launch two consecutive opening attacks.

Note: much of this lost territory was regained by French (October onwards).

FRENCH INNER FORTRESSES STRENGTHEN DEFENCES.

This map shows the extent of the German advance between 21 February and 1 July (when the Allied attack on the Somme front commenced).

GERMAN LINES

- Maucourt
- Beaumont
- Ornes
- Damloup
- ★ Ft. Tavannes
- ★ Ft. Douaumont
- ★ Ft. Vaux
- ★ Ft. Souville
- ★ Ft. St. Michel
- ★ Ft. Belleville
- ★ Ft. Belrupt
- Louvemont
- ★ Ft. Thiaumont
- Bras
- Haumont
- Champneuville
- Charny
- Brabant
- Champ
- *Côtes de Meuse*
- ★ Ft. Vacherauville
- ★ Ft. Marre
- Marre
- Thierville
- Consenvoye
- *MEUSE*
- Forges
- Drillancourt
- Chattancourt
- ★ Ft. Bois Bourrus
- ★ Ft. Choisel
- ★ Ft. Chana
- ★ Ft. Chaume
- ★ Ft. Sartelles

VERDUN

MEUSE

to Bar-le-Duc

LINES

FRENCH

- Bethincourt
- *Le Mort Homme*
- Esnes
- Malancourt
- Montfaucon
- Avocourt

FRENCH OUTER FORTRESS ZONE GUARDING VERDUN.

AREA OVERRUN BY GERMANS

KEY
- •••• German lines on 21 March.
- − − − German lines on 1 July.

Miles
0 1 2 3

© Arthur Banks 1975

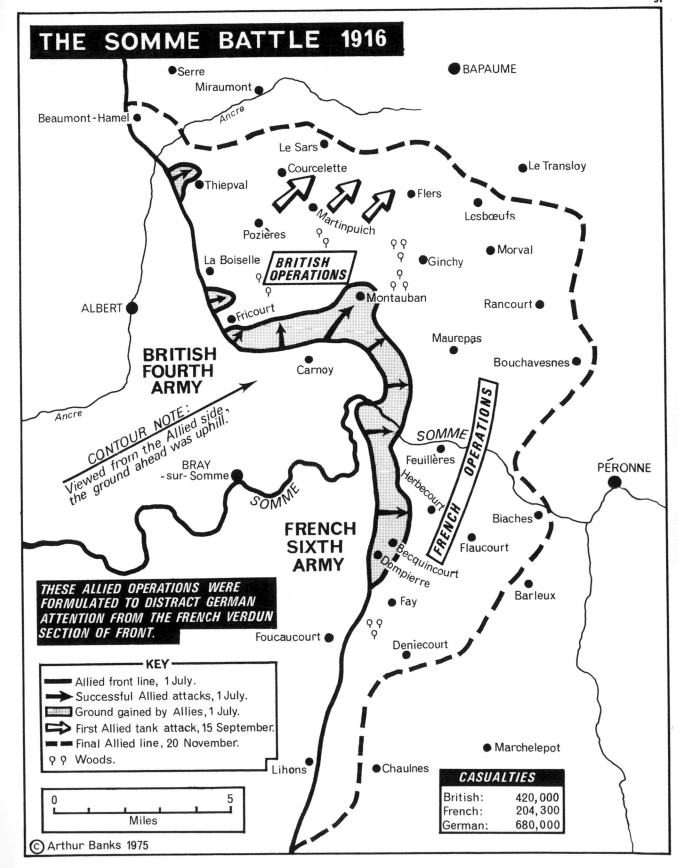

THE SOMME BATTLE 1916

BAPAUME

Serre

Miraumont

Ancre

Beaumont-Hamel

Le Sars

Le Transloy

Courcelette

Thiepval

Flers

Martinpuich

Lesbœufs

Pozières

La Boiselle

Ginchy

Morval

BRITISH OPERATIONS

Montauban

Rancourt

ALBERT

Fricourt

Maurepas

Bouchavesnes

BRITISH FOURTH ARMY

Carnoy

CONTOUR NOTE:
Viewed from the Allied side,
the ground ahead was uphill.

Ancre

SOMME

Feuillères

FRENCH OPERATIONS

PÉRONNE

BRAY -sur- Somme

Herbecourt

SOMME

Biaches

FRENCH SIXTH ARMY

Becquincourt

Flaucourt

Dompierre

Barleux

THESE ALLIED OPERATIONS WERE FORMULATED TO DISTRACT GERMAN ATTENTION FROM THE FRENCH VERDUN SECTION OF FRONT.

Fay

Foucaucourt

Deniecourt

KEY

Allied front line, 1 July.

Successful Allied attacks, 1 July.

Ground gained by Allies, 1 July.

First Allied tank attack, 15 September.

Final Allied line, 20 November.

Woods.

Marchelepot

Lihons

Chaulnes

0					5

Miles

CASUALTIES	
British:	420,000
French:	204,300
German:	680,000

© Arthur Banks 1975

to Baranovichi (100 miles) RUSSIAN FOURTH ARMY

THE BRUSILOV OFFENSIVE JUNE-OCTOBER 1916

Pripet

Stokhod

ARMY GROUP LINSINGEN *(4 JUNE)*

ABORTIVE ATTACKS 100 MILES TO NORTH (IN JUNE AND JULY)

RUSSIAN THIRD ARMY *(Lesh)*

EVERT (Commander: Russian Centre Army Group)

FOURTH AUSTRIAN ARMY *(Archduke Josef Ferdinand)*

Kovel

Goryn

Lutsk

Sluch

● Krilov

Rovno ●

FIRST AUSTRIAN ARMY *(Pulhallo von Brlog)*

Dubno ●

Styr

HQ, RUSSIAN EIGHTH ARMY

R U S S I A

BRUSILOV'S PLANS
To spread heavy pressure over the whole front simultaneously rather than to concentrate at fixed points, thus preventing the enemy switching reserves from point to point at will.

SECOND AUSTRIAN ARMY *(Böhm-Ermolli)*

Brody

RUSSIAN EIGHTH ARMY *(Kaledin)* (11 INF. & 4 CAV. DIVISIONS)

BRUSILOV'S G.H.Q.

Lemberg ●

SOUTHERN 'GERMAN' ARMY *(von Bothmer)*

Brzezany ●

Tarnopol ●

Volochisk ●

RUSSIAN ELEVENTH ARMY *(Sakharov)* (8 INF. & 1 CAV. DIVISIONS)

BRUSILOV (Commander: Russian S.W. Army Group)

Dniester

AUSTRIA-HUNGARY

HQ, RUSSIAN ELEVENTH ARMY

HQ, RUSSIAN SEVENTH ARMY

RUSSIAN SEVENTH ARMY *(Shcherbachev)* (7 INF. & 3½ CAV. DIVISIONS)

ACTING IN CONCERT

SEVENTH AUSTRIAN ARMY *(Pflanzer-Baltin)*

Stanislau ●

Gusyatin ●

HQ, RUSSIAN NINTH ARMY

RUSSIAN NINTH ARMY *(Lechitsky)* 10 INF. & 4 CAV. DIVISIONS

TOTAL DIVISIONS 4 JUNE = 38.

Kolomea ●

CARPATHIAN MTS.

Kamenets-Podolski ●

NOTE: BRUSILOV'S DIVISIONS 4 JUNE.

0   30
Miles

Kuty ●

Czernowitz ●

Pruth

The Brusilov Offensive was the most competent Russian operation of the war. It weakened the offensives of the Central Powers at Verdun and in Italy, and without German assistance being forthcoming, Austria probably would have collapsed. It was a direct cause of the Habsburg Empire's disintegration. On both sides casualties were colossal, over two million men being involved. The offensive halted through sheer exhaustion on the Russian side, and discontent in the rear areas eventually led to the Russian Revolution.

Kimpolung

Sereth

R U M A N I A

KEY
━━━ Russian front line 4 June.
╍╍╍ Russian front line 10 October.
▒ Ground gained by Russians.
◀ Main Russian advances.
+++ Double track railways.
⊻⊻ Pripet marshes.
⊠ Russian Army H.Q.
⊠ Russian Army Group G.H.Q.

DIVISIONAL COMPARISONS. Most Russian divisions had 16 battalions, the remainder 12. Austrian divisions had 12 battalions: German had 9.

© Arthur Banks 1973

THE RUMANIAN CAMPAIGN 1916

KEY TO BOTH MAPS
- Rumanian forces.
- Advances of the Central Powers with commanders named.
- ★ Important Rumanian fortresses.
- Russian forces.

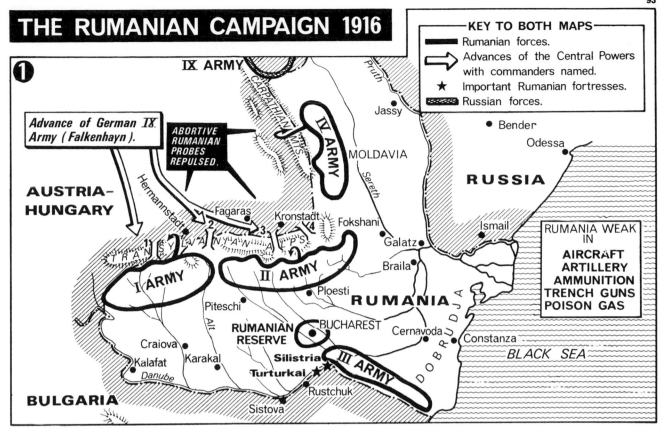

①

Advance of German IX Army (Falkenhayn).

ABORTIVE RUMANIAN PROBES REPULSED.

IX ARMY

IV ARMY

MOLDAVIA

AUSTRIA-HUNGARY

RUSSIA

Jassy

Bender

Odessa

Fagaras   Kronstadt   Fokshani

Hermannstadt   Galatz

TRANSYLVANIAN ALPS

I ARMY   II ARMY   Braila

Ismail

RUMANIA

RUMANIA WEAK IN
AIRCRAFT
ARTILLERY
AMMUNITION
TRENCH GUNS
POISON GAS

Piteschi   Ploesti

RUMANIAN RESERVE   BUCHAREST

Craiova   Cernavoda   Constanza

Karakal   **Silistria**   III ARMY   DOBRUDJA   BLACK SEA

Kalafat   **Turturkai** ★

Danube   Rustchuk

BULGARIA   Sistova

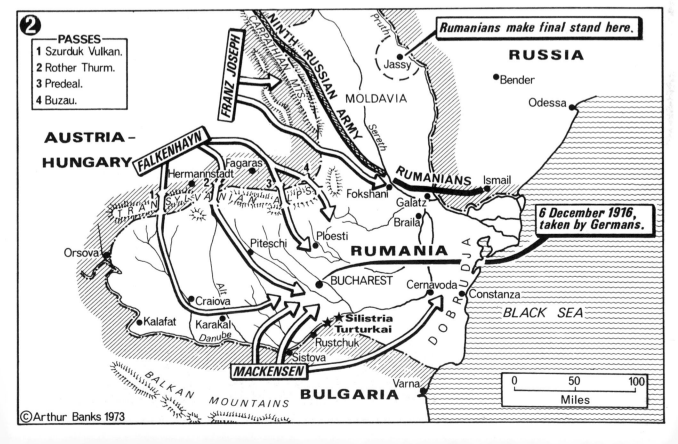

②

PASSES
1. Szurduk Vulkan.
2. Rother Thurm.
3. Predeal.
4. Buzau.

FRANZ JOSEPH

NINTH RUSSIAN ARMY

CARPATHIAN MTS.

Rumanians make final stand here.

AUSTRIA-HUNGARY

MOLDAVIA   RUSSIA

FALKENHAYN   Jassy   Bender

Hermannstadt   Fagaras   Odessa

TRANSYLVANIAN ALPS   Fokshani   **RUMANIANS**   Ismail

6 December 1916, taken by Germans.

Orsova   Galatz

Piteschi   Braila

Ploesti   RUMANIA

Craiova   BUCHAREST   Cernavoda

Kalafat   Karakal   ★ **Silistria**   Constanza   BLACK SEA

Danube   **Turturkai**   DOBRUDJA

Rustchuk

Sistova

MACKENSEN

BALKAN MOUNTAINS   Varna

BULGARIA

0   50   100
Miles

© Arthur Banks 1973

"THIRD YPRES"(PASSCHENDAELE):JULY – NOVEMBER 1917

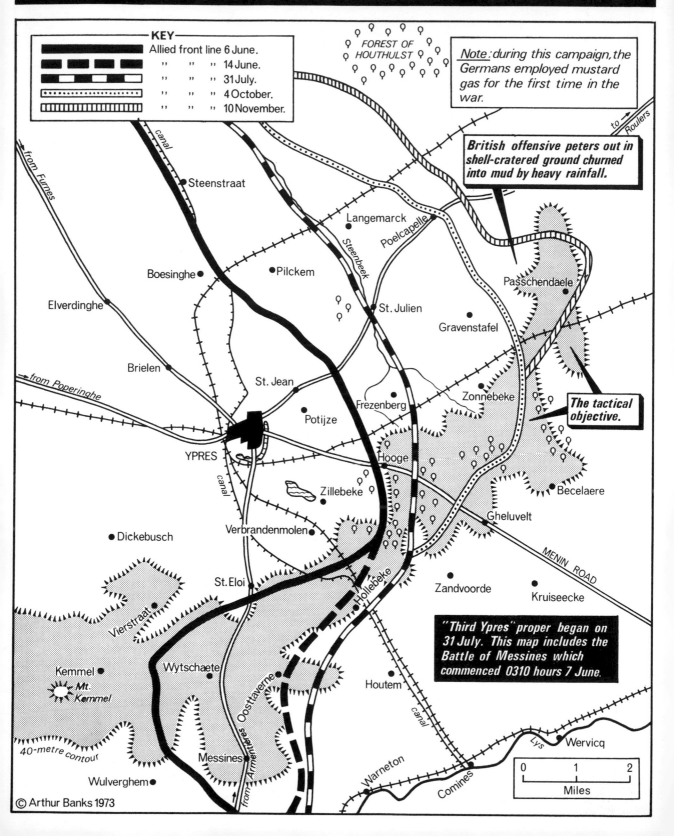

KEY

Allied front line 6 June.
,, ,, ,, 14 June.
,, ,, ,, 31 July.
,, ,, ,, 4 October.
,, ,, ,, 10 November.

FOREST OF HOUTHULST

Note: during this campaign, the Germans employed mustard gas for the first time in the war.

British offensive peters out in shell-cratered ground churned into mud by heavy rainfall.

to Roulers

canal

Steenstraat

Langemarck

Poelcapelle

Boesinghe

Pilckem

Steenbeek

Passchendaele

Elverdinghe

St. Julien

Gravenstafel

from Furnes

Brielen

St. Jean

Zonnebeke

The tactical objective.

from Poperinghe

Potijze

Frezenberg

YPRES

Hooge

Becelaere

Zillebeke

Gheluvelt

Dickebusch

Verbrandenmolen

MENIN ROAD

St. Eloi

Zandvoorde

Kruiseecke

Vierstraat

Hollebeke

"Third Ypres" proper began on 31 July. This map includes the Battle of Messines which commenced 0310 hours 7 June.

Kemmel

Mt. Kemmel

Wytschaete

Oosttaverne

Houtem

canal

from Armentières

Lys

Wervicq

40-metre contour

Messines

Warneton

Comines

Wulverghem

0	1	2

Miles

© Arthur Banks 1973

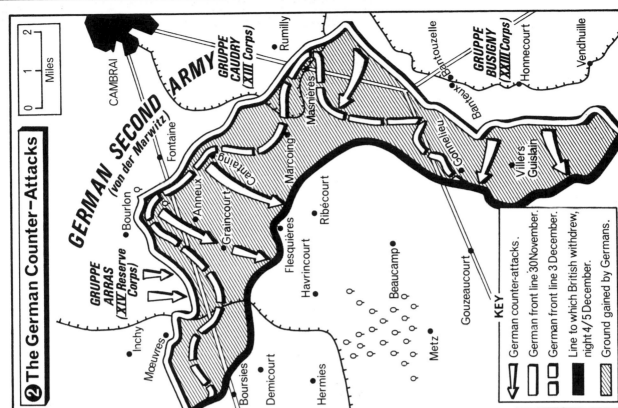

② The German Counter-Attacks

GERMAN SECOND ARMY (von der Marwitz)

GRUPPE ARRAS (XIV Reserve Corps)

GRUPPE CAUDRY (XIII Corps)

GRUPPE BUSIGNY (XXIII Corps)

CAMBRAI
Rumilly
Bantouzelle
Honnecourt
Vendhuille
Masnières
Baateux
Fontaine
Marcoing
Cantaing
Gonnelieu
Villers Guislain
Bourlon
Anneux
Graincourt
Flesquières
Ribécourt
Beaucamp
Gouzeaucourt
Inchy
Moeuvres
Boursies
Demicourt
Hermies
Havrincourt
Metz

KEY

German counter-attacks.	(arrow)
German front line 30 November.	
German front line 3 December.	
Line to which British withdrew, night 4/5 December.	
Ground gained by Germans.	

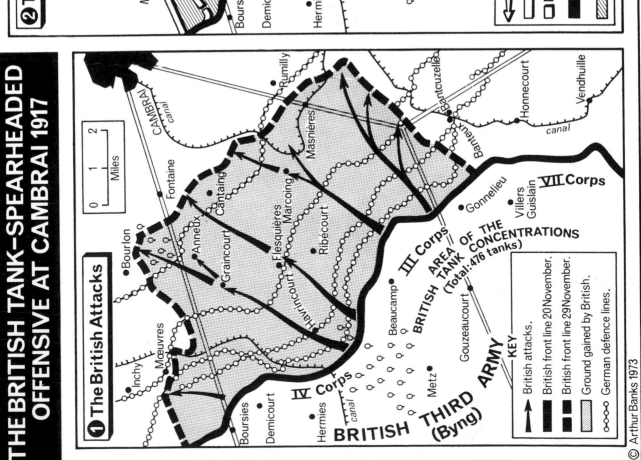

THE BRITISH TANK-SPEARHEADED OFFENSIVE AT CAMBRAI 1917

① The British Attacks

CAMBRAI
canal
Rumilly
Bantuzelle
Honnecourt
Vendhuille
canal
Masnières
Baateux
Fontaine
Cantaing
Marcoing
Gonnelieu
VII Corps
Villers Guislain
Bourlon
Anneux
Graincourt
Flesquières
Ribecourt
III Corps
AREA OF THE TANK CONCENTRATIONS
(Total:476 tanks)
BRITISH
Inchy
Moeuvres
Havrincourt
Beaucamp
Gouzeaucourt
Boursies
Demicourt
canal
Metz
IV Corps
Hermies

BRITISH THIRD (Byng) ARMY

KEY

British attacks.	(arrow)
British front line 20 November.	
British front line 29 November.	
Ground gained by British.	
German defence lines.	oooo

© Arthur Banks 1973

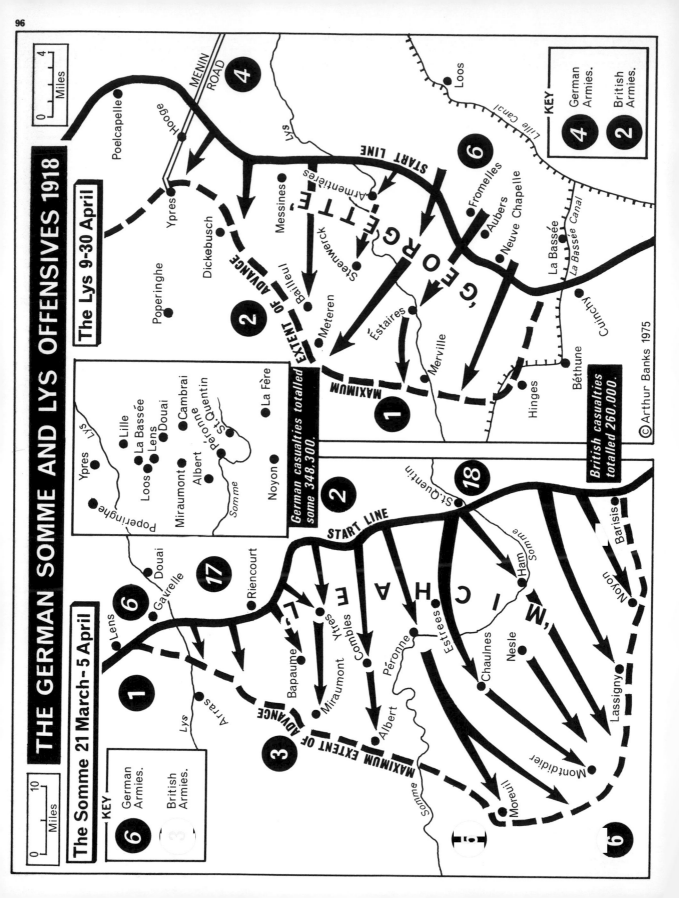

THE GERMAN SOMME AND LYS OFFENSIVES 1918

The Lys 9–30 April

KEY

④ German Armies.

② British Armies.

German casualties totalled some 348,300.

British casualties totalled 260,000.

© Arthur Banks 1975

The Somme 21 March–5 April

KEY

⑥ German Armies.

③ British Armies.

THE GERMAN AISNE AND MATZ OFFENSIVES 1918

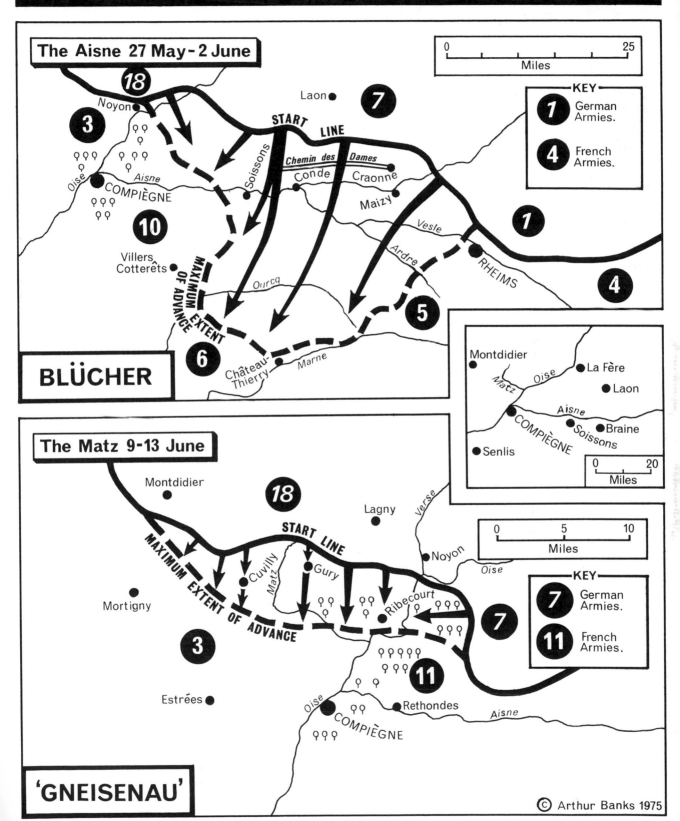

The Aisne 27 May – 2 June

0 — Miles — 25

KEY
1 German Armies.
4 French Armies.

Laon

18
Noyon
3
7
START LINE
Chemin des Dames
Conde
Craonne
Soissons
Maizy
Oise
Aisne
COMPIÈGNE
10
Vesle
1
Villers Cotterêts
MAXIMUM EXTENT OF ADVANCE
Ardre
RHEIMS
Ourcq
4
6
Château-Thierry
Marne
5

BLÜCHER

Montdidier
Matz
Oise
La Fère
Laon
Aisne
COMPIÈGNE
Soissons
Braine
Senlis
0 — Miles — 20

The Matz 9-13 June

Montdidier
18
Lagny
Verse
START LINE
Noyon
Oise
0 — 5 — Miles — 10

KEY
7 German Armies.
11 French Armies.

Mortigny
MAXIMUM EXTENT OF ADVANCE
Cuvilly
Matz
Gury
Ribecourt
7
3
Estrées
Oise
COMPIÈGNE
11
Rethondes
Aisne

'GNEISENAU'

© Arthur Banks 1975

THE ALLIED OFFENSIVES 18 JULY–11 NOVEMBER 1918

KEY

Allied line on 18 July.
Allied line on 25 August.
Allied line on 15 October.
Allied line on 6 November.
Allied line on 11 November.
Allied army boundaries.
German defence lines.

GERMANY

EIFEL

Trier

Saarbrücken

Dieuze

Malmédy

Spa

GERMAN O.H.L.

Liége

Namur

Meuse

Dinant

ARDENNES

Bastogne

Neufchâteau

Arlon

LUXEMBOURG

LUXEMBOURG

Longwy

Montmédy

Diedenhofen

Metz

Nancy

Toul

St. Mihiel

12 Sept.

AMERICANS

12 Sept.

Verdun

Bar-le-Duc

St. Dizier

26 Sept.

26 Sept.

Vitry-le-François

Charleville-Mézières

Rethel

KRIEMHILD

BRUNHILD

Moselle

Louvain

BRUSSELS

BELGIUM

Malines

ANTWERP

Schelde

Audenarde

Tournai

Courtrai

Ghent

Thielt

Bruges

Ostend

Zeebrugge

NORTH SEA

HOLLAND

Calais

Dunkirk

Nieuport

KING ALBERT'S H.Q.

BELGIANS

Ypres

28 Sept.

28 Sept.

Hondschoote

Hazebrouck

Cassel

St. Omer

Aire

Armentières

LILLE

Béthune

La Bassée

St. Pol

27 Sept.

27 Sept.

Lens

Douai

Scarpe

Cambrai

27 Sept.

SIEGFRIED

Arras

Bapaume

Albert

Doullens

8 Aug.

8 Aug.

Montdidier

Somme

Abbeville

Aumale

Beauvais

Clermont

Compiègne

Creil

Chantilly

Senlis

Pontoise

PARIS

Meaux

La Ferté

Coulommiers

FOCH'S H.Q.

FRENCH

Bombon

Provins

PETAIN'S G.Q.G.

Montmirail

Château Thierry

Soissons

Aisne

Fismes

Chauny

Ham

Noyon

Roye

Nesle

Chaulnes

Péronne

Chaulnes

SIEGFRIED

HERMANN

HUNDING

CHEMIN DES DAMES

Laon

Marle

Guise

La Cateau

Le Cateau

Vervins

Hirson

Avesnes

GERMAN O.H.L.

Maubeuge

Mons

Ath

Charleroi

Sambre

MOVED 5 SEPTEMBER

FLANDERN

WOTAN

Lys

BRITISH

HAIG'S G.H.Q.

Montreuil

Boulogne

Dormans

18 July

Rheims

Épernay

Châlons-sur-Marne

Fère Champenoise

Marne

Château Thierry

18 July

18 July

Montmirail

FRANCE

Miles

0   50

© Arthur Banks 1973

THE ALLIED ADVANCE INTO GERMANY 1918

© Arthur Banks 1975

Map labels:

GERMANY

HOLLAND

BELGIUM

FRANCE

A L L I E S

Neutral zone

BRITISH

AMERICAN Rhine

FRENCH

Rhine

EIFEL

ARDENNES

LUX.

Gie

Frankfurt

Mainz

Mannheim

Worms

Speier

Strassburg

Coblenz

Cologne

Düren

Liége

Namur

Hasselt

BRUSSELS

Arnhem

Ghent

Bruges

Lille

Mons

Cambrai

Luxembourg

Metz

Nancy

Verdun

Rheims

PARIS

Dunkirk

ZONE 1 (French)

ZONE 2 (American)

ZONE 3 (British)

ZONE 4 (Belgian)

Line 12 Dec.

Line 8 Dec.

Line 1 Dec.

Line 18 Nov.

ARMISTICE LINE 11 November

50

0

Miles

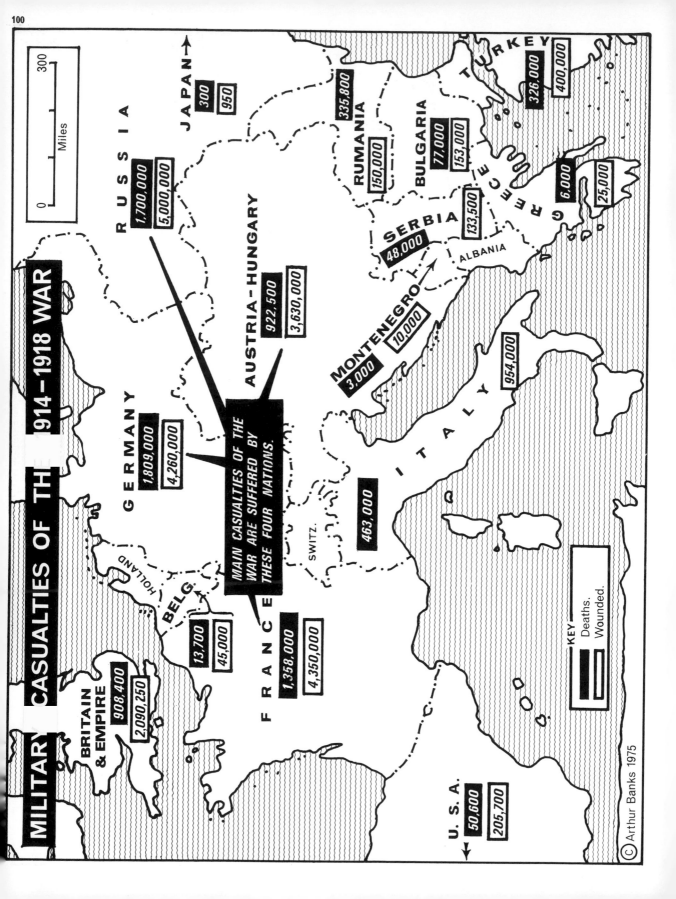

MILITARY CASUALTIES OF THE 1914–1918 WAR

MAIN CASUALTIES OF THE WAR ARE SUFFERED BY THESE FOUR NATIONS.

KEY
Deaths.
Wounded.

RUSSIA
1,700,000
5,000,000

JAPAN →
300
950

RUMANIA
335,800
150,000

BULGARIA
77,000
153,000

TURKEY
326,000
400,000

GREECE
6,000
25,000

SERBIA
48,000

AUSTRIA-HUNGARY
922,500
3,630,000

MONTENEGRO
3,000
10,000

133,500

ALBANIA

GERMANY
1,809,000
4,260,000

ITALY
954,000
463,000

SWITZ.

BELG.
13,700
45,000

HOLLAND

FRANCE
1,358,000
4,350,000

BRITAIN & EMPIRE
908,400
2,090,250

U.S.A.
50,600
205,700

© Arthur Banks 1975

300 · Miles · 0

CIVILIAN CASUALTIES AND EXPENDITURE 1914–18

KEY
- ▬ Deaths.
- ☐ Financial cost ($ millions).

NOTE THE HIGH RUSSIAN LOSSES. BRITISH, GERMAN, AND FRENCH EXPENDITURE IS HIGHER THAN THAT OF THE UNITED STATES.

Scale: 0 — 300 Miles

TURKEY 2,000,000 / 3,500

RUSSIA 2,000,000 / 26,000 — casualties

JAPAN → 600 / 1,000

280,000 / 3,000

RUMANIA 275,000 / 1,000

BULGARIA 132,000 / 1,000

SERBIA 70,000 / 3,000

GREECE 700

ALBANIA

MONTENEGRO 707 / 1,000

24,000

AUSTRIA–HUNGARY 300,000

GERMANY 500,000 / 60,000 — cost of war

SWITZ. 3,000 / 18,000

HOLLAND 30,000 / 10,000

BELG. cost of war

FRANCE 40,000 / 49,000 — cost of war

cost of war

ITALY

BRITAIN & EMPIRE 31,000 / 60,000

U.S.A. 1,000 / 33,000

© Arthur Banks 1975

V

THE INTER-WAR YEARS

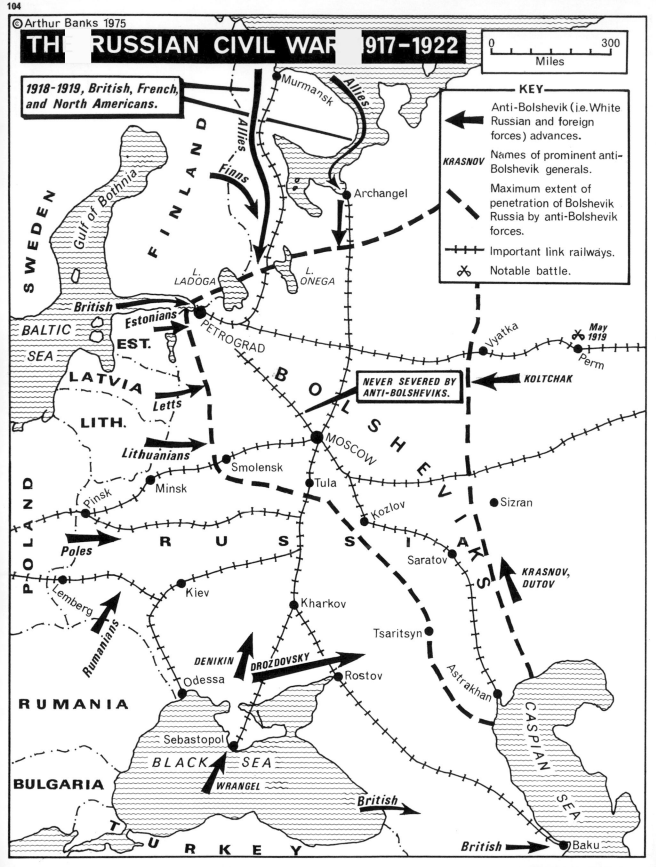

© Arthur Banks 1975

THE RUSSIAN CIVIL WAR 1917-1922

0 — 300
Miles

1918-1919, British, French, and North Americans.

KEY

Anti-Bolshevik (i.e. White Russian and foreign forces) advances.

KRASNOV — Names of prominent anti-Bolshevik generals.

Maximum extent of penetration of Bolshevik Russia by anti-Bolshevik forces.

—+—+— Important link railways.

✂ Notable battle.

Murmansk

Allies

Allies

Finns

Archangel

SWEDEN

FINLAND

Gulf of Bothnia

L. LADOGA

L. ONEGA

British

Estonians

BALTIC SEA

EST.

PETROGRAD

B O L S H E V I K

Vyatka

✂ **May 1919**

Perm

LATVIA

Letts

NEVER SEVERED BY ANTI-BOLSHEVIKS.

← *KOLTCHAK*

LITH.

Lithuanians

Smolensk

MOSCOW

Minsk

Tula

Sizran

Pinsk

POLAND

R U S S I A N S

Poles

Kozlov

Saratov

KRASNOV, DUTOV

Lemberg

Kiev

Kharkov

Rumanians

Tsaritsyn

Odessa

DENIKIN

DROZDOVSKY →

Rostov

Astrakhan

RUMANIA

CASPIAN SEA

Sebastopol

B L A C K   S E A

WRANGEL

British →

BULGARIA

T U R K E Y

British → Baku

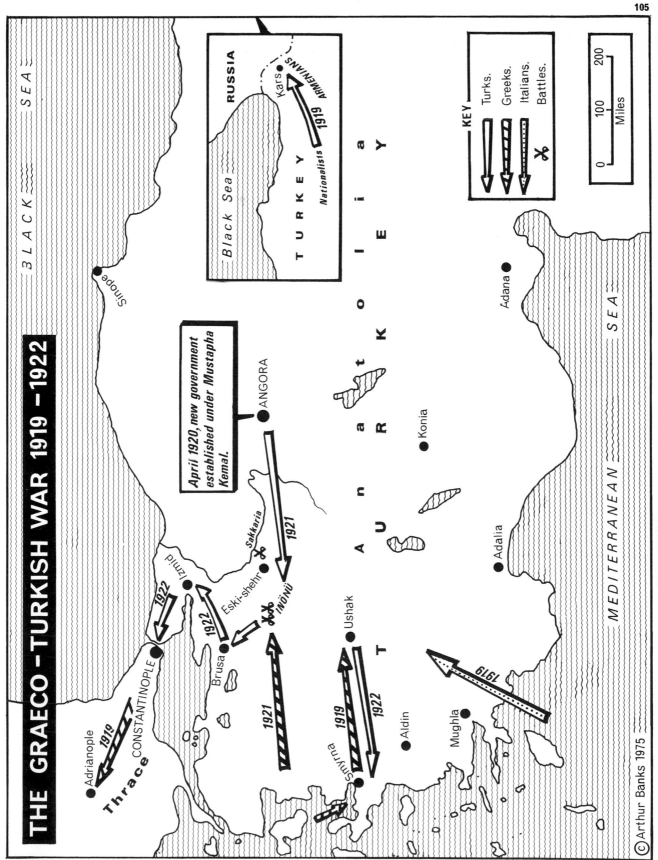

THE GRAECO–TURKISH WAR 1919–1922

KEY

Turks.
Greeks.
Italians.
Battles.

200
100
0 100 200
Miles

April 1920, new government established under Mustapha Kemal.

RUSSIA

Kars

1919 ARMENIANS

T U R K E Y
Nationalists

Black Sea

Sinope

ANGORA

A n a t o l i a   T U R K E Y

Adana

Konia

Adalia

Izmid

Sakkaria

Eski-shehr

Inönü

Brusa

Ushak

1921

1922

1919

1922

1919

Smyrna

Aldin

Mughla

1919

CONSTANTINOPLE

Adrianople

1919

Thrace

BLACK SEA

MEDITERRANEAN SEA

© Arthur Banks 1975

105

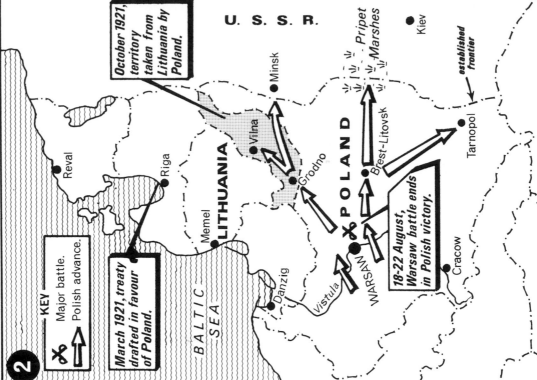

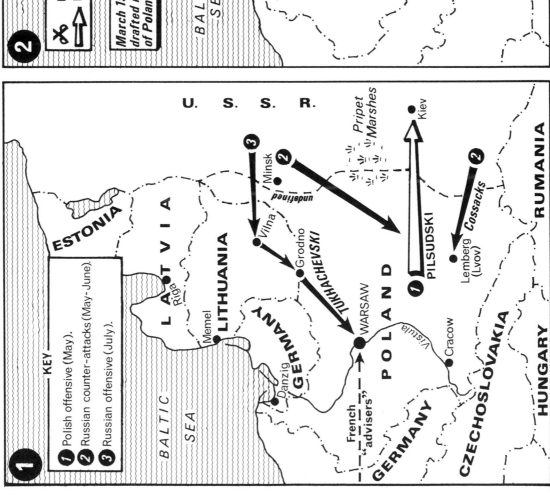

THE WEIMAR REPUBLIC

BALTIC SEA

Memel

East Prussia

Danzig

POLISH "CORRIDOR"

P o s e n

Katowice

Kolberg

Breslau

Oder

NORTH SEA

BERLIN

Elbe

Dresden

Leipzig

WEIMAR

Erfurt

Nuremberg

Munich

Hamburg

NORTH SCHLESWIG

Hanover

Bremen

Weser

Münster

Cassel

Frankfurt

Stuttgart

Rhine

Cologne

Coblenz

Mainz

SAAR

KEY
Germany's losses.

0   100
Miles

1919, new Republican Constitution formed: Chancellor (rather than President) is main figure.

1920, Hitler forms National Socialist Party. 1923, "putsch" ends in failure: 1924, Hitler is imprisoned: he writes "MEIN KAMPF."

1923, American occupation force returns home.

This map shows Germany in 1919, following the Treaty of Versailles.

© Arthur Banks 1975

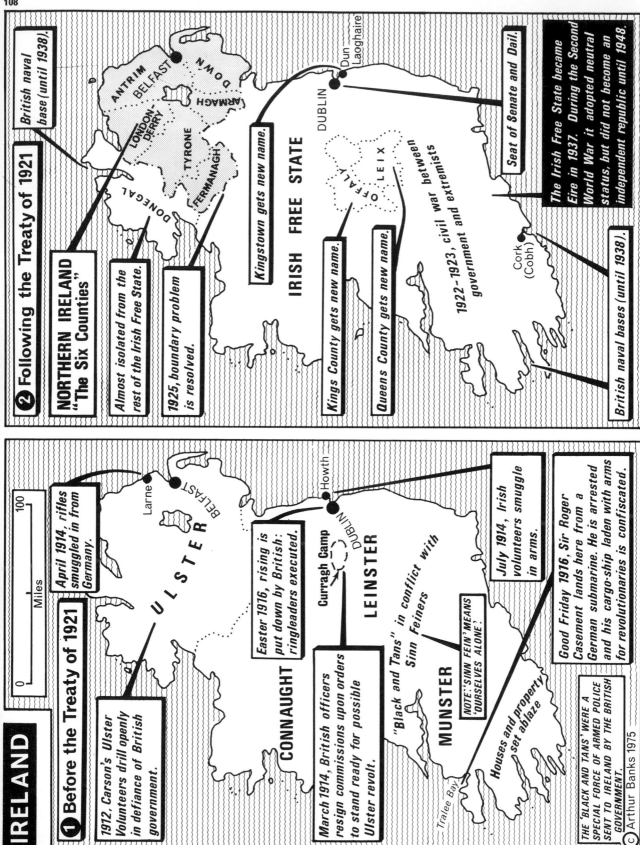

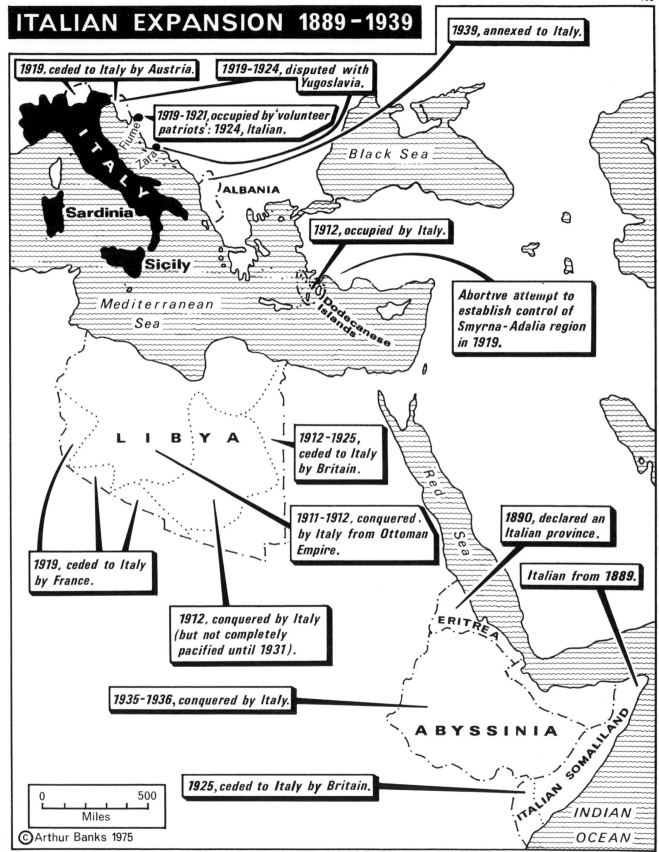

ITALIAN EXPANSION 1889-1939

1939, annexed to Italy.

1919, ceded to Italy by Austria.

1919-1924, disputed with Yugoslavia.

1919-1921, occupied by 'volunteer patriots': 1924, Italian.

ITALY

Fiume

Zara

ALBANIA

Black Sea

Sardinia

Sicily

1912, occupied by Italy.

Mediterranean Sea

Dodecanese Islands

Abortive attempt to establish control of Smyrna-Adalia region in 1919.

L I B Y A

1912-1925, ceded to Italy by Britain.

1911-1912, conquered by Italy from Ottoman Empire.

1890, declared an Italian province.

1919, ceded to Italy by France.

Italian from 1889.

Red Sea

ERITREA

1912, conquered by Italy (but not completely pacified until 1931).

1935-1936, conquered by Italy.

A B Y S S I N I A

ITALIAN SOMALILAND

1925, ceded to Italy by Britain.

INDIAN OCEAN

0   500
Miles

© Arthur Banks 1975

EUROPE IN 1925

Note the extent of Germany: also, Austria-Hungary no longer exists as such. Russia is now U.S.S.R.

500

Miles

0

U. S. S. R.

Caspian Sea

Black Sea

T U R K E Y

FINLAND

EST.

LATVIA

LITH.

GERM.

POLAND

RUMANIA

BULGARIA

GREECE

ALB.

YUGOSLAVIA

HUNGARY

AUSTRIA

CZECH.

GERMANY

NORWAY

SWEDEN

Baltic Sea

DENMARK

NETH.

BELGIUM

LUX.

FRANCE

SWITZ.

ITALY

BRITISH ISLES

ATLANTIC OCEAN

North Sea

Mediterranean Sea

SPAIN

PORTUGAL

© Arthur Banks 1975

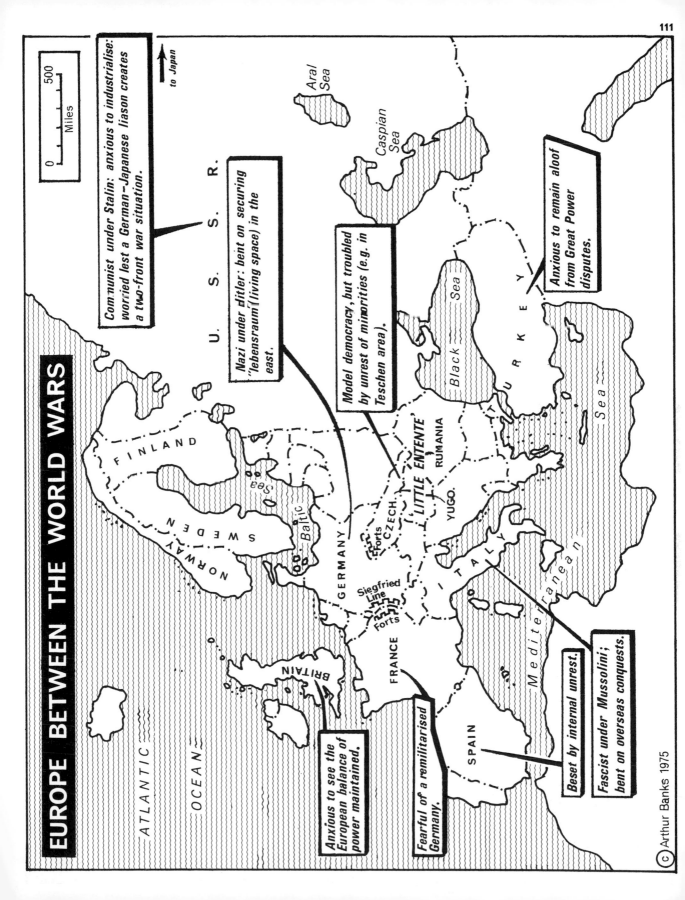

EUROPE BETWEEN THE WORLD WARS

Communist under Stalin: anxious to industrialise; worried lest a German–Japanese liason creates a two-front war situation.

Nazi under Hitler: bent on securing "lebensraum" (living space) in the east.

Model democracy, but troubled by unrest of minorities (e.g. in Teschen area).

Anxious to remain aloof from Great Power disputes.

Anxious to see the European balance of power maintained.

Fearful of a remilitarised Germany.

Beset by internal unrest.

Fascist under Mussolini; bent on overseas conquests.

to Japan

500

Miles

0

Aral Sea

Caspian Sea

U. S. S. R.

Black Sea

T U R K E Y

FINLAND

Baltic Sea

SWEDEN

NORWAY

LITTLE ENTENTE

RUMANIA

CZECH.

YUGO.

Forts

GERMANY

Siegfried Line

Forts

I T A L Y

Mediterranean Sea

BRITAIN

FRANCE

SPAIN

ATLANTIC

OCEAN

© Arthur Banks 1975

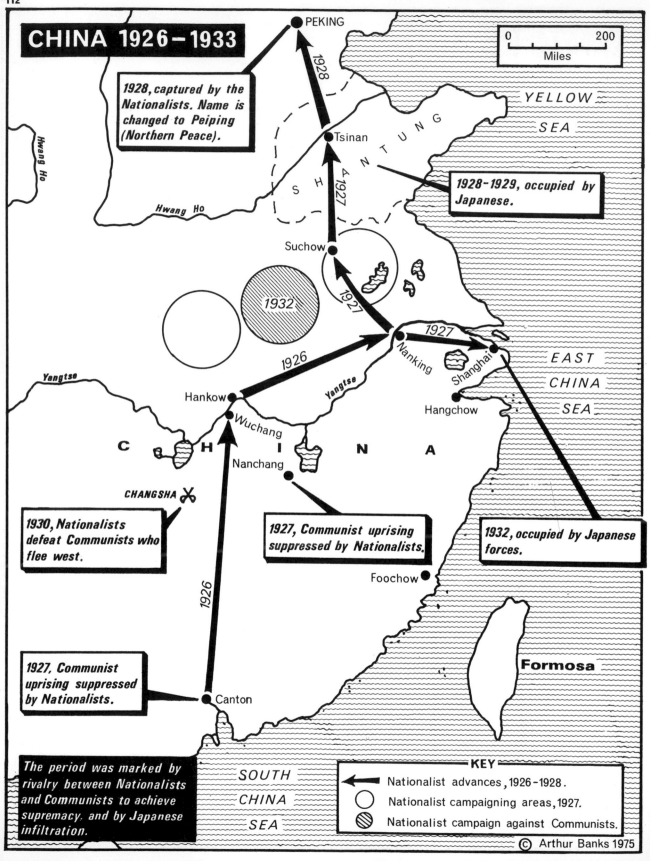

112

CHINA 1926-1933

1928, captured by the Nationalists. Name is changed to Peiping (Northern Peace).

0 — 200
Miles

YELLOW
SEA

Hwang Ho

Hwang Ho

S H A N T U N G

1928
PEKING

Tsinan

1927

1928-1929, occupied by Japanese.

Suchow

1932

1926

1927

Nanking

1927

Shanghai

EAST
CHINA
SEA

Hankow

Yangtse

Hangchow

Yangtse

Wuchang

C   H   I   N   A

Nanchang

1926

CHANGSHA ✂

1930, Nationalists defeat Communists who flee west.

1927, Communist uprising suppressed by Nationalists.

1932, occupied by Japanese forces.

Foochow

1927, Communist uprising suppressed by Nationalists.

Canton

Formosa

The period was marked by rivalry between Nationalists and Communists to achieve supremacy. and by Japanese infiltration.

SOUTH
CHINA
SEA

— KEY —

Nationalist advances, 1926-1928.

Nationalist campaigning areas, 1927.

Nationalist campaign against Communists.

© Arthur Banks 1975

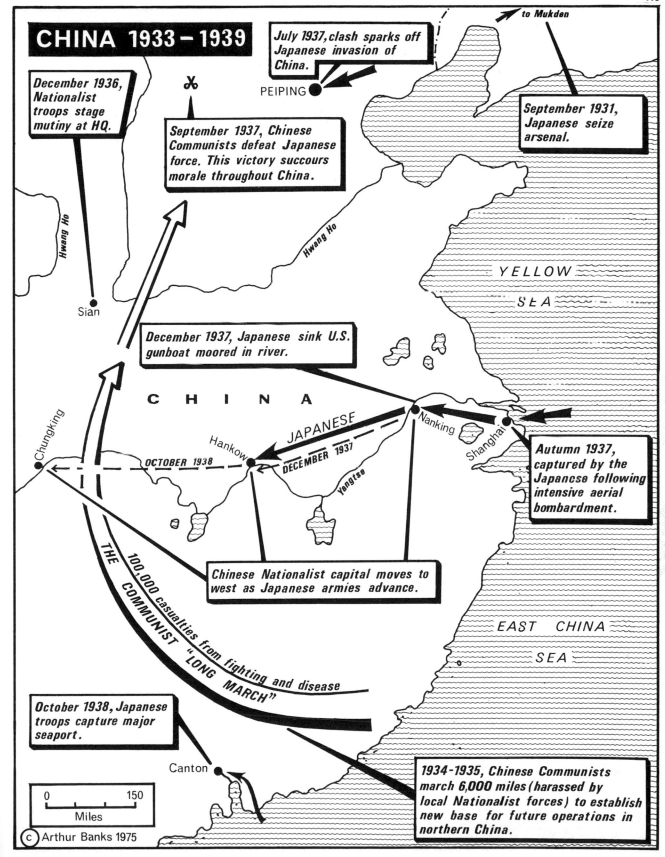

113

CHINA 1933 - 1939

July 1937, clash sparks off Japanese invasion of China.

PEIPING

to Mukden

September 1931, Japanese seize arsenal.

December 1936, Nationalist troops stage mutiny at HQ.

September 1937, Chinese Communists defeat Japanese force. This victory succours morale throughout China.

Hwang Ho

Hwang Ho

YELLOW SEA

Sian

December 1937, Japanese sink U.S. gunboat moored in river.

C H I N A

JAPANESE

Nanking

Shanghai

Chungking

Hankow

OCTOBER 1938

DECEMBER 1937

Yangtse

Autumn 1937, captured by the Japanese following intensive aerial bombardment.

Chinese Nationalist capital moves to west as Japanese armies advance.

100,000 casualties from fighting and disease

THE COMMUNIST "LONG MARCH"

EAST CHINA SEA

October 1938, Japanese troops capture major seaport.

Canton

0   150
Miles

© Arthur Banks 1975

1934-1935, Chinese Communists march 6,000 miles (harassed by local Nationalist forces) to establish new base for future operations in northern China.

114

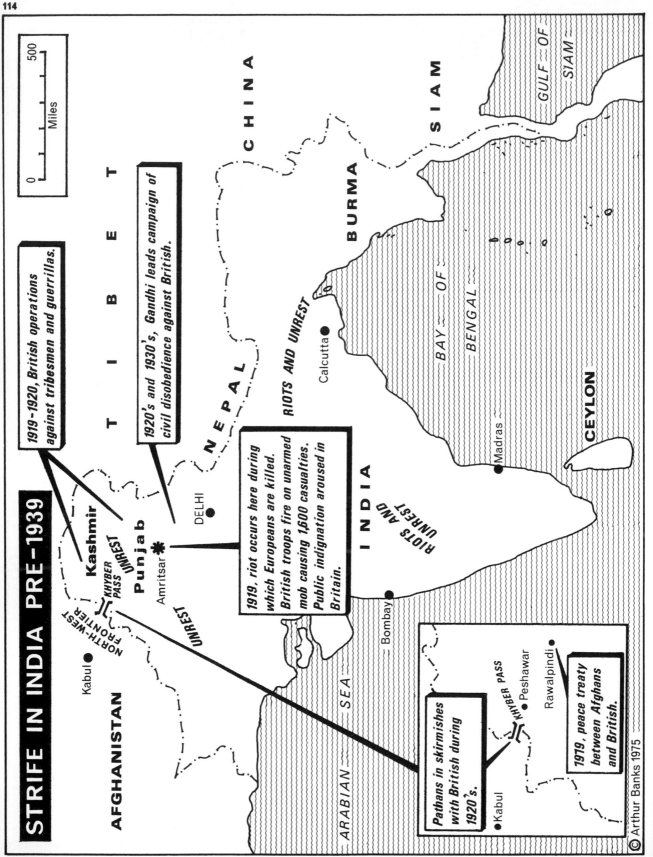

STRIFE IN INDIA PRE–1939

1919–1920, British operations against tribesmen and guerrillas.

1920's and 1930's, Gandhi leads campaign of civil disobedience against British.

1919, riot occurs here during which Europeans are killed. British troops fire on unarmed mob causing 1,600 casualties. Public indignation aroused in Britain.

Pathans in skirmishes with British during 1920's.

1919, peace treaty between Afghans and British.

500

Miles

0

T I B E T

C H I N A

N E P A L

BURMA

SIAM

GULF OF SIAM

RIOTS AND UNREST

Calcutta

BAY OF BENGAL

CEYLON

Madras

I N D I A

RIOTS AND UNREST

Kashmir

Punjab

Amritsar

DELHI

KHYBER PASS

NORTH-WEST FRONTIER

UNREST

UNREST

Kabul

AFGHANISTAN

ARABIAN SEA

Bombay

KHYBER PASS

Peshawar

Rawalpindi

Kabul

© Arthur Banks 1975

SPAIN: THE AXIS TRAINING GROUND 1936-1939

September 1937, nine-power conference held at Nyon in Switzerland: anti-submarine naval patrol zones established.

Mid-1937, submarines of "unknown" origin attack British, French, Soviet, and Spanish Government shipping.

The Spanish Civil War between the Nationalists and Republicans attracted foreign contingents and volunteers to both sides. The Nationalists were the victors. Total casualties: at least 750,000.

KEY

- Ⓡ Military revolts, 1936.
- Spanish Nationalist advances.
- Spanish government moves from Madrid to east coast.
- Spanish Nationalist naval blockade (from Nov. 1937).
- ✷ Important battles.
- ✳ Heavily bombed by Germans.

Non-interventionist policy.

26 January 1939, falls to Nationalists.

December 1937-February 1938, bitter fighting here.

March 1937, Italian reverses.

28 March 1939, both cities surrender to Nationalists: civil war ends.

May 1937, shelled by German pocket-battleship: bombed by German Air Force.

July 1936, Franco arrives here to command Spanish Nationalist forces.

April 1937, devastated by German aircraft.

Nationalist HQ.

Besieged at intervals, 1936-1939.

1928, dictatorship established.

F R A N C E

Andorra

MEDITERRANEAN SEA

Balearic Islands

Barcelona

Vinaroz

Valencia

Ebro

Teruel

Brihuega
Guadalajara

Guernica

Bilbao

BURGOS Ⓡ

OVIEDO Ⓡ

Duero

MADRID

TOLEDO

S P A I N

Tagus

Badajoz

SEVILLE Ⓡ

Guadalquivir

Malaga

Almeria

CADIZ Ⓡ

Tangier

SPANISH MOROCCO

Melilla

P O R T U G A L

LISBON

Nov. 1936

1937-1938

1936

1936

1936

1937

1938

1939

1939

Oct. 1937

© Arthur Banks 1975

0   100
Miles

VI
THE SECOND
WORLD WAR

HITLER'S ROAD TO WAR 1936–1939

KEY

卐 Hitler's "Third Reich".

- - - Training ground for Luftwaffe (in Spain).

① Hitler's first "exploratory" move (1936).

② Austria annexed (1938).

③ Sudetenland annexed (later, western Czechoslovakia, 1939).

④ Memel annexed (1939).

▨ Territories gained by Hitler (1936-1939).

⑤ Danzig attacked (September 1939).

MUSSOLINI
Hitler's "ally and friend"

© Arthur Banks 1975

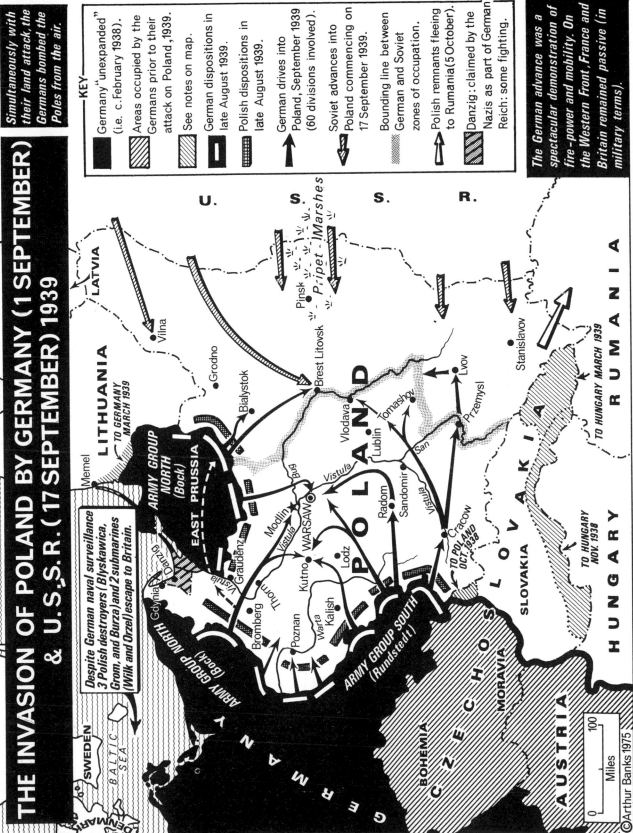

THE INVASION OF POLAND BY GERMANY (1 SEPTEMBER) & U.S.S.R. (17 SEPTEMBER) 1939

Simultaneously with their land attack, the Germans bombed the Poles from the air.

KEY

- Germany "unexpanded" (i.e. c.February 1938).
- Areas occupied by the Germans prior to their attack on Poland, 1939.
- German dispositions in late August 1939.
- See notes on map.
- Polish dispositions in late August 1939.
- German drives into Poland, September 1939 (60 divisions involved).
- Soviet advances into Poland commencing on 17 September 1939.
- Bounding line between German and Soviet zones of occupation.
- Polish remnants fleeing to Rumania (5 October).
- Danzig: claimed by the Nazis as part of German Reich: some fighting.

The German advance was a spectacular demonstration of fire-power and mobility. On the Western Front, France and Britain remained passive (in military terms).

Despite German naval surveillance 3 Polish destroyers (Blyskawica, Grom, and Burza) and 2 submarines (Wilk and Orzel) escape to Britain.

U. S. S. R.

Pripet - Marshes

SWEDEN

BALTIC SEA

DENMARK

GERMANY

ARMY GROUP NORTH (Bock)

EAST PRUSSIA

ARMY GROUP NORTH (Bock)

Memel
TO GERMANY MARCH 1939

LITHUANIA

LATVIA

Vilna

Grodno

Bialystok

Brest Litovsk

Pinsk

Lvov

Stanislavov

Vlodava

Tomashov

Lublin

San

Przemysl

Gdynia
Danzig
Graudenz
Thorn
Bromberg
Poznan
Warta
Kalish
Lodz
Kutno
Modlin
Vistula
WARSAW
Radom
Sandomir
Vistula
Cracow
TO POLAND OCT. 1938

Bug

Vistula

POLAND

ARMY GROUP SOUTH (Rundstedt)

TO POLAND NOV. 1938

C Z E C H O S L O V A K I A

SLOVAKIA

BOHEMIA

MORAVIA

AUSTRIA

HUNGARY

TO HUNGARY MARCH 1939

TO HUNGARY MARCH 1939

RUMANIA

0   100
Miles

©Arthur Banks 1975

THE CRUISE OF 'ADMIRAL GRAF SPEE' 21 AUGUST–13 DECEMBER 1939

KEY
Track of German pocket-battleship 'Admiral Graf Spee', with dates.

❶ The Quarry – 'Admiral Graf Spee'

Note: in an attempt to confuse the British Admiralty, 'Graf Spee' frequently displayed false name-plates of the other two German pocket-battleships, the 'Admiral Scheer' and 'Deutschland'.

During 'Graf Spee's' voyage, her supplies were replenished by the tanker 'Altmark'.

Total tonnage of merchant shipping sunk by 'Graf Spee' during her 115-day cruise as a commerce raider amounted to 50,089 gross tons.

Note: Allied naval groups hunting the 'Graf Spee' are shown by their official force designations, thus.... **F** **G** **H** etc.

NORTH AMERICA

EUROPE

Wilhelmshaven
GERMANY

23 Aug.
25 Aug.
27 Aug.
21 Aug.
29 Aug.
31 Aug.
2 Sept.
4 Sept.
6 Sept.
8 Sept.

ATLANTIC OCEAN

AFRICA

SOUTH AMERICA

INDIAN OCEAN

L
F
N
M
K
J
G
H
I

30 Sept.
29 Sept.
10 Sept.
3 Oct.
10 Oct.
8 Oct.
7 Oct.
5 Oct.
13 Oct.
23 Oct.
22 Oct.
2 Dec.
27 Sept.
17 Sept.
7 Dec.
3 Dec.
2 Dec.
4 Dec.
24 Nov.
28 Oct.
7 Dec.
1 Nov.
20 Nov.
15 Nov.
14 Nov.
8 Nov.

13 Dec.
Plate

13 December 1939, the Battle of the River Plate.

VICTIMS OF THE 'GRAF SPEE'
❶ SS 'Clement' ❷ SS 'Newton Beech' ❸ SS 'Ashlea' ❹ SS 'Huntsman'
❺ SS 'Trevanion' ❻ SS 'Africa Shell' ❼ SS 'Doric Star' ❽ SS 'Tairoa' ❾ SS 'Streonshalh'

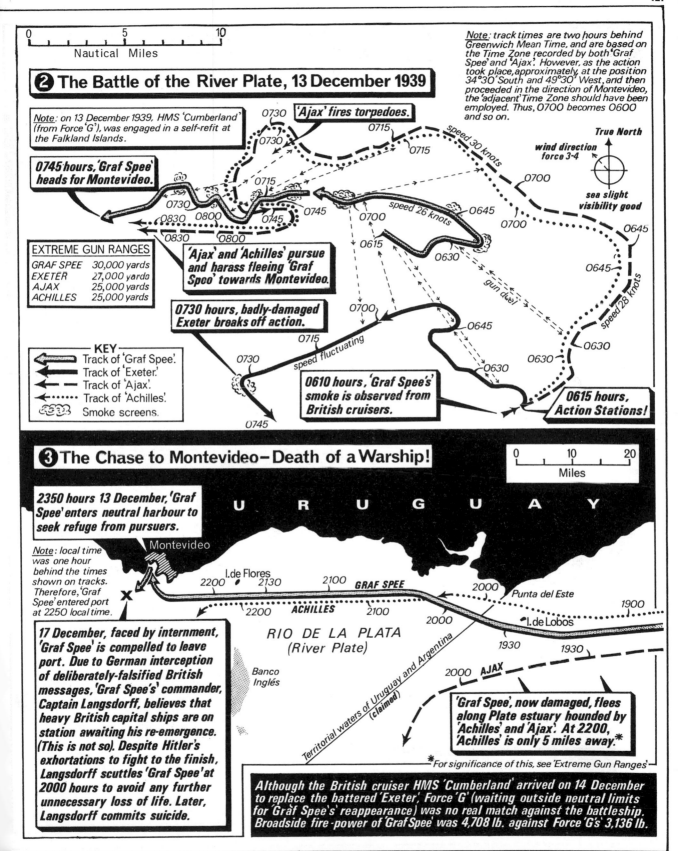

THE SOVIET–FINNISH WAR 30 NOVEMBER 1939 – 12 MARCH 1940

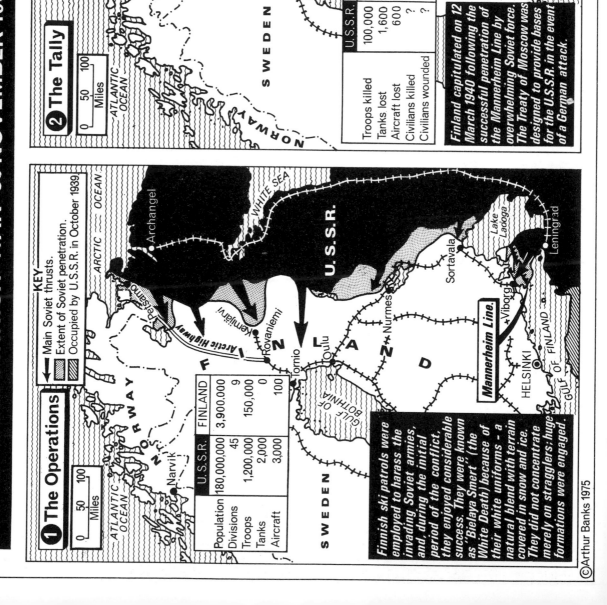

① The Operations

KEY
- → Main Soviet thrusts.
- ▨ Extent of Soviet penetration.
- ▩ Occupied by U.S.S.R. in October 1939.

Scale: 0 50 100 Miles

	U.S.S.R.	FINLAND
Population	180,000,000	3,900,000
Divisions	45	9
Troops	1,200,000	150,000
Tanks	2,000	0
Aircraft	3,000	100

Finnish ski patrols were employed to harass the invading Soviet armies, and, during the initial period of the conflict, they enjoyed considerable success. They were known as 'Bielaya Smert' (the White Death) because of their white uniforms – a natural blend with terrain covered in snow and ice. They did not concentrate merely on stragglers; huge formations were engaged.

Labels: ATLANTIC OCEAN, ARCTIC OCEAN, WHITE SEA, Narvik, Archangel, Petsamo, NORWAY, SWEDEN, F I N L A N D, U.S.S.R., Kemijärvi, Rovaniemi, Tornio, Oulu, Nurmes, Sortavala, Lake Ladoga, Viborg, HELSINKI, Leningrad, GULF OF BOTHNIA, GULF OF FINLAND, **Mannerheim Line.**, Arctic Highway

② The Tally

Scale: 0 50 100 Miles

U.S.S.R. secures access to Norwegian border.

Proposed rail link to Sweden.

Ceded to U.S.S.R. (×3)

U.S.S.R. secures thirty-year lease on port.

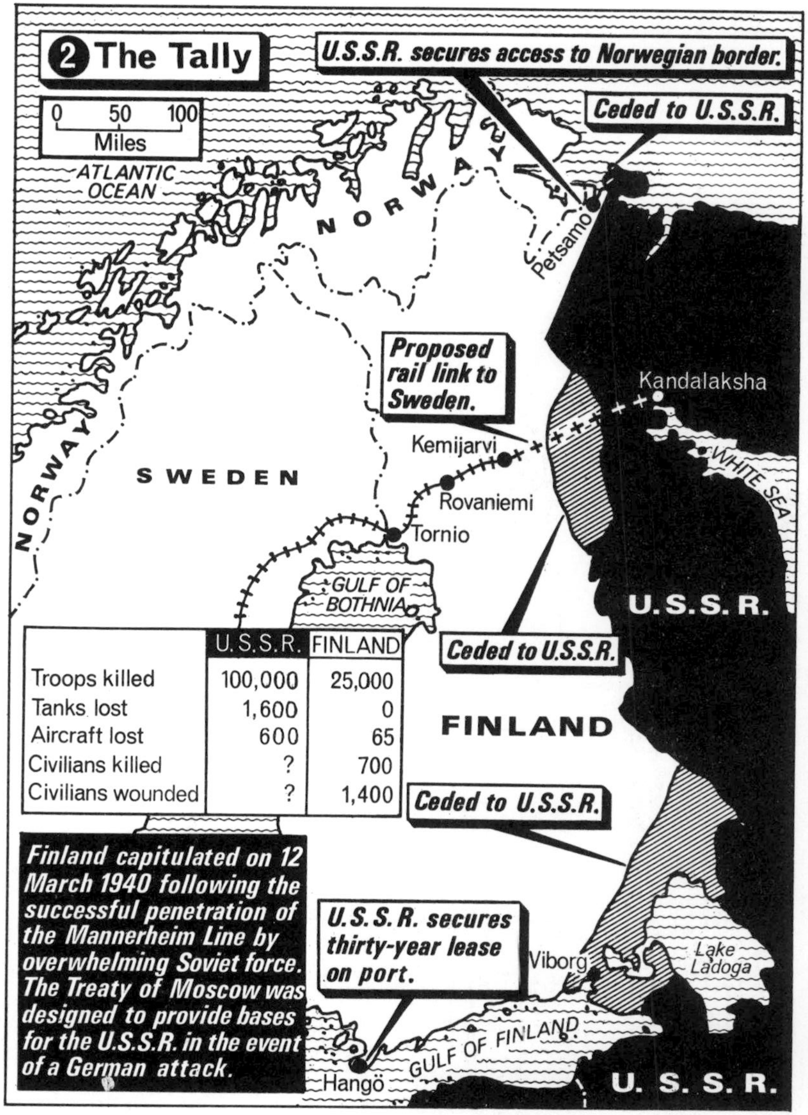

	U.S.S.R.	FINLAND
Troops killed	100,000	25,000
Tanks lost	1,600	0
Aircraft lost	600	65
Civilians killed	?	700
Civilians wounded	?	1,400

Finland capitulated on 12 March 1940 following the successful penetration of the Mannerheim Line by overwhelming Soviet force. The Treaty of Moscow was designed to provide bases for the U.S.S.R. in the event of a German attack.

Labels: ATLANTIC OCEAN, WHITE SEA, Kandalaksha, Petsamo, NORWAY, SWEDEN, FINLAND, U.S.S.R., Kemijärvi, Rovaniemi, Tornio, Viborg, Hangö, Lake Ladoga, GULF OF BOTHNIA, GULF OF FINLAND

© Arthur Banks 1975

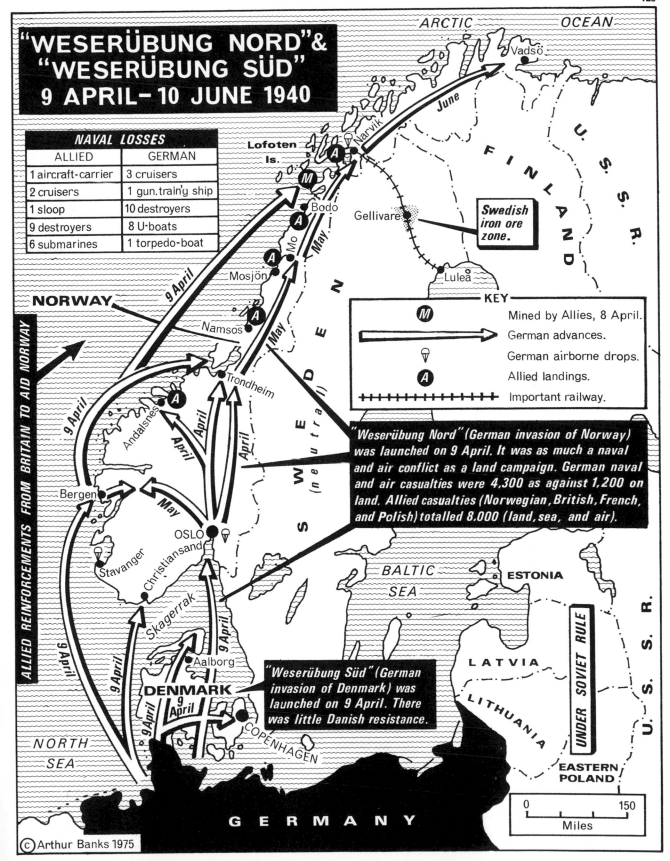

"WESERÜBUNG NORD" & "WESERÜBUNG SÜD" 9 APRIL – 10 JUNE 1940

NAVAL LOSSES

ALLIED	GERMAN
1 aircraft-carrier	3 cruisers
2 cruisers	1 gun.train'g ship
1 sloop	10 destroyers
9 destroyers	8 U-boats
6 submarines	1 torpedo-boat

ARCTIC OCEAN

Vadsö

Narvik

Lofoten Is.

M

Bodo

Gellivare

Mo

Mosjön

Namsos

Trondheim

Andalsnes

Bergen

Stavanger

Christiansand

OSLO

Aalborg

DENMARK
9 April

COPENHAGEN

NORWAY

S W E D E N (neutral)

F I N L A N D

U. S. S. R.

Swedish iron ore zone.

Lulea

ALLIED REINFORCEMENTS FROM BRITAIN TO AID NORWAY

June

May

May

May

April

April

May

9 April

9 April

9 April

9 April

9 April

9 April

Skagerrak

NORTH SEA

BALTIC SEA

ESTONIA

LATVIA

LITHUANIA

UNDER SOVIET RULE

U. S. S. R.

EASTERN POLAND

KEY

- **M** Mined by Allies, 8 April.
- → German advances.
- German airborne drops.
- **A** Allied landings.
- +++ Important railway.

"Weserübung Nord" (German invasion of Norway) was launched on 9 April. It was as much a naval and air conflict as a land campaign. German naval and air casualties were 4,300 as against 1,200 on land. Allied casualties (Norwegian, British, French, and Polish) totalled 8,000 (land, sea, and air).

"Weserübung Süd" (German invasion of Denmark) was launched on 9 April. There was little Danish resistance.

G E R M A N Y

0   150
Miles

© Arthur Banks 1975

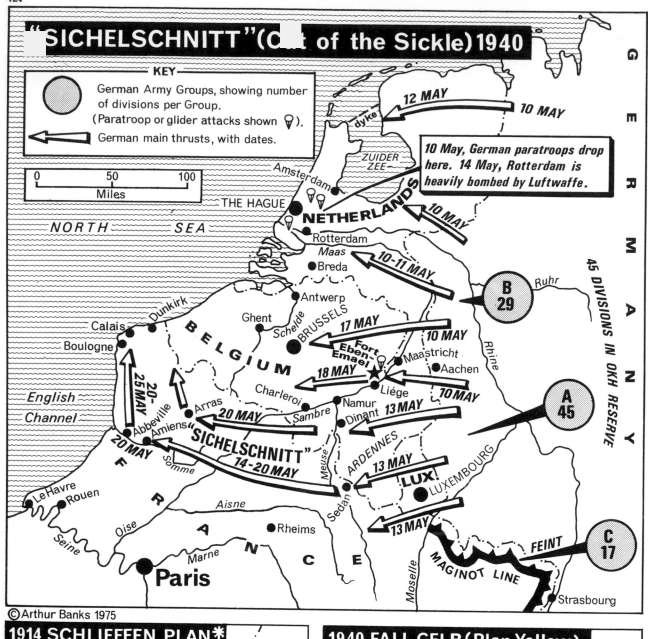

"SICHELSCHNITT" (Cut of the Sickle) 1940

KEY

○ German Army Groups, showing number of divisions per Group. (Paratroop or glider attacks shown ♟).

← German main thrusts, with dates.

0 — 50 — 100
Miles

10 May, German paratroops drop here. 14 May, Rotterdam is heavily bombed by Luftwaffe.

NORTH SEA

Amsterdam
THE HAGUE
NETHERLANDS
Rotterdam
Maas
Breda
Antwerp
Ghent
Schelde BRUSSELS
Dunkirk
Calais
Boulogne

English Channel

BELGIUM
Fort Eben-Emael
Charleroi
Liége
Namur
Dinant
Arras
Abbeville
Amiens
Sambre
"SICHELSCHNITT"
14-20 MAY
Somme
ARDENNES
Meuse
Sedan

F R A N C E

Le Havre
Rouen
Aisne
Oise
Seine
Rheims
Marne
Paris

Maastricht
Aachen
Rhine
LUX.
LUXEMBOURG
Moselle
MAGINOT LINE
Strasbourg

B 29 — *Ruhr*
A 45
C 17 — FEINT

45 DIVISIONS IN OKH RESERVE

G E R M A N Y

12 MAY · 10 MAY · *dyke*
ZUIDER ZEE
10 MAY
10-11 MAY
17 MAY
10 MAY
18 MAY
10 MAY
20 MAY
13 MAY
20-25 MAY
13 MAY
13 MAY

© Arthur Banks 1975

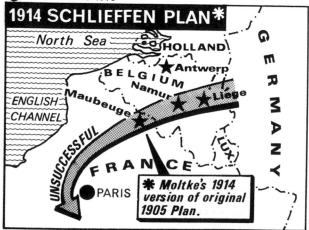

1914 SCHLIEFFEN PLAN *

North Sea
HOLLAND
BELGIUM · Antwerp
Maubeuge · Namur · Liége
ENGLISH CHANNEL
G E R M A N Y
LUX.
F R A N C E
UNSUCCESSFUL
PARIS

* Moltke's 1914 version of original 1905 Plan.

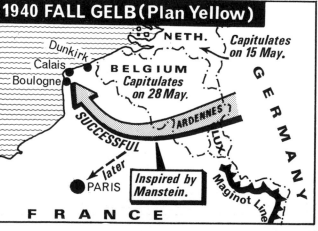

1940 FALL GELB (Plan Yellow)

NETH. *Capitulates on 15 May.*
Dunkirk
Calais
Boulogne
BELGIUM *Capitulates on 28 May.*
ARDENNES
SUCCESSFUL
G E R M A N Y
LUX.
later
PARIS
Maginot Line
F R A N C E

Inspired by Manstein.

OPERATIONS IN THE VICINITY OF DUNKIRK IN 1940

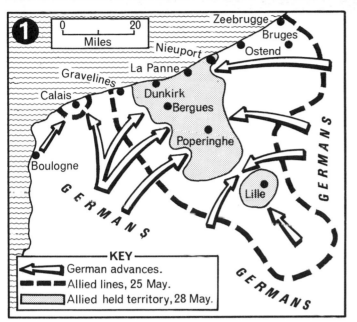

1

Miles 0 — 20

Zeebrugge
Bruges
Ostend
Nieuport
La Panne
Gravelines
Calais
Dunkirk
Bergues
Poperinghe
Boulogne

GERMANS
GERMANS
GERMANS
GERMANS

Lille

— KEY —
← German advances.
╍ ╍ Allied lines, 25 May.
▒ Allied held territory, 28 May.

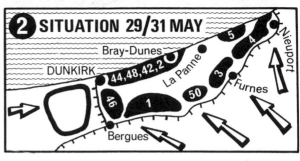

2 SITUATION 29/31 MAY

Bray-Dunes
DUNKIRK
44,48,42,2
46
1
50
La Panne
3
Furnes
5
4
Nieuport
Bergues

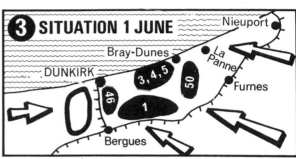

3 SITUATION 1 JUNE

Nieuport
Bray-Dunes
DUNKIRK
46
1
3,4,5
50
La Panne
Furnes
Bergues

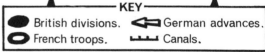

— KEY —
⬭ British divisions. ← German advances.
◯ French troops. ⊢⊢⊢ Canals.

THE FALL OF FRANCE JUNE 1940

ENGLAND
Dunkirk
BELGIUM
GERMANY
ENGLISH CHANNEL
Cherbourg
LUX.
Brest
Nantes
PARIS
FRANCE
BAY OF BISCAY
Royan
Vichy
Lyons
SWITZ.
Grenoble
ITALY
Toulouse
Marseilles
Toulon
SPAIN
MEDITERRANEAN SEA

— KEY —
▲▲▲ Maginot Line.
⬅ German advances.
⬅ Italian attacks (20 June).
━○━ Line reached by Germans at the armistice (22 June).
▩ Trapped French troops.

Operation "DYNAMO"

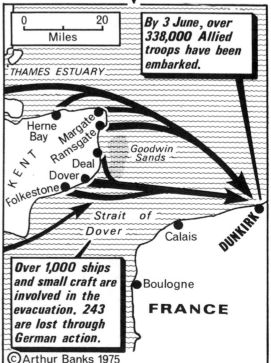

Miles 0 — 20

By 3 June, over 338,000 Allied troops have been embarked.

THAMES ESTUARY
Herne Bay
Margate
Ramsgate
Goodwin Sands
KENT
Deal
Dover
Folkestone
Strait of Dover
Calais
DUNKIRK
Boulogne
FRANCE

Over 1,000 ships and small craft are involved in the evacuation. 243 are lost through German action.

© Arthur Banks 1975

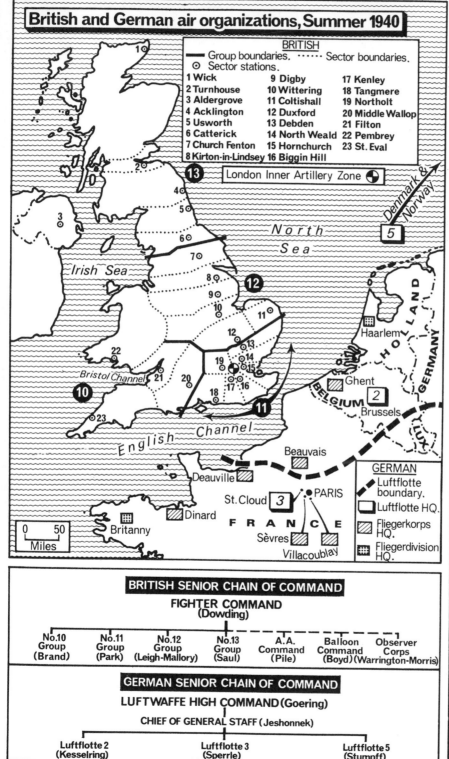

THE BATTLE OF BRITAIN 1940

British and German air organizations, Summer 1940

BRITISH
— Group boundaries. ⋯⋯ Sector boundaries.
⊙ Sector stations.

1 Wick	9 Digby	17 Kenley
2 Turnhouse	10 Wittering	18 Tangmere
3 Aldergrove	11 Coltishall	19 Northolt
4 Acklington	12 Duxford	20 Middle Wallop
5 Usworth	13 Debden	21 Filton
6 Catterick	14 North Weald	22 Pembrey
7 Church Fenton	15 Hornchurch	23 St. Eval
8 Kirton-in-Lindsey	16 Biggin Hill	

London Inner Artillery Zone

North Sea

Irish Sea

Bristol Channel

English Channel

Denmark & Norway

HOLLAND

GERMANY

BELGIUM

Haarlem

Ghent

Brussels

Beauvais

Deauville

Dinard

Britanny

St. Cloud

PARIS

Sèvres

Villacoublay

FRANCE

GERMAN
▬ ▬ Luftflotte boundary.
☐ Luftflotte HQ.
▨ Fliegerkorps HQ.
▦ Fliegerdivision HQ.

Miles 0 50

BRITISH SENIOR CHAIN OF COMMAND

FIGHTER COMMAND
(Dowding)

| No.10 Group (Brand) | No.11 Group (Park) | No.12 Group (Leigh-Mallory) | No.13 Group (Saul) | A.A. Command (Pile) | Balloon Command (Boyd) | Observer Corps (Warrington-Morris) |

GERMAN SENIOR CHAIN OF COMMAND

LUFTWAFFE HIGH COMMAND (Goering)

CHIEF OF GENERAL STAFF (Jeshonnek)

| Luftflotte 2 (Kesselring) | Luftflotte 3 (Sperrle) | Luftflotte 5 (Stumpff) |

© Arthur Banks 1975

GERMAN OFFENSIVE PLANS

1. RECONNAISSANCE
Initial phase for Luftwaffe to probe R.A.F. defences, and gain general knowledge of the unfamiliar airspace.

2. BATTLE WITH R.A.F.
This phase to be a "direct clash" fight to eliminate Fighter Command and its airfields.

3. DESTRUCTION OF BRITAIN'S WAR ECONOMY
An offensive against urban centres in general and London in particular.

BRITISH DEFENSIVE PLANS

1. R.A.F. Fighter Command to concentrate on the destruction of enemy bombers: "fighter only" clashes to be avoided.

2. Protection of airfields and the important radiolocation sites.

BRITISH RADIOLOCATION NET

Miles 0 200

NORWAY

BRITAIN

HOLL

BELG

FRANCE

KEY
▤ High altitude cover.
▨ Low altitude cover.

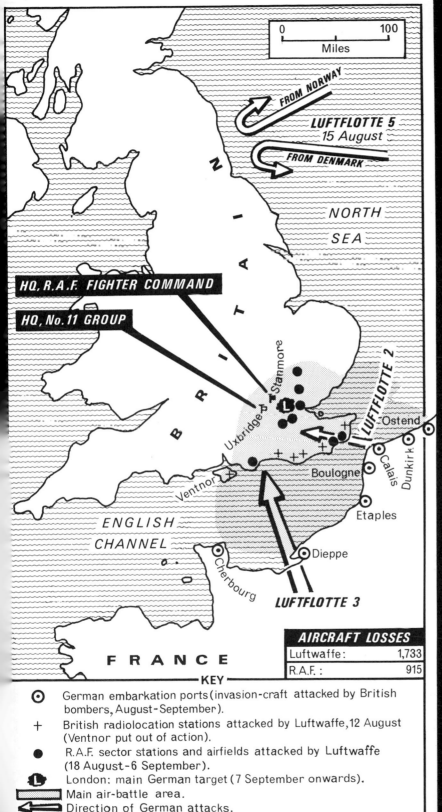

FROM NORWAY

LUFTFLOTTE 5
15 August

FROM DENMARK

NORTH SEA

HQ, R.A.F. FIGHTER COMMAND

HQ, No.11 GROUP

B R I T A I N

Stanmore

L

Uxbridge

Ventnor

ENGLISH CHANNEL

Cherbourg

LUFTFLOTTE 3

LUFTFLOTTE 2

Ostend

Calais
Dunkirk

Boulogne

Etaples

Dieppe

F R A N C E

AIRCRAFT LOSSES
| Luftwaffe: | 1,733 |
| R.A.F. : | 915 |

KEY

⊙ German embarkation ports (invasion-craft attacked by British bombers, August–September).

+ British radiolocation stations attacked by Luftwaffe, 12 August (Ventnor put out of action).

● R.A.F. sector stations and airfields attacked by Luftwaffe (18 August–6 September).

L London: main German target (7 September onwards).

▨ Main air-battle area.

⬅ Direction of German attacks.

© Arthur Banks 1975

DAILY AIRCRAFT LOSSES

The main period of the battle was from 13 August (Adler Tag or 'Eagle Day') until 15 September (the day when the Germans made their heaviest attack).

KEY
German losses shown thus: ■
British losses shown thus: □

Note:— On some days flying was restricted, or aircraft grounded because of bad weather. These days are shown thus: ▨

Date	German	British
13 AUGUST	45	13
14 August	▨	
15 August	75	34
16 August	45	21
17 August	▨	
18 August	71	27
19 August	▨	
20 August	▨	
21 August	▨	
22 August	▨	
23 August	▨	
24 August	38	22
25 August	20	16
26 August	41	31
27 August	3	0
28 August	30	20
29 August	17	9
30 August	36	26
31 August	41	39
1 September	14	15
2 September	35	31
3 September	16	16
4 September	25	17
5 September	23	20
6 September	35	23
7 September	41	28
8 September	15	2
9 September	28	19
10 September	3	0
11 September	29	25
12 September	4	0
13 September	4	1
14 September	14	14
15 SEPTEMBER	60	26
Totals	**808**	**495**

GERMAN PLANS FOR INVADING BRITAIN 1940

Code-named "Operation Sealion", these plans were postponed (indefinitely) following Luftwaffe's failure to gain air-mastery over England in the Battle of Britain.

Plans for a landing front from Ramsgate to Lyme Regis were considered but discounted.

N O R T H   S E A

German-occupied

F R A N C E

Dunkirk

to Ostend

Calais

Boulogne

Etaples

Dieppe

Strait of Dover

Margate

Ramsgate

Deal

Dover

Folkestone

Hythe

Dymchurch

Rye

Hastings

Bexhill

Eastbourne

Newhaven

Uckfield

Brighton

Worthing

Bognor Regis

Canterbury

Ashford

Tenterden

Etchingham

Gravesend

Maldon

LONDON

Guildford

Portsmouth

Southampton

Thames Estuary

Thames

E N G L A N D

Isle of Wight

E N G L I S H   C H A N N E L

to Lyme Regis

to line of the River Severn's estuary

Oxford

SIXTEENTH ARMY

NINTH ARMY

ARMY GROUP "A"

XIII

VII

XXXVIII

VIII

KEY
- Embarkation ports.
- First objective.
- Second objective.
- Proposed lodgment area.
- Paratroop drop zone.
- Corps attacks.

0 — 20 Miles

© Arthur Banks 1975

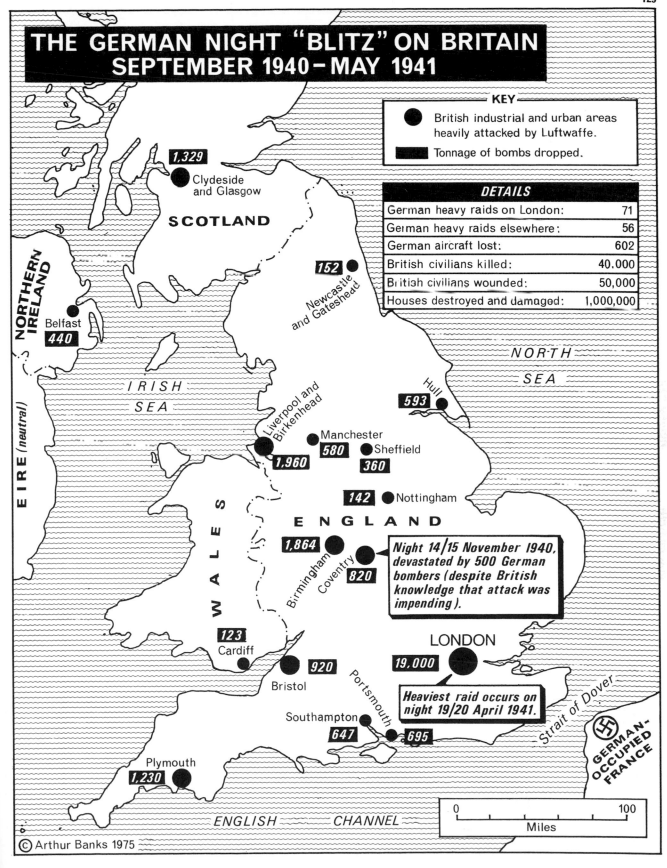

THE GERMAN NIGHT "BLITZ" ON BRITAIN SEPTEMBER 1940 – MAY 1941

KEY

● British industrial and urban areas heavily attacked by Luftwaffe.

▬ Tonnage of bombs dropped.

DETAILS	
German heavy raids on London:	71
German heavy raids elsewhere:	56
German aircraft lost:	602
British civilians killed:	40,000
British civilians wounded:	50,000
Houses destroyed and damaged:	1,000,000

1,329 Clydeside and Glasgow

SCOTLAND

NORTHERN IRELAND

Belfast **440**

152 Newcastle and Gateshead

NORTH SEA

IRISH SEA

Hull **593**

EIRE *(neutral)*

Liverpool and Birkenhead **1,960**

Manchester **580**

Sheffield **360**

142 Nottingham

ENGLAND

WALES

Birmingham **1,864**

Coventry **820**

Night 14/15 November 1940, devastated by 500 German bombers (despite British knowledge that attack was impending).

123 Cardiff

Bristol **920**

Portsmouth

LONDON

19,000

Heaviest raid occurs on night 19/20 April 1941.

Southampton **647**

695

Strait of Dover

GERMAN-OCCUPIED FRANCE

Plymouth **1,230**

ENGLISH CHANNEL

0		100

Miles

© Arthur Banks 1975

SECOND BATTLE OF THE ATLANTIC

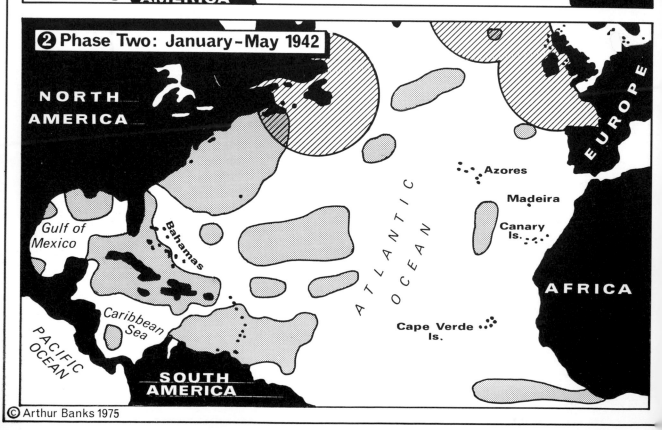

❶ Phase One: July 1940 – April 1941

GREEN-LAND

ICELAND

BRITISH ISLES

NORTH AMERICA

NEWFOUNDLAND

Lorient

EUROPE

Azores

•Bermuda

Madeira

Gulf of Mexico

Bahamas

Canary Is.

ATLANTIC OCEAN

AFRICA

PACIFIC OCEAN

West Indies

Caribbean Sea

Cape Verde Is.

SOUTH AMERICA

❷ Phase Two: January – May 1942

NORTH AMERICA

EUROPE

Azores

Madeira

Gulf of Mexico

Bahamas

Canary Is.

ATLANTIC OCEAN

AFRICA

Caribbean Sea

Cape Verde Is.

PACIFIC OCEAN

SOUTH AMERICA

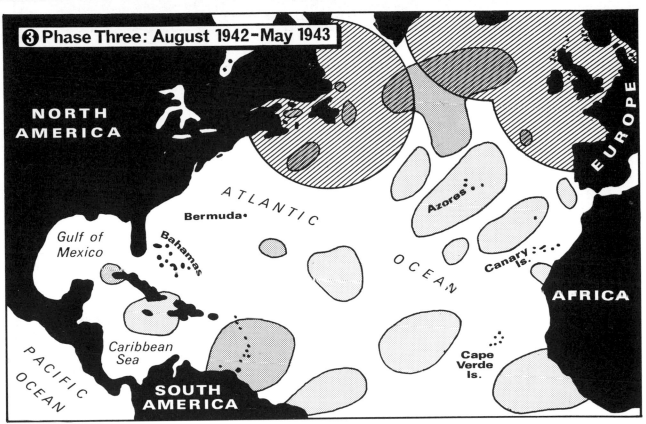

❸ Phase Three: August 1942–May 1943

NORTH AMERICA

ATLANTIC

Bermuda

Gulf of Mexico

Bahamas

Azores

Canary Is.

AFRICA

EUROPE

OCEAN

PACIFIC OCEAN

Caribbean Sea

SOUTH AMERICA

Cape Verde Is.

KEY

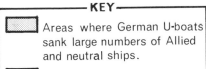

Areas where German U-boats sank large numbers of Allied and neutral ships.

Ranges of Allied land-based air cover.

Lorient. First German U-boat base on Atlantic coast (operational from July 1940).

Allied convoy routes.

Allied bases.

These map sections illustrate phases of the naval fight in the vital north Atlantic theatre. The German assault against Allied merchant shipping was three-pronged: via U-boats, surface raiders, and long-range aircraft. 1,163 U-boats were involved (often in 'pack' formations) of which 784 were sunk. Allied (plus neutral) losses totalled 2,826 ships (a tonnage of 14,680,000).

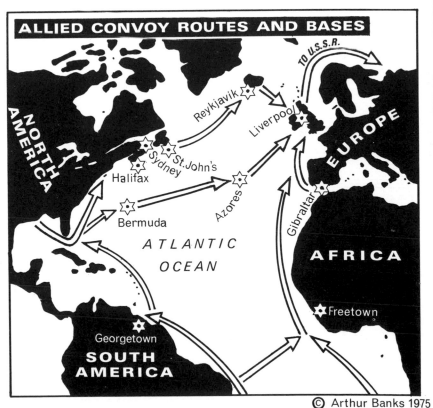

ALLIED CONVOY ROUTES AND BASES

TO U.S.S.R.

NORTH AMERICA

Reykjavik

Liverpool

EUROPE

St.John's
Sydney

Halifax

Azores

Gibraltar

Bermuda

ATLANTIC OCEAN

AFRICA

Freetown

Georgetown

SOUTH AMERICA

© Arthur Banks 1975

THE MEDITERRANEAN AND NORTH AFRICA 1940–1941

BLACK SEA

March 1941, battle off Cape Matapan: British sink three Italian cruisers and two Italian destroyers, but battleship "Vittorio Veneto" escapes.

September 1940, British fleet attacks targets and repels Italian E-boat sortie.

December 1941, Italian-manned slow-speed torpedoes ("pigs") incapacitate two British battleships in harbour.

March 1941, German aircraft drop accoustic and magnetic mines in Suez Canal, closing it for three weeks.

Alexandria

E G Y P T

Rhodes

Scarpanto

Crete

Aegean Sea

March 1941, British troops to Greece

Sidi Barrani

Bardia

Tobruk

Derna

Msus

Beda Fomm

Benghazi

El Agheila

L I B Y A

KEY
- ▬ Italian-held territory.
- ➔ British advances.
- ✂ Important naval clash.
- ✂ Important tank clash.

ALBANIA

Tyrrhenian Sea

Taranto

Malta

Sicily

MEDITERRANEAN SEA

Following hesitant Italian advance into Egypt in September 1940, British launch counter-offensive in December. This develops into full-scale advance and victory: British take 130,000 prisoners.

November 1940, British carrier-borne aircraft inflict heavy damage on Italian naval units.

February 1941, Rommel arrives here to command German Afrika Korps in Libya.

Tripoli

Castel Benito Airfield

TUNISIA

Adriatic Sea

I T A L Y

Sardinia

Corsica

Genoa

February 1941, bombarded by British Force "H"(from Gibraltar).

February 1941, British 'U'-class submarines commence operations against Axis shipping plying between Italy and Libya.

0   200
⊢──┴──┴──┤
Miles

© Arthur Banks 1975

BRITISH NAVAL LOSSES OFF GREECE AND CRETE 1941

0   200
Miles

KEY

✴ British warships sunk or badly damaged.

✱ British transports   „   „   „   „   .

26 May, H.M.S. "Formidable" (sole British aircraft-carrier in area dominated by 500 Axis aircraft) is dive-bombed and put out of action.

THE TOLL	
Warships sunk:	*9*
Warships seriously damaged:	*7*
Warships damaged:	*6*

© Arthur Banks 1975

ROMMEL IN NORTH AFRICA 1941–1942

❶ His advance.
❷ His retreat.
❸ His second advance.

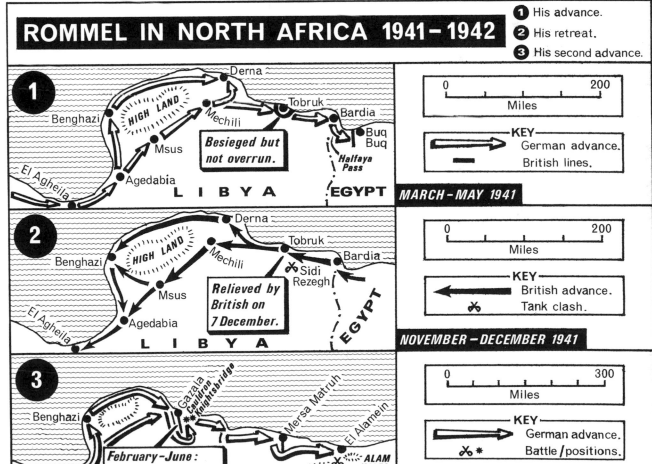

❶

Besieged but not overrun.

MARCH – MAY 1941

0   200
Miles

KEY
➡ German advance.
▬ British lines.

❷

Relieved by British on 7 December.

NOVEMBER – DECEMBER 1941

0   200
Miles

KEY
◀ British advance.
✄ Tank clash.

❸

February–June: stalemate situation.

JANUARY – JULY 1942

0   300
Miles

KEY
➡ German advance.
✄ ✱ Battle / positions.

SECURING THE BALKAN FLANK SPRING 1941

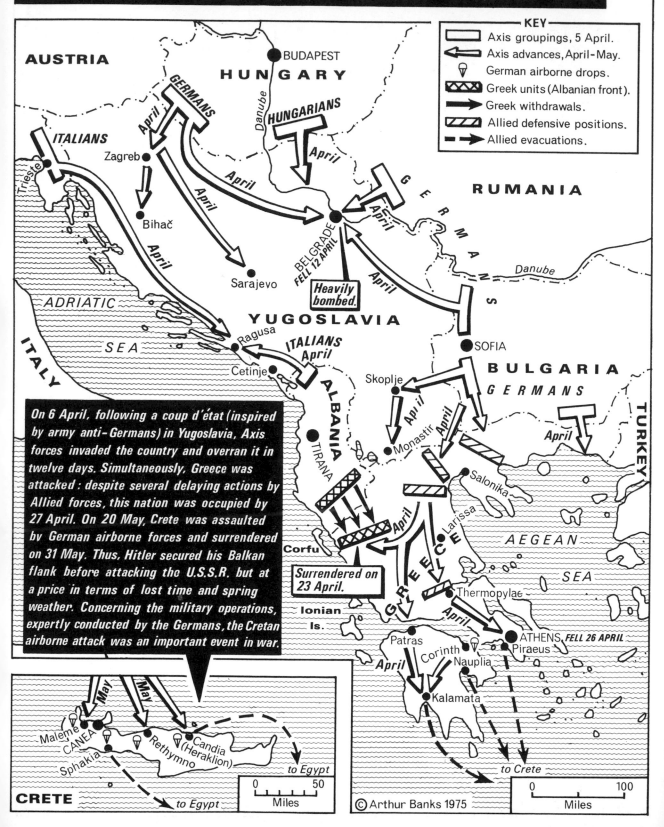

KEY
- Axis groupings, 5 April.
- Axis advances, April–May.
- German airborne drops.
- Greek units (Albanian front).
- Greek withdrawals.
- Allied defensive positions.
- Allied evacuations.

AUSTRIA

BUDAPEST

HUNGARY

GERMANS

April

HUNGARIANS

April

ITALIANS

Trieste

Zagreb

April

April

Bihač

April

RUMANIA

GERMANS

April

Danube

BELGRADE
FELL 12 APRIL

Heavily bombed.

Sarajevo

ADRIATIC

SEA

YUGOSLAVIA

Ragusa

ITALIANS
April

Cetinje

SOFIA

BULGARIA

GERMANS

ITALY

ALBANIA

TIRANA

Skoplje

April

Monastir

April

Salonika

TURKEY

April

On 6 April, following a coup d'état (inspired by army anti-Germans) in Yugoslavia, Axis forces invaded the country and overran it in twelve days. Simultaneously, Greece was attacked: despite several delaying actions by Allied forces, this nation was occupied by 27 April. On 20 May, Crete was assaulted by German airborne forces and surrendered on 31 May. Thus, Hitler secured his Balkan flank before attacking the U.S.S.R. but at a price in terms of lost time and spring weather. Concerning the military operations, expertly conducted by the Germans, the Cretan airborne attack was an important event in war.

Corfu

Surrendered on 23 April.

Ionian
Is.

Larissa

AEGEAN

SEA

G
R
E
E
C
E

April

Thermopylae

April

Patras

Corinth

Nauplia

ATHENS *FELL 26 APRIL*
Piraeus

April

Kalamata

to Crete

CRETE

Maleme

May

May

CANEA

Rethymno

Candia
(Heraklion)

Sphakia

to Egypt

to Egypt

0   50
Miles

© Arthur Banks 1975

0   100
Miles

to Crete

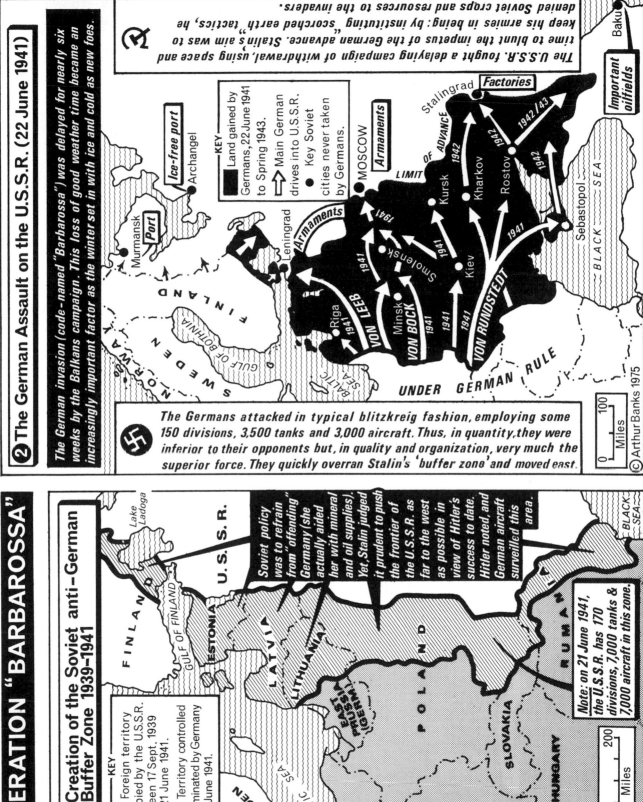

OPERATION "BARBAROSSA"

① Creation of the Soviet anti–German Buffer Zone 1939–1941

KEY

- Foreign territory occupied by the U.S.S.R. between 17 Sept. 1939 and 21 June 1941.
- Territory controlled or dominated by Germany on 21 June 1941.

Soviet policy was to refrain from "offending" Germany (she actually aided her with mineral and oil supplies). Yet, Stalin judged it prudent to push the frontier of the U.S.S.R. as far to the west as possible in view of Hitler's success to date. Hitler noted, and German aircraft surveilled this area.

Note: on 21 June 1941, the U.S.S.R. has 170 divisions, 7,000 tanks & 7,000 aircraft in this zone.

Lake Ladoga

U.S.S.R.

FINLAND

GULF OF FINLAND

ESTONIA

LATVIA

LITHUANIA

EAST PRUSSIA (GERM.)

POLAND

SLOVAKIA

HUNGARY

RUMANIA

GERMANY

SWEDEN

BALTIC SEA

BLACK SEA

0 — 200 Miles

② The German Assault on the U.S.S.R. (22 June 1941)

The German invasion (code-named "Barbarossa") was delayed for nearly six weeks by the Balkans campaign. This loss of good weather time became an increasingly important factor as the winter set in with ice and cold as new foes.

The U.S.S.R. fought a delaying campaign of withdrawal, using space and time to blunt the impetus of the German advance. Stalin's aim was to keep his armies in being; by instituting "scorched earth" tactics, he denied Soviet crops and resources to the invaders.

KEY

- Land gained by Germans, 22 June 1941 to Spring 1943.
- Main German drives into U.S.S.R.
- Key Soviet cities never taken by Germans.

Ice-free port — Archangel

Port — Murmansk

Factories

Armaments

Important oilfields — Baku

FINLAND

SWEDEN

NORWAY

GULF OF BOTHNIA

BALTIC SEA

Leningrad

Riga 1941

Minsk 1941

Smolensk 1941

Kiev 1941

MOSCOW

Kursk 1942

Kharkov 1942

Rostov 1942

Stalingrad

Sebastopol

BLACK SEA

LIMIT OF ADVANCE

VON LEEB

VON BOCK

VON RUNDSTEDT

1941 / 1942 / 1942/43

UNDER GERMAN RULE

The Germans attacked in typical blitzkreig fashion, employing some 150 divisions, 3,500 tanks and 3,000 aircraft. Thus, in quantity, they were inferior to their opponents but, in quality and organization, very much the superior force. They quickly overran Stalin's 'buffer zone' and moved east.

0 — 100 Miles

© Arthur Banks 1975

THE JAPANESE ASSAULT ON PEARL HARBOR 1941

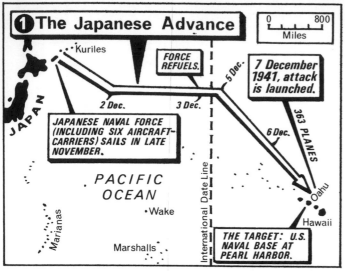

① The Japanese Advance

Kuriles

FORCE REFUELS.

5 Dec.

7 December 1941, attack is launched.

2 Dec.

3 Dec.

6 Dec.

363 PLANES

0 — 800
Miles

JAPAN

JAPANESE NAVAL FORCE (INCLUDING SIX AIRCRAFT-CARRIERS) SAILS IN LATE NOVEMBER.

PACIFIC OCEAN

Oahu

Hawaii

• Wake

International Date Line

Marianas

Marshalls

THE TARGET: U.S. NAVAL BASE AT PEARL HARBOR.

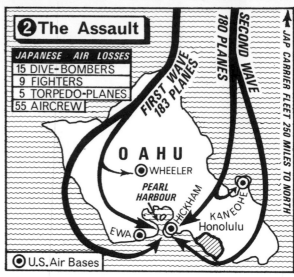

② The Assault

JAPANESE · AIR · LOSSES
15	DIVE-BOMBERS
9	FIGHTERS
5	TORPEDO-PLANES
55	AIRCREW

180 PLANES

SECOND WAVE

FIRST WAVE 183 PLANES

JAP CARRIER FLEET 250 MILES TO NORTH

O A H U

⊙ WHEELER

PEARL HARBOUR

HICKHAM

EWA ⊙

KANEOHE

Honolulu

⊙ U.S. Air Bases

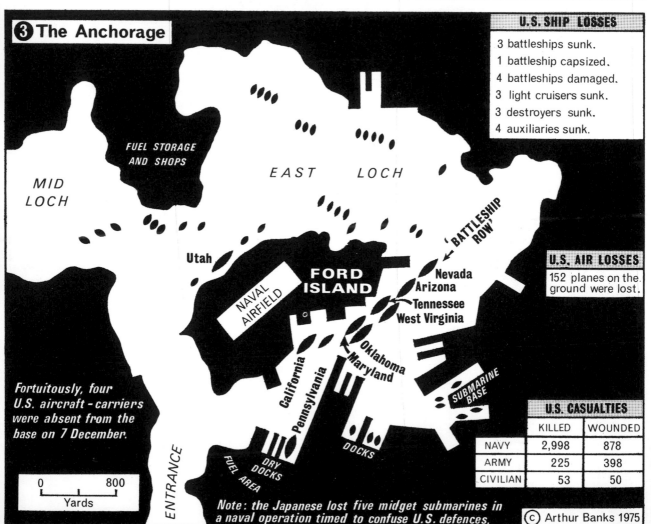

③ The Anchorage

FUEL STORAGE AND SHOPS

MID LOCH

EAST LOCH

Utah

NAVAL AIRFIELD

FORD ISLAND

'BATTLESHIP ROW'

Nevada
Arizona
Tennessee
West Virginia

Oklahoma
Maryland

California

Pennsylvania

SUBMARINE BASE

DOCKS

DRY DOCKS

FUEL AREA

ENTRANCE

Fortuitously, four U.S. aircraft-carriers were absent from the base on 7 December.

0 — 800
Yards

U.S. SHIP LOSSES

3 battleships sunk.
1 battleship capsized.
4 battleships damaged.
3 light cruisers sunk.
3 destroyers sunk.
4 auxiliaries sunk.

U.S. AIR LOSSES

152 planes on the ground were lost.

U.S. CASUALTIES

	KILLED	WOUNDED
NAVY	2,998	878
ARMY	225	398
CIVILIAN	53	50

Note: the Japanese lost five midget submarines in a naval operation timed to confuse U.S. defences.

ⓒ Arthur Banks 1975

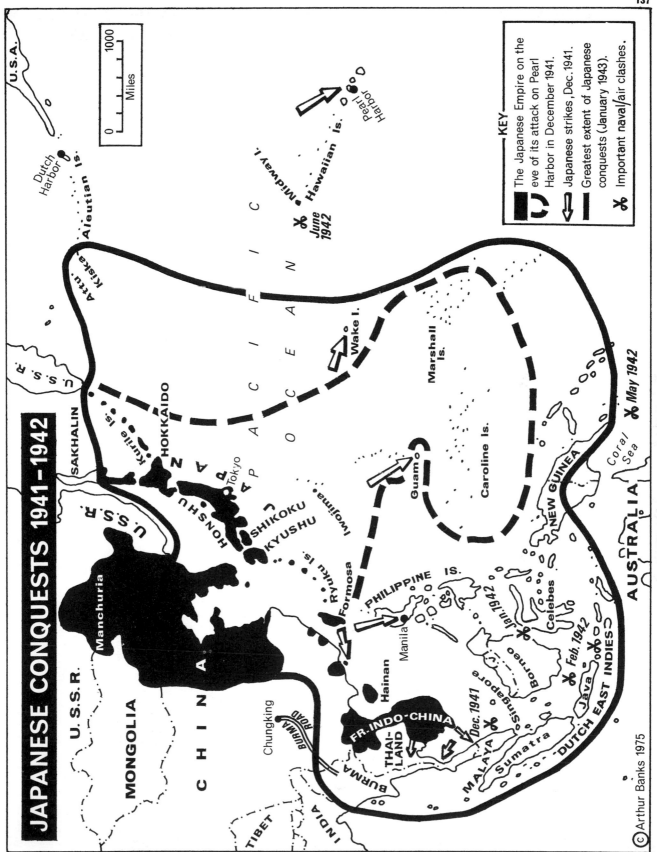

JAPANESE CONQUESTS 1941-1942

KEY

The Japanese Empire on the eve of its attack on Pearl Harbor in December 1941.

Japanese strikes, Dec. 1941.

Greatest extent of Japanese conquests (January 1943).

Important naval/air clashes.

U.S.A.

Dutch Harbor

Aleutian Is.

Attu · Kiska

Midway I.

June 1942

Hawaiian Is.

Pearl Harbor

P A C I F I C   O C E A N

Wake I.

Marshall Is.

Caroline Is.

May 1942

Coral Sea

NEW GUINEA

AUSTRALIA

U.S.S.R.

SAKHALIN

Kurile Is.

HOKKAIDO

J A P A N

HONSHU

Tokyo

SHIKOKU

KYUSHU

Iwojima

Ryukyu Is.

Formosa

Guam

PHILIPPINE IS.

Manila

Jan. 1942

Celebes

Feb. 1942

Borneo

Java

DUTCH EAST INDIES

Sumatra

Singapore

Dec. 1941

MALAYA

Hainan

FR.-INDO-CHINA

THAI-LAND

BURMA

BURMA ROAD

Chungking

U.S.S.R.

MONGOLIA

Manchuria

C H I N A

TIBET

INDIA

© Arthur Banks 1975

THE JAPANESE ASSAULT ON BURMA 1942

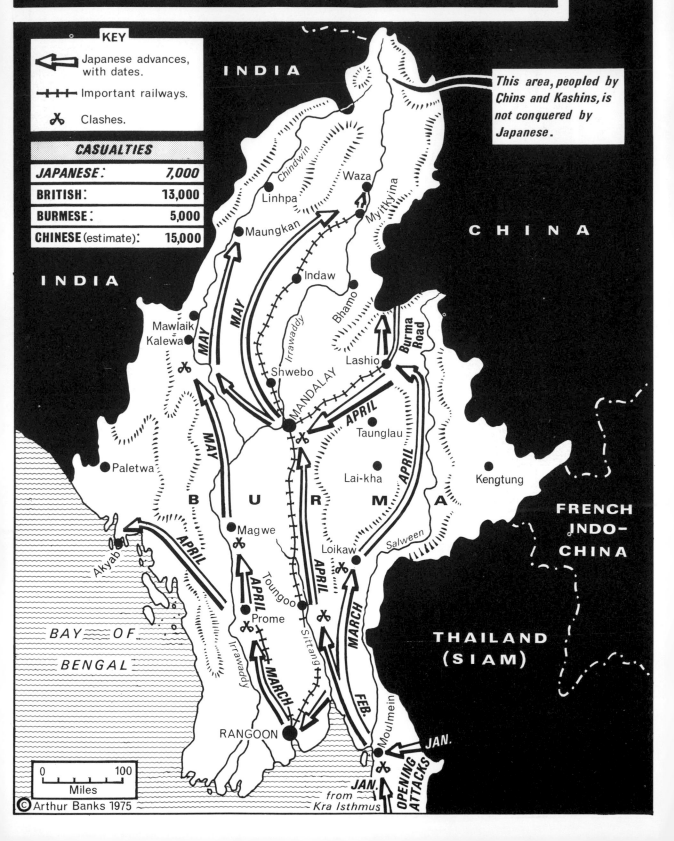

KEY

⬅ Japanese advances, with dates.

╂╂╂ Important railways.

✂ Clashes.

CASUALTIES	
JAPANESE:	7,000
BRITISH:	13,000
BURMESE:	5,000
CHINESE (estimate):	15,000

This area, peopled by Chins and Kashins, is not conquered by Japanese.

INDIA

INDIA

CHINA

Chindwin

Waza

Linhpa

Myitkyina

Maungkan

Indaw

Bhamo

Irrawaddy

Mawlaik
Kalewa

MAY

MAY

Shwebo

Lashio

Burma Road

MANDALAY

APRIL

Taunglau

MAY

Paletwa

Lai-kha

Kengtung

B U R M A

APRIL

Magwe

Loikaw

Salween

FRENCH
INDO-
CHINA

Akyab

APRIL

Toungoo

APRIL

Prome

Sittang

MARCH

Irrawaddy

BAY OF
BENGAL

MARCH

FEB.

THAILAND
(SIAM)

Moulmein

JAN.

RANGOON

0   100
Miles

JAN.
from
Kra Isthmus

OPENING
ATTACKS

© Arthur Banks 1975

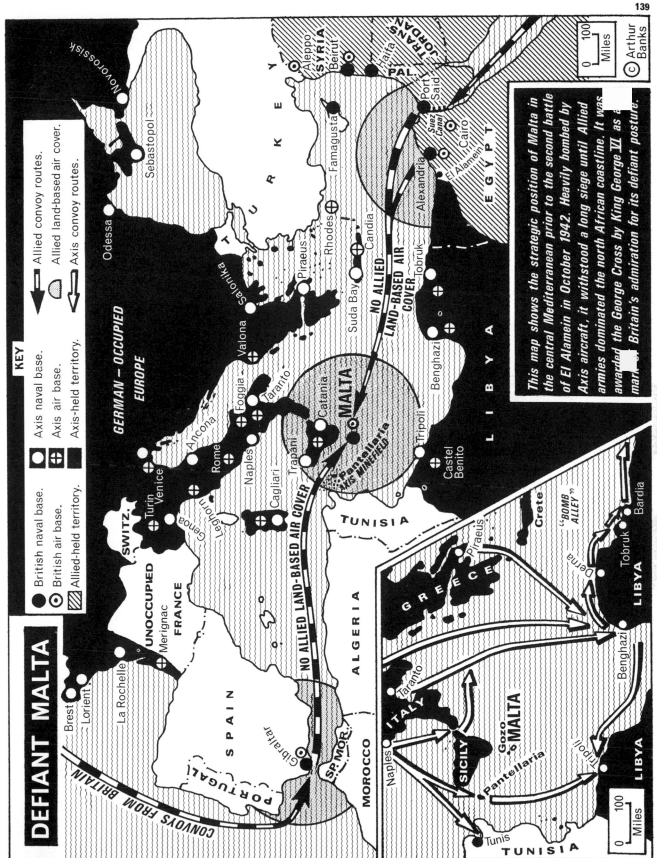

DEFIANT MALTA

KEY

- ● Axis naval base.
- ⊕ Axis air base.
- ■ Axis-held territory.
- ● British naval base.
- ⊙ British air base.
- ▨ Allied-held territory.

→ Allied convoy routes.
◗ Allied land-based air cover.
⇨ Axis convoy routes.

This map shows the strategic position of Malta in the central Mediterranean prior to the second battle of El Alamein in October 1942. Heavily bombed by Axis aircraft, it withstood a long siege until Allied armies dominated the north African coastline. It was awarded the George Cross by King George VI as a mark of Britain's admiration for its defiant posture.

GERMAN – OCCUPIED EUROPE

CONVOYS FROM BRITAIN

Brest
Lorient
La Rochelle
Merignac
UNOCCUPIED FRANCE
SWITZ.
Turin
Venice
Genoa
Leghorn
Rome
Ancona
Foggia
Naples
Taranto
Cagliari
SPAIN
Gibraltar
SP. MOR.
MOROCCO
PORTUGAL
ALGERIA
TUNISIA
NO ALLIED LAND-BASED AIR COVER

Catania
Trapani
MALTA
Pantelleria
H.M.S WINGFIELD
Tripoli
Castel Benito
LIBYA
Benghazi
Tobruk
NO ALLIED LAND-BASED AIR COVER

EGYPT
El Alamein
Alexandria
Cairo
Port Said
Suez Canal
PAL.
SYRIA
Beirut
Aleppo
TRANS-JORDAN
Haifa

TURKEY
Famagusta
Rhodes
Candia
Suda Bay
Piraeus
Salonika
Valona
Novorossisk
Sebastopol
Odessa

0 100
Miles
© Arthur Banks

GREECE
Piraeus
Crete
"BOMB ALLEY"
Derna
Tobruk
Bardia
LIBYA
Benghazi

ITALY
Naples
Taranto
SICILY
Gozo
MALTA
Pantelleria
Tripoli
LIBYA
Tunis
TUNISIA

0 100
Miles

ALLIED AID TO THE U.S.S.R.

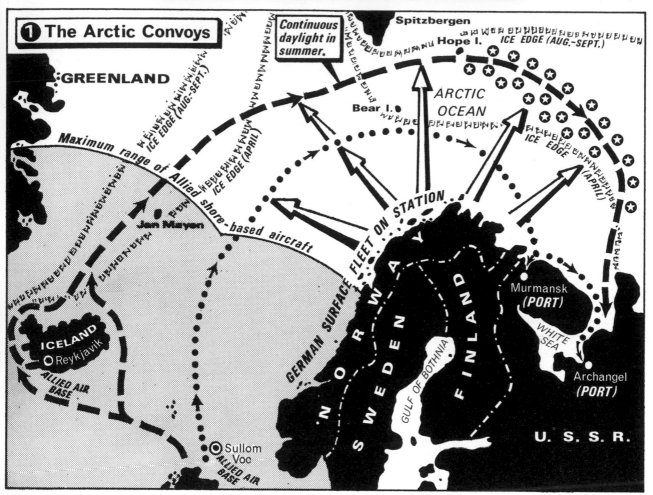

1 The Arctic Convoys

Continuous daylight in summer.

GREENLAND — Spitzbergen — Hope I. — ICE EDGE (AUG.-SEPT.) — ARCTIC OCEAN — Bear I. — ICE EDGE (APRIL) — Maximum range of Allied shore-based aircraft — Jan Mayen — ICELAND — Reykjavik — ALLIED AIR BASE — Sullom Voe ALLIED AIR BASE — GERMAN SURFACE FLEET ON STATION — NORWAY — SWEDEN — FINLAND — GULF OF BOTHNIA — Murmansk (PORT) — WHITE SEA — Archangel (PORT) — U.S.S.R.

2 The Caspian Route

0 300 Miles

Black Sea — GERMAN LAND THREAT — Astrakhan — U.S.S.R. CASPIAN SEA — U.S.S.R. — Baku — Tehran — PERSIA (IRAN) — IRAQ — ALLIED AID — Basra — Persian Gulf

© Arthur Banks 1975

KEY

- Tracks of Allied summer convoys.
- Tracks of Allied winter convoys.
- Area overflown by Allied land-based aircraft.
- German air and U-boat attacks.
- Area where convoy PQ 17 was massacred after scattering in July 1942.

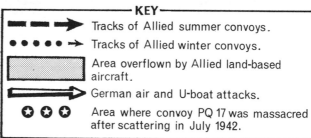

Anglo–American aid to the U.S.S.R. equalled about 5% of Soviet internal production. It included over 20,000 aircraft, 13,000 tanks, food, clothing, medical supplies, petroleum, and electronic equipment. It went via two main routes (see maps). 40 Allied convoys made the northern journey despite German interference in transit (815 merchant ships sailed: 98 were sunk). The Caspian route, although safer, was indirect from the west

140

EUROPE UNDER THE AXIS 1942

KEY

Axis powers, associates, and territories under their rule.

Vichy France and French territories.

Mediterranean territories.

Neutral countries.

Unconquered by Axis powers.

This map shows Europe at the peak of German and Italian power.

U. S. S. R.

FINLAND

Leningrad

MOSCOW

Stalingrad

ESTONIA

LATVIA

LITH.

East. Prussia

POLAND

SWEDEN

Baltic Sea

NORWAY

DEN.

Berlin

GERMANY

CZECHO-

SLOVAKIA

AUSTRIA

HUNGARY

RUMANIA

Black Sea

BULGARIA

YUGOSLAVIA

ALB.

GREECE

T U R K E Y

Cyprus

Crete

North Sea

NETH.

BEL.

LUX.

FRANCE

SWITZ.

I T A L Y

Rome

Corsica

Sardinia

Sicily

Mediterranean Sea

BRITAIN

LONDON

EIRE

Vichy

SPAIN

ALGERIA

TUNISIA

Miles

0   300

© Arthur Banks 1975

STRATEGY: VIEWPOINTS AND INTENTIONS AUTUMN 1942

0   300
Miles

THE SOVIET VIEW

Fighting desperately for survival, the Soviets want a 'second front' to be created in western Europe to divert German armies from their own front. Also, they desire a huge increase in war matériel from the Anglo/Americans. They are anxious to keep Japan in a state of non-belligerency lest they become involved in a 'two-front war' situation.

KEY

- ■ Axis- dominated territory.
- ▦ Vichy France and African territories.
- ⊡ Against the Axis.
- □ Neutral states.

THE GERMAN VIEW

Noting the progress of their two drives to the east (Caucasus and north Africa), the Germans consider that a massive 'pincer' operation to link these fronts is possible (this aim influences the 31 August attack at Alam Halfa).

NOTE: HITLER CONSIDERS AN ALLIED LANDING IN NORWAY TO BE A DISTINCT POSSIBILITY.

GERMAN "GRAND DESIGN"

CASPIAN SEA

Stalingrad

U. S. S. R.

Moscow

Leningrad

CAUCASUS

BLACK SEA

TURKEY

El Alamein

ALAM HALFA

EGYPT

FINLAND

N O R W A Y

S W E D E N

BALTIC SEA

NORTH SEA

BRITAIN

SWITZ.

ITALY

MEDITERRANEAN SEA

LIBYA

Toulon

Algiers

Oran

SPAIN

PORT.

THE AMERICAN VIEW

With vast resources, both in manpower and matériel, the Americans favour an early invasion of western Europe to force the Germans into a 'direct clash' situation to eliminate them from the war. Once this has been achieved, the whole might of the United States can be switched to the Pacific to deal with Japan.

In January 1942, at the Washington "Arcadia" Conference, Roosevelt and Churchill agree that the war against Germany gets first priority.

THE BRITISH VIEW

With limited resources (and the 19 August Dieppe raid experience in mind), the British favour a policy of weakening German strength by operations in the Mediterranean.

THE GERMAN REBUFF AT ALAM HALFA
31 AUGUST – 2 SEPTEMBER 1942

This battle was decisive: German expansion in the area was ended.

KEY

- British minefields.
- British dummy minefields.
- Axis minefields.
- British divisional defences.
- Axis divisional defences.
- British tank formations.
- Axis tank units.
- Axis drives.
- Axis feints.
- British moves.
- Ridges.
- Tracks.

Sidi Abd el Rahman

KIDNEY RIDGE

XXI CORPS

164 Div.

Trento Div.

Ramcke Div.

COASTAL ROAD

9 Australian Div.

El Alamein

ARABS' GULF

26 Bde. Aust.

El Imayid

HQ XXX CORPS

1 South African Div.

X CORPS

Bologna Div.

Brescia Div.

QARET EL ABD

5 Indian Div.

RUWEISAT RIDGE

2 New Zealand Div.

31 Aug.

23 Armd. Bde.

22 Armd. Bde.

HQ XIII CORPS

ALAM HALFA

10 Armd. Div.

44 Div.

1 Sept.

15 Pz. Div.

8 Armd. Bde.

90 Light Div.

31 Aug.

90 Lt. Div.

21 Div.

7 Sept.

XX

XX

7 Motor. Bde.

RAGIL

DAK

DAK

MAIN DRIVE

31 Aug.

4 Armd. Bde.

31 Aug.

31 Aug.

DAK

Recce Group

31 Aug.

7 Armd. Div.

31 Aug.

QARET EL HIMEIMAT

SAMAKET GABALLA

SCORE SHEET		
DETAILS	AXIS	BRITISH
CASUALTIES	2,910	1,640
TANKS LOST	49	68
GUNS LOST	55	18

0 — 5 Miles

© Arthur Banks 1975

QATTARA DEPRESSION (impassable)

OPERATION "TORCH" NOVEMBER 1942

FORCE 'H'

2 capital ships
2 fleet carriers
3 cruisers
17 destroyers

British covering force in case Italian Fleet sorties out.

EASTERN TASK FORCE

Construction:	American/British
Land cmdr.:	Ryder (U.S.)
Naval cmdr.:	Burrough (Br.)
Troops:	33,000
Ships:	56

CENTRAL TASK FORCE

Construction:	American
Land cmdr.:	Fredendall (U.S.)
Naval cmdr.:	Troubridge (Br.)
Troops:	39,000
Ships:	57

WESTERN TASK FORCE

Construction:	American
Land cmdr.:	Patton (U.S.)
Naval cmdr.:	Hewitt (U.S.)
Troops:	35,000
Ships:	94

ALLIED COMMAND STRUCTURE

EISENHOWER
(Commander-in-Chief)

CUNNINGHAM (NAVAL Cdr.)

CLARK (DEPUTY C-in-C)

DOOLITTLE / **WELSH** (AIR Cdrs.)

PATTON (LAND Cdr. WEST)

FREDENDALL (LAND Cdr. CENTRE)

RYDER (LAND Cdr. EAST)

THE AXIS RESPONSE

Axis Powers rush troops and aircraft to Tunisia.

BRITISH

El Alamein

ITALY

Sicily

Tunis

Tripoli

Algiers

Oran

ALLIES

"TORCH"

Mediterranean Sea

ALGERIA

Algiers

Oran

SPAIN

PORTUGAL

Gibraltar

Tangier

Span. Morocco

MOROCCO

Mehdia
Rabat
Fedala
Casablanca
Safi

ATLANTIC OCEAN

TWO ASSAULT CONVOYS FROM BRITAIN

ASSAULT CONVOY FROM U.S.A.

0   200

© Arthur Banks 1975

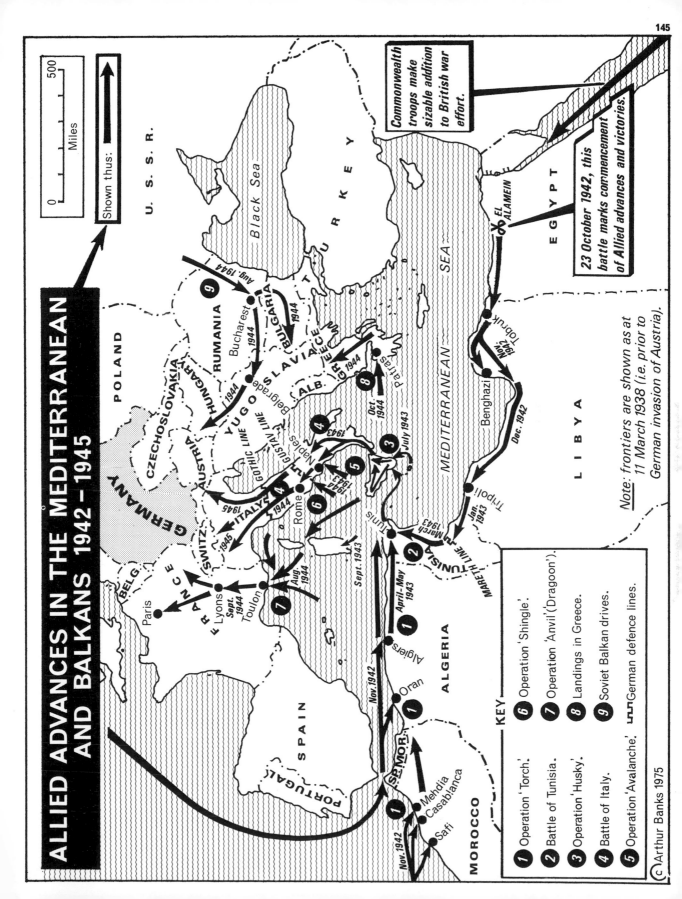

ALLIED ADVANCES IN THE MEDITERRANEAN AND BALKANS 1942–1945

Commonwealth troops make sizable addition to British war effort.

23 October 1942, this battle marks commencement of Allied advances and victories.

Note: frontiers are shown as at 11 March 1938 (i.e. prior to German invasion of Austria).

500 / 0 Miles

Shown thus:

U.S.S.R.

Black Sea

TURKEY

POLAND

CZECHOSLOVAKIA

HUNGARY

RUMANIA

Bucharest 1944

BULGARIA 1944

Aug. 1944

Belgrade 1944

YUGOSLAVIA

ALB.

GREECE

Patras

Oct. 1944

AUSTRIA

GERMANY

SWITZ.

GOTHIC LINE

GUSTAV LINE

ITALY

Naples 1943

Rome

1944 1943

1944 1945

1945

1945

Aug. 1944

Sept. 1944

FRANCE

Paris

Lyons Sept. 1944

Toulon

BELG.

Tunis

July 1943

March 1943

Jan. 1943

Tripoli

MARETH LINE

TUNISIA

Sept. 1943

April–May 1943

Algiers

Nov. 1942

Oran

ALGERIA

SPAIN

PORTUGAL

SP. MOR.

Mehdia
Casablanca
Safi

Nov. 1942

MOROCCO

EL ALAMEIN

EGYPT

Tobruk Nov. 1942

Benghazi

Dec. 1942

MEDITERRANEAN SEA

LIBYA

KEY

1 Operation 'Torch'.
2 Battle of Tunisia.
3 Operation 'Husky'.
4 Battle of Italy.
5 Operation 'Avalanche'.
6 Operation 'Shingle'.
7 Operation 'Anvil' ('Dragoon').
8 Landings in Greece.
9 Soviet Balkan drives.
⌐⌐⌐ German defence lines.

© Arthur Banks 1975

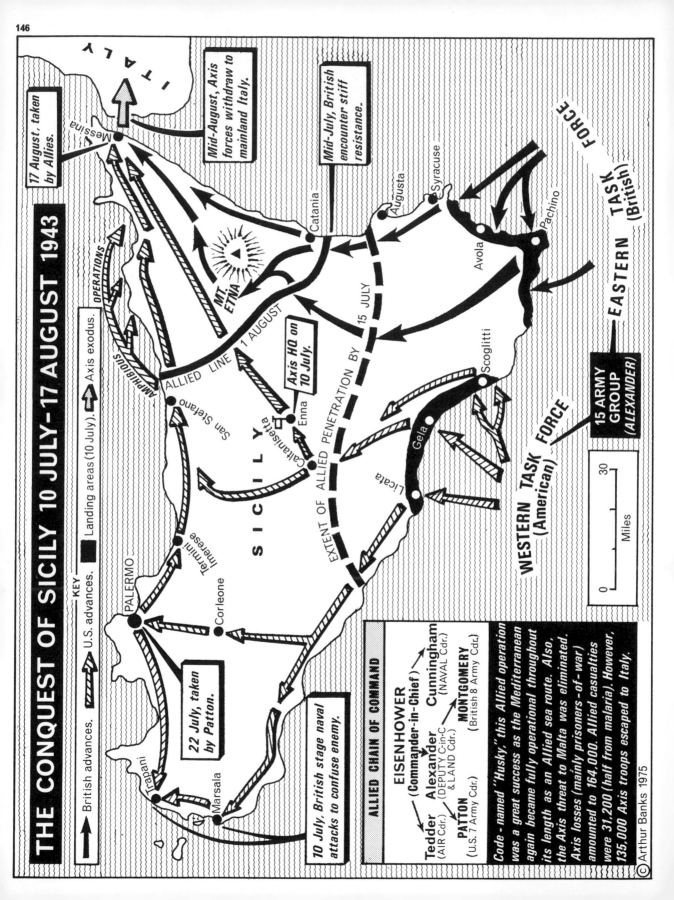

THE CONQUEST OF SICILY 10 JULY–17 AUGUST 1943

ITALY

17 August, taken by Allies.

Mid-August, Axis forces withdraw to mainland Italy.

Mid-July, British encounter stiff resistance.

Messina

Catania

Augusta

Syracuse

Pachino

Avola

EASTERN TASK FORCE (British)

Axis HQ on 10 July.

EXTENT OF ALLIED PENETRATION BY 15 JULY

MT. ETNA

ALLIED LINE 1 AUGUST

AMPHIBIOUS OPERATIONS

San Stefano

Enna

Caltanissetta

Scoglitti

Gela

Licata

WESTERN TASK FORCE (American)

15 ARMY GROUP (ALEXANDER)

SICILY

Termini Imerese

PALERMO

Corleone

22 July, taken by Patton.

Trapani

Marsala

10 July, British stage naval attacks to confuse enemy.

KEY
→ British advances.
▱ U.S. advances.
■ Landing areas (10 July).
⇧ Axis exodus.

0   30
Miles

ALLIED CHAIN OF COMMAND

EISENHOWER (Commander-in-Chief)

Tedder (AIR Cdr.)

Alexander (DEPUTY C-in-C & LAND Cdr.)

Cunningham (NAVAL Cdr.)

PATTON (U.S. 7 Army Cdr.)

MONTGOMERY (British 8 Army Cdr.)

Code-named "Husky," this Allied operation was a great success as the Mediterranean again became fully operational throughout its length as an Allied sea route. Also, the Axis threat to Malta was eliminated. Axis losses (mainly prisoners-of-war) amounted to 164,000. Allied casualties were 31,200 (half from malaria). However, 135,000 Axis troops escaped to Italy.

© Arthur Banks 1975

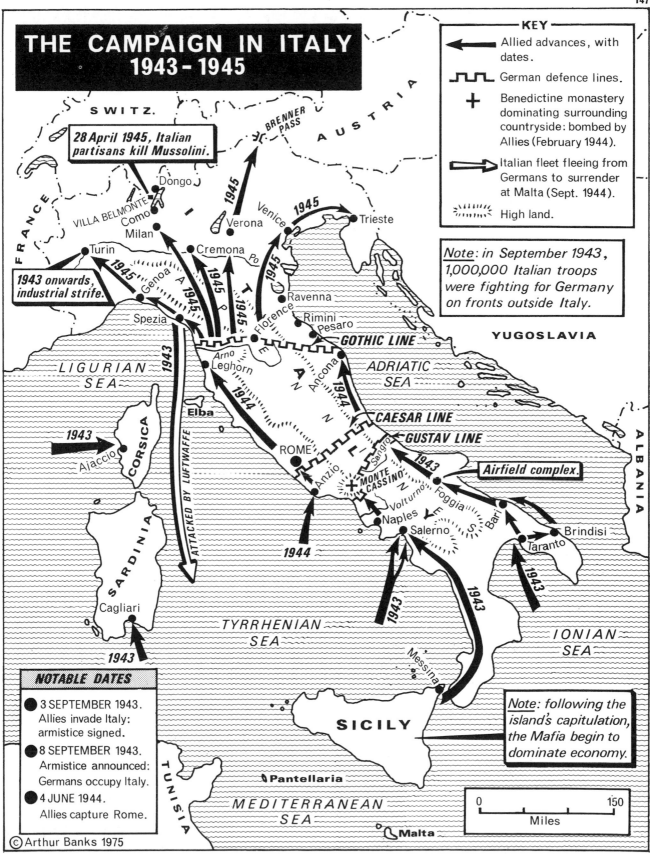

THE CAMPAIGN IN ITALY 1943 – 1945

KEY

← Allied advances, with dates.

⊓⊔ German defence lines.

✚ Benedictine monastery dominating surrounding countryside: bombed by Allies (February 1944).

⇨ Italian fleet fleeing from Germans to surrender at Malta (Sept. 1944).

〜〜 High land.

Note: in September 1943, 1,000,000 Italian troops were fighting for Germany on fronts outside Italy.

28 April 1945, Italian partisans kill Mussolini.

1943 onwards, industrial strife.

GOTHIC LINE

CAESAR LINE

GUSTAV LINE

Airfield complex.

ATTACKED BY LUFTWAFFE

MONTE CASSINO

Note: following the island's capitulation, the Mafia begin to dominate economy.

NOTABLE DATES

● 3 SEPTEMBER 1943. Allies invade Italy: armistice signed.

● 8 SEPTEMBER 1943. Armistice announced: Germans occupy Italy.

● 4 JUNE 1944. Allies capture Rome.

© Arthur Banks 1975

SWITZ. BRENNER PASS AUSTRIA

FRANCE

Dongo VILLA BELMONTE Como Milan Turin Cremona Verona Venice Trieste YUGOSLAVIA

Genoa Spezia Po Ravenna Florence Rimini Pesaro ANCONA Ancona ADRIATIC SEA ALBANIA

LIGURIAN SEA Arno Leghorn Elba

CORSICA Ajaccio ROME Anzio Sangro 1943 Naples Volturno Foggia Bari Brindisi Taranto

SARDINIA Cagliari TYRRHENIAN SEA Salerno IONIAN SEA

Messina

SICILY

Pantellaria

TUNISIA MEDITERRANEAN SEA Malta

0 — 150 Miles

THE CARRIER CLASH IN MID-PACIFIC IN JUNE 1943

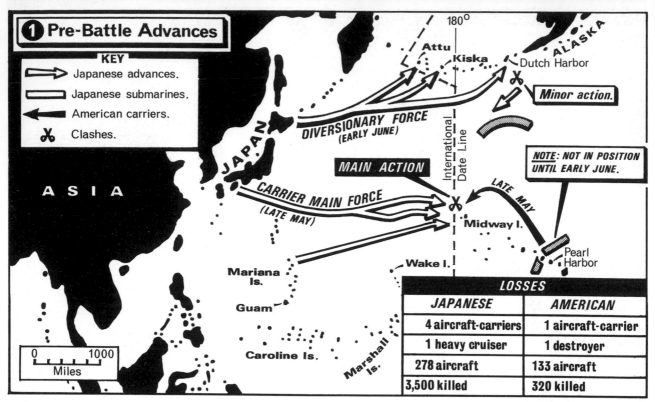

① Pre-Battle Advances

KEY
- ⇨ Japanese advances.
- ▭ Japanese submarines.
- ◀ American carriers.
- ✂ Clashes.

ALASKA
Attu
Kiska
Dutch Harbor
180°

Minor action.

DIVERSIONARY FORCE (EARLY JUNE)

International Date Line

JAPAN

ASIA

MAIN ACTION

CARRIER MAIN FORCE (LATE MAY)

NOTE: NOT IN POSITION UNTIL EARLY JUNE.

LATE MAY

Midway I.

Pearl Harbor

Mariana Is.

Guam

Wake I.

Caroline Is.

Marshall Is.

0 —— 1000
Miles

LOSSES

	JAPANESE	AMERICAN
	4 aircraft-carriers	1 aircraft-carrier
	1 heavy cruiser	1 destroyer
	278 aircraft	133 aircraft
	3,500 killed	320 killed

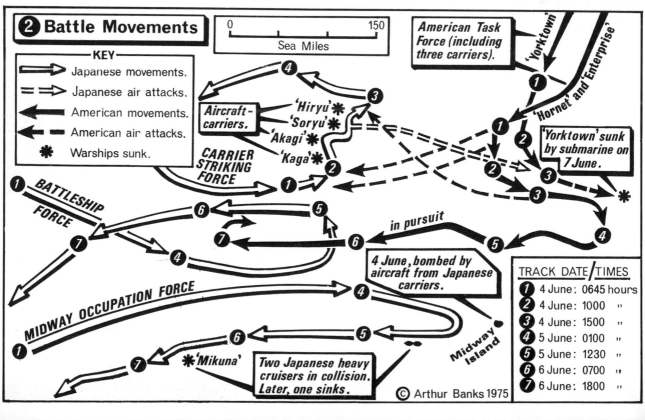

② Battle Movements

0 —— 150
Sea Miles

American Task Force (including three carriers).

'Yorktown'

'Hornet and Enterprise'

KEY
- ⇨ Japanese movements.
- ⇢ Japanese air attacks.
- ◀ American movements.
- ◀--- American air attacks.
- ✳ Warships sunk.

Aircraft-carriers.
'Hiryu' ✳
'Soryu' ✳
'Akagi' ✳
'Kaga' ✳

CARRIER STRIKING FORCE

'Yorktown' sunk by submarine on 7 June.

BATTLESHIP FORCE

in pursuit

4 June, bombed by aircraft from Japanese carriers.

MIDWAY OCCUPATION FORCE

Midway Island

✳ 'Mikuna'
Two Japanese heavy cruisers in collision. Later, one sinks.

© Arthur Banks 1975

TRACK DATE/TIMES
- ① 4 June: 0645 hours
- ② 4 June: 1000 "
- ③ 4 June: 1500 "
- ④ 5 June: 0100 "
- ⑤ 5 June: 1230 "
- ⑥ 6 June: 0700 "
- ⑦ 6 June: 1800 "

ALLIED ADVANCES IN BURMA 1944-1945

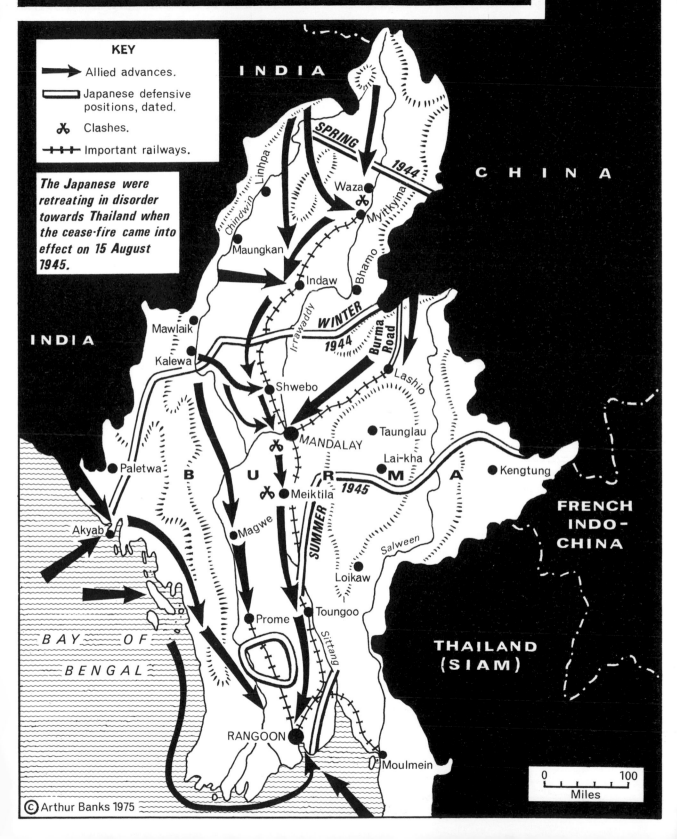

KEY

→ Allied advances.

▭ Japanese defensive positions, dated.

✂ Clashes.

┽┽┽ Important railways.

The Japanese were retreating in disorder towards Thailand when the cease-fire came into effect on 15 August 1945.

INDIA

CHINA

SPRING 1944

Waza

Myitkyina

Bhamo

Maungkan

Indaw

WINTER 1944

Burma Road

Lashio

INDIA

Mawlaik

Kalewa

Shwebo

MANDALAY

Taunglau

Lai-kha

Kengtung

Paletwa

B U R M A 1945

Meiktila

Magwe

Akyab

Loikaw

Salween

FRENCH INDO-CHINA

BAY OF BENGAL

SUMMER

Prome

Toungoo

Sittang

THAILAND (SIAM)

RANGOON

Moulmein

0   100
Miles

Chindwin

Linhpa

Irrawaddy

© Arthur Banks 1975

THE LIBERATION OF WESTERN EUROPE 1944

Allied Pre-Invasion Strategy

BOGUS ALLIED RADIO ACTIVITY

Strait of Dover

Dunkirk

PAS DE CALAIS

Lille

Allies intent on misleading Germans that invasion will occur in this area.

Portsmouth

Weymouth

ENGLISH CHANNEL

Intended landing areas (weaker in defence than Pas de Calais). Also, main embarkation ports in England further away from German spy-plane activity.

GERMANS PREPARING 'V' LAUNCH SITES

Amiens

Cherbourg

Le Havre

Seine

IMPORTANT RAILWAYS, ROADS, AND BRIDGES

AREAS HEAVILY BOMBED BY ALLIES PRIOR TO 6 JUNE 1944.

0   30
Miles

Caen

NORMANDY

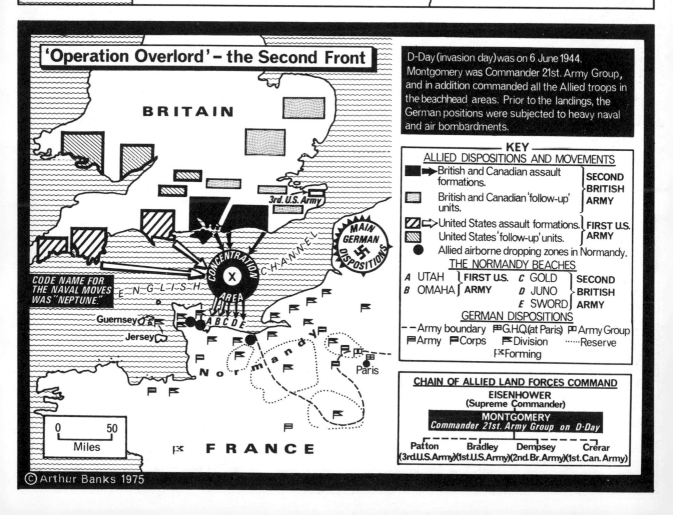

'Operation Overlord' – the Second Front

BRITAIN

3rd. U.S. Army

CODE NAME FOR THE NAVAL MOVES WAS "NEPTUNE."

ENGLISH CHANNEL

CONCENTRATION AREA

MAIN GERMAN DISPOSITIONS

Guernsey

Jersey

A B C D E

Normandy

Paris

0   50
Miles

FRANCE

D-Day (invasion day) was on 6 June 1944. Montgomery was Commander 21st. Army Group, and in addition commanded all the Allied troops in the beachhead areas. Prior to the landings, the German positions were subjected to heavy naval and air bombardments.

KEY
ALLIED DISPOSITIONS AND MOVEMENTS

■➔ British and Canadian assault formations. } SECOND BRITISH ARMY

▨ British and Canadian 'follow-up' units.

▨➔ United States assault formations. } FIRST U.S. ARMY

▨ United States 'follow-up' units.

● Allied airborne dropping zones in Normandy.

THE NORMANDY BEACHES

A UTAH } FIRST U.S. ARMY
B OMAHA

C GOLD } SECOND BRITISH ARMY
D JUNO
E SWORD

GERMAN DISPOSITIONS

- - Army boundary   ▭ G.H.Q.(at Paris)   ▭ Army Group
▭ Army   ▭ Corps   ▭ Division   ⋯⋯ Reserve
▭ Forming

CHAIN OF ALLIED LAND FORCES COMMAND

EISENHOWER
(Supreme Commander)

MONTGOMERY
Commander 21st. Army Group on D-Day

Patton	Bradley	Dempsey	Crerar
(3rd.U.S.Army)	(1st.U.S.Army)	(2nd.Br.Army)	(1st.Can. Army)

© Arthur Banks 1975

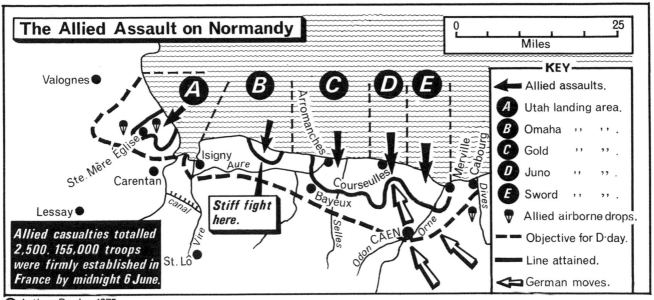

The Allied Assault on Normandy

0 — 25
Miles

KEY
- ← Allied assaults.
- (A) Utah landing area.
- (B) Omaha ,, ,, .
- (C) Gold ,, ,, .
- (D) Juno ,, ,, .
- (E) Sword ,, ,, .
- Allied airborne drops.
- --- Objective for D·day.
- — Line attained.
- ⇐ German moves.

Valognes

Ste. Mère Eglise

Isigny   Aure

Carentan

Lessay

canal

Vire

St. Lô

Arromanches   Courseulles   Bayeux   Selles   CAEN   Odon   Orne   Dives   Merville   Cabourg

Stiff fight here.

Allied casualties totalled 2,500. 155,000 troops were firmly established in France by midnight 6 June.

© Arthur Banks 1975

The Liberation of Northern France and the Low Countries

KEY
- Allied lodgment area by 31 July 1944.
- → Allied drives 1944/1945.
- Important Allied airborne drop (ending in failure).
- ΛΛΛΛ German 'West Wall' (Siegfried Line).
- ⇐ German 'V' attack against Britain 1944/1945.
- Important industrial or mining areas.

BRITAIN

LONDON

English   Channel

Amsterdam   N E T H.   Arnhem   G E R M A N Y   RUHR

THE HAGUE   Ostend   Antwerp   B E L G I U M   BRUSSELS   Remagen   Rhine

Cherbourg   Dieppe   Le Havre   Rouen   LUX.   SAAR

Caen   Falaise   Seine   PARIS   F R A N C E

Brest   Seine

Lorient   St. Nazaire   Orléans   Basle

Loire   Nantes   SWITZ.

19 June, fierce storm wrecks an artificial harbour off coast.

Allies pursue a "broad front" policy of advance.

These ports remain in German hands until end of war in May 1945.

August, Germans escape Allied trap situation.

DEVERS (from the south)

0 — 100
Miles

BATTLE OF THE BULGE 16 DECEMBER 1944 - 16 JANUARY 1945

Rhine

Bonn

FIFTEENTH ARMY

G E R M A N Y

SIXTH SS PZ ARMY

FIFTH PZ ARMY

SEVENTH ARMY

Echternach

Night 16/17 December, German paratroops drop here.

LXVII

Aachen

I SS PZ

II SS PZ

Monschau

Eupen

Malmedy

St. Vith

LXVI

Ardennes

Allied link-up.

LUX.

Stubbornly defended by American troops throughout the battle.

NETH.

Maastricht

Verviers

Stavelot

U.S.

M ARMY

Liège

FIRST

Ourthe

VII Corps

Houffalize

LVIII PZ

XLVII PZ 16 JAN.

Marche

Bastogne

THIRD U.S. ARMY

B E L G I U M

Meuse

XXX Corps

St. Trond

Louvain

Namur

Meuse

Celles

petrol shortage

Dinant

BRUSSELS

Charleroi

Sambre

SCORE SHEET		
DETAILS	GERMANS	ALLIES
CASUALTIES	100,000	82,500
TANKS LOST	800	700
GUNS LOST	350	300

Miles

0 — 20

This Hitler-inspired Ardennes attack delayed the Allied advance into Germany by six weeks.

KEY

- German line, 16 December 1944.
- German thrusts.
- German line, 23 December 1944.
- U.S. advances, January 1945.
- British & Commonwealth advances, January 1945.
- British corps concentration.
- British reconnaissance patrols.
- U.S. corps concentration.

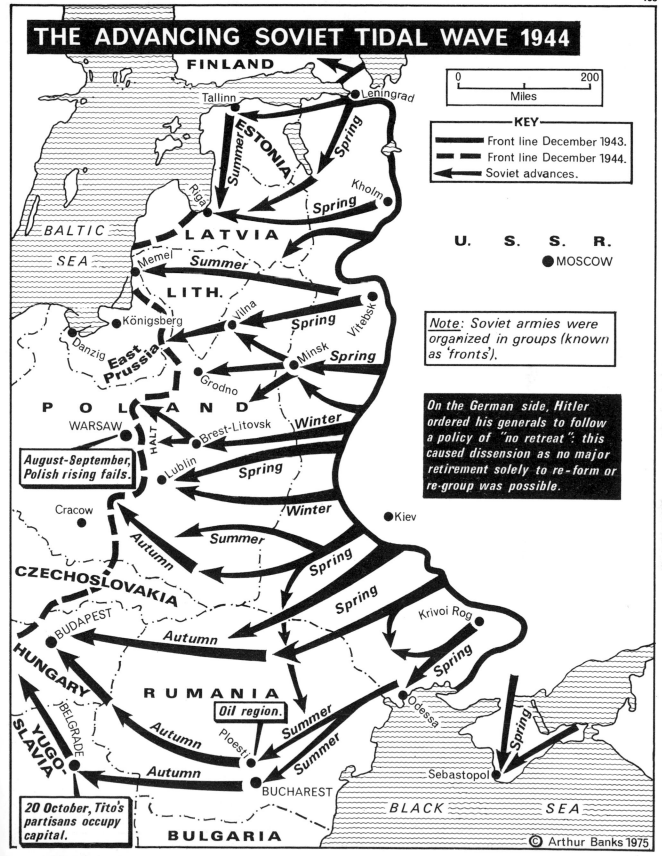

THE ADVANCING SOVIET TIDAL WAVE 1944

KEY
— Front line December 1943.
--- Front line December 1944.
◄— Soviet advances.

0 — 200
Miles

U. S. S. R.
● MOSCOW

Note: Soviet armies were organized in groups (known as 'fronts').

On the German side, Hitler ordered his generals to follow a policy of "no retreat": this caused dissension as no major retirement solely to re-form or re-group was possible.

FINLAND

Tallinn
Leningrad

ESTONIA
Summer
Spring

Riga
Kholm
Spring

BALTIC SEA

LATVIA

Memel
Summer

LITH.
Vilna
Spring
Vitebsk

Königsberg
Minsk
Spring

Danzig
Grodno

East Prussia

P O L A N D

WARSAW
Brest-Litovsk
Winter
HALT

August-September, Polish rising fails.

Lublin
Spring

Cracow
Winter

Autumn
Summer

Kiev

CZECHOSLOVAKIA

Spring

BUDAPEST
Spring

Krivoi Rog

Autumn

HUNGARY

Spring

YUGO-SLAVIA
BELGRADE

R U M A N I A

Oil region.

Ploesti
Summer
Summer

Odessa

Spring

Autumn
BUCHAREST

Sebastopol

20 October, Tito's partisans occupy capital.

BULGARIA

BLACK SEA

© Arthur Banks 1975

© Arthur Banks 1975

DENMARK

SWEDEN

GERMANY AT BAY JANUARY–MAY 1945

Note: frontiers shown as they were in early 1938 (prior to the German annexation of Austria and the Sudetenland).

BALTIC SEA

Memel

Königsberg

NORTH SEA

Flensburg

Kiel Canal

Kiel

Lübeck

Rostock

Kolberg

Danzig

East Prussia

CHERNYAKHOVSKY

RENDULIC

ROKOSSOVSKY

Allenstein

Hamburg

Elbe

Stettin

HIMMLER

Oder

ZHUKOV

Posen

Vistula

Warsaw

NETHERLANDS

BLASKOWITZ

Bremen

Lüneburg

Hanover

Brunswick

Berlin

Frankfurt

Oder

Lodz

Arnhem

MONTGOMERY

Magdeburg

ZHUKOV

P O L A N D

BRADLEY

Kassel

Neisse

Breslau

KONIEV

Cracow

Vistula

Cologne

BRADLEY

Erfurt

Leipzig

Dresden

G E R M A N Y

C Z E C H O S L O V A K I A

Frankfurt

Main

Prague

Elbe

SCHÖRNER

BELG LUX

MODEL

DEVERS

Mainz

Nuremberg

PETROV

Brünn

FRANCE

Danube

Danube

Vienna

MALINOVSKY

Budapest

HAUSSER

Stuttgart

Augsburg

Berchtesgaden

Salzburg

A U S T R I A

WOHLER

H U N G A R Y

Basle

Innsbruck

Szeged

Berne

TOLBUKHIN

SWITZERLAND

Brenner Pass

Y U G O S L A V I A

Como

Milan

KESSELRING

Zagreb

WEICHS

Turin

Po

Venice

Trieste

Danube

Belgrade

CLARK

Pola

ADRIATIC

GULF OF GENOA

Genoa

Florence

SEA

I T A L Y

FRANCE

0   50   100
Miles

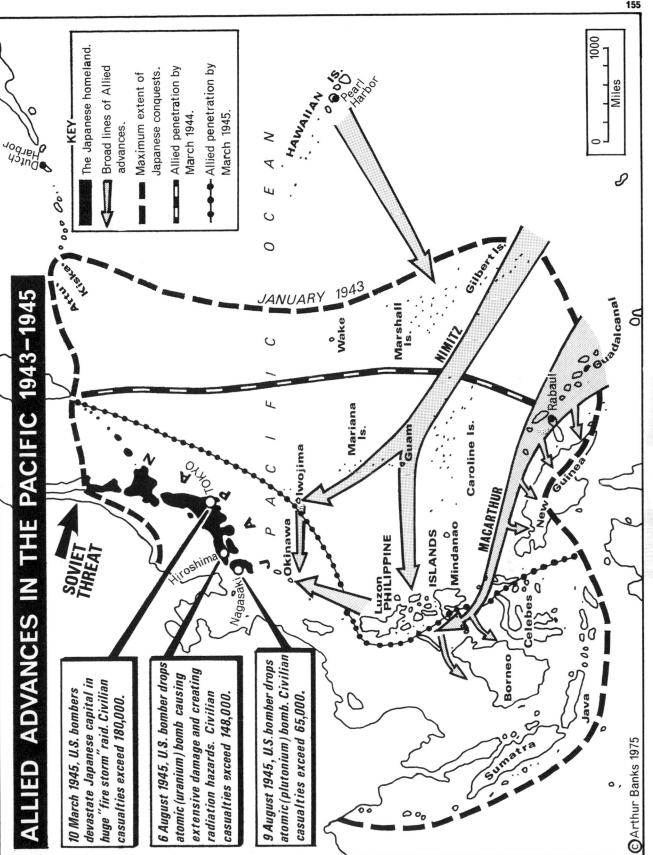

ALLIED ADVANCES IN THE PACIFIC 1943–1945

KEY

- The Japanese homeland.
- Broad lines of Allied advances.
- Maximum extent of Japanese conquests.
- Allied penetration by March 1944.
- Allied penetration by March 1945.

Dutch Harbor

HAWAIIAN IS.

Pearl Harbor

P A C I F I C   O C E A N

JANUARY 1943

Attu
Kiska

Wake

Marshall Is.

Gilbert Is.

NIMITZ

Guadalcanal

Rabaul

Mariana Is.

Guam

Caroline Is.

New Guinea

MACARTHUR

SOVIET THREAT

TOKYO

J A P A N

Hiroshima

Nagasaki

Iwojima

Okinawa

Luzon

PHILIPPINE ISLANDS

Mindanao

Borneo

Celebes

Java

Sumatra

10 March 1945, U.S. bombers devastate Japanese capital in huge "fire storm" raid. Civilian casualties exceed 180,000.

6 August 1945, U.S. bomber drops atomic (uranium) bomb causing extensive damage and creating radiation hazards. Civilian casualties exceed 148,000.

9 August 1945, U.S. bomber drops atomic (plutonium) bomb. Civilian casualties exceed 65,000.

1000
Miles
0

© Arthur Banks 1975

155

THE RECONQUEST OF THE PHILIPPINES 1944-1945

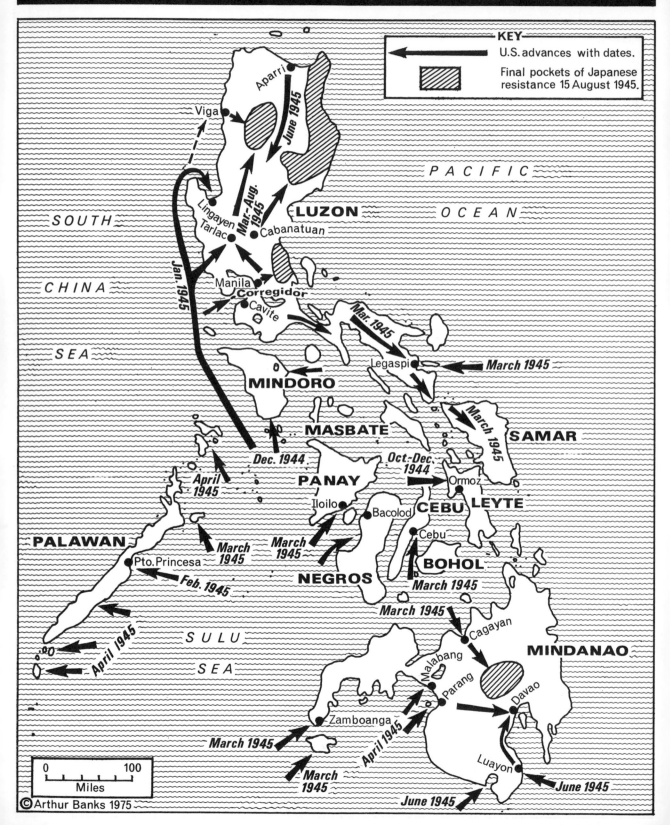

KEY

U.S. advances with dates.

Final pockets of Japanese resistance 15 August 1945.

Aparri

Viga

June 1945

PACIFIC

OCEAN

LUZON

SOUTH

Lingayen

Mar.-Aug. 1945

Tarlac

Cabanatuan

CHINA

Jan. 1945

Manila

Corregidor

Cavite

Mar. 1945

SEA

Legaspi

March 1945

MINDORO

March 1945

MASBATE

SAMAR

Oct.-Dec. 1944

April 1945

PANAY

Ormoz

Dec. 1944

Iloilo

CEBU

LEYTE

Bacolod

PALAWAN

Cebu

Pto. Princesa

March 1945

March 1945

BOHOL

Feb. 1945

NEGROS

March 1945

March 1945

Cagayan

SULU

MINDANAO

SEA

April 1945

Malabang

Parang

Davao

Zamboanga

Luayon

March 1945

April 1945

June 1945

March 1945

June 1945

0   100

Miles

© Arthur Banks 1975

THE OKINAWA CAMPAIGN 1 APRIL–22 JUNE 1945

Note: the British Royal Navy aided the U.S. Fifth Fleet during the naval operations.

KEY
- U.S. advances.
- ⊕ Japanese airfields.
- Japanese defence lines.
- ▧ Final Japanese pocket.

Iheya

Izena

Ie-Shima

Aha

Tako

Bise

Nago

OKINAWA

PACIFIC OCEAN

East China Sea

Hagushi

Shuri

Naha

June

May

Tsugen

U.S. feint attacks (1 April)

U.S. III MARINE AMPHIBIOUS CORPS (Geiger)

1 April

U.S. XXIV CORPS (Hodge)

Kerama

0 ___ 10 Miles

CASUALTIES

Japanese troops:	125,000
Japanese sailors:	3,700
Japanese airmen:	7,800
U.S. troops:	40,000
U.S. sailors:	9,600
U.S. airmen:	1,200

HISTORICAL NOTE
IN 1281, KUBLAI KHAN'S MONGOL FLEET INVADING JAPAN WAS DISPERSED BY A 'DIVINE WIND' (KAMI KAZE): see Vol 1, page 152.

Both campaigns were marked by a large number of attacks on Allied warships by enemy kamikaze suicidal pilots.

THE IWOJIMA CAMPAIGN 19 FEBRUARY–16 MARCH 1945

KEY
- U.S. advances.
- Line on 19 February.
- Line on 24 February.
- Line on 1 March.
- Line on 11 March.
- ▧ Final Japanese pockets.

U.S. CASUALTIES

Killed:	6,900
Wounded:	18,000

Only 220 Japanese troops (out of a total of 22,000) surrender.

Nishi

AIRFIELD

AIRFIELD

MT. SURIBACHI

PACIFIC OCEAN

19 February

4 Marine Div.

3 Marine Div.

5 Marine Div.

U.S. 3 AMPHIBIOUS CORPS (Schmidt)

FIFTH

0 ___ 1 Mile

© Arthur Banks 1975

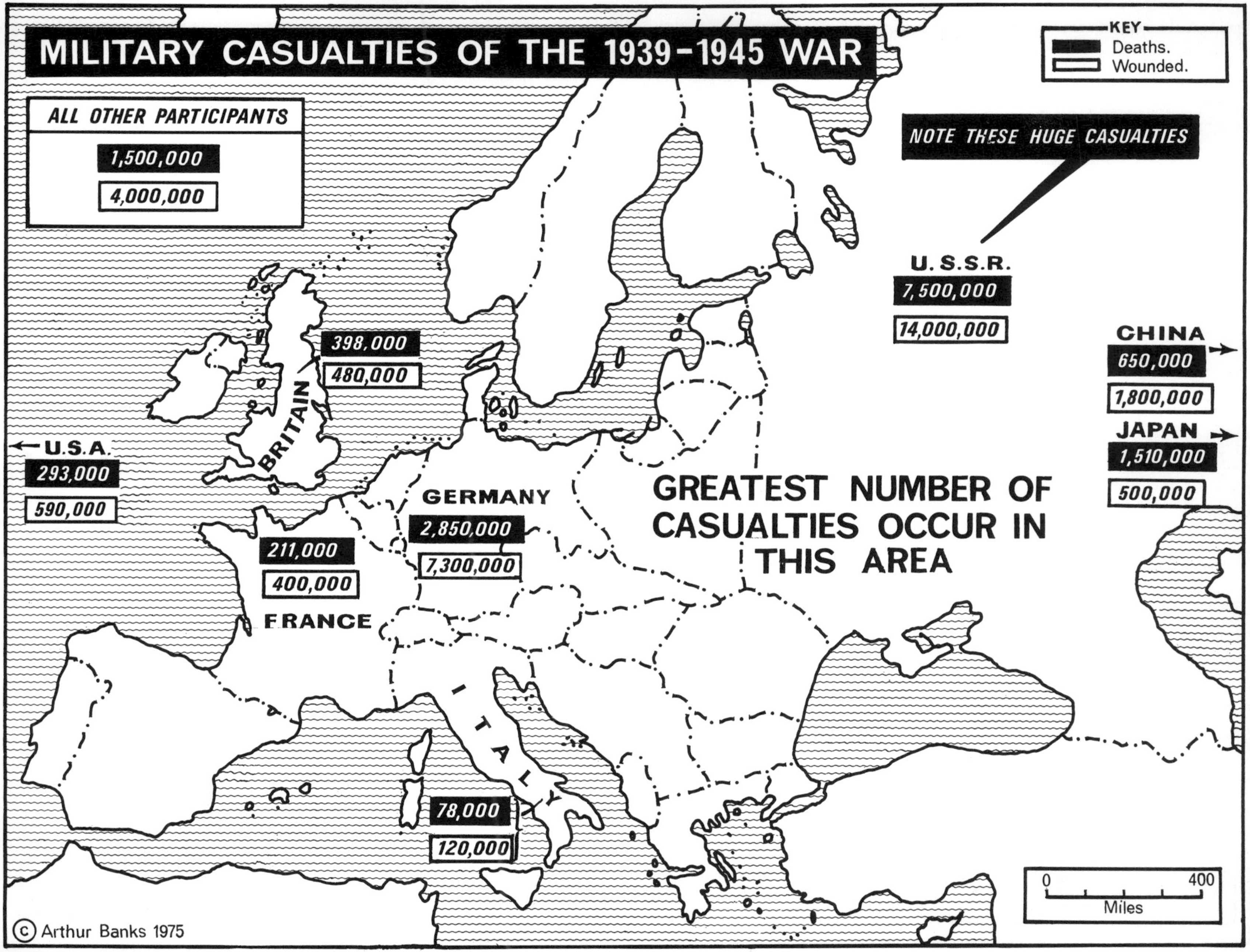
MILITARY CASUALTIES OF THE 1939-1945 WAR
KEY
Deaths.
Wounded.
ALL OTHER PARTICIPANTS
1,500,000
4,000,000
NOTE THESE HUGE CASUALTIES
U.S.S.R.
7,500,000
14,000,000
CHINA
650,000
1,800,000
JAPAN
1,510,000
500,000
U.S.A.
293,000
590,000
BRITAIN
398,000
480,000
GERMANY
2,850,000
7,300,000
FRANCE
211,000
400,000
ITALY
78,000
120,000
GREATEST NUMBER OF CASUALTIES OCCUR IN THIS AREA
0
400
Miles
© Arthur Banks 1975

CIVILIAN CASUALTIES AND EXPENDITURE 1939-1945

KEY
Deaths.
Cost ($ millions).

JAPAN →
300,000
100,000

CHINA →
1,000,000
no figs. available

U.S.S.R.
15,000,000
200,000

NOTE THESE HIGH CIVILIAN CASUALTIES

Approximately 6,000,000 Jews in Germany and 4,500,000 Poles were killed (1939-1945).

POLAND

GERMANY
500,000
300,000

I T A L Y
80,000
50,000

BRITAIN
70,000
150,000

FRANCE
110,000
100,000

ALL OTHER PARTICIPANTS
15,000,000 ?
350,000

U.S.A. →
1,000 ?
350,000

NOTE THESE HIGH EXPENDITURES

400
Miles
0

© Arthur Banks 1975

THE WORLD'S SUPERPOWERS 1945

UNION OF SOVIET SOCIALIST REPUBLICS

Possessor of the largest army in the world and virtually self-sufficient in raw materials. However, due to German occupation, much of her industry is in ruins. She does not possess the over-riding weapon of all, the atomic bomb.

UNITED STATES OF AMERICA

Sole possessor of the atomic bomb makes her the world's leading military power: she possesses the largest air force and navy in the world. Furthermore, she is the world's leading industrial and manufacturing nation. Her homeland has remained inviolate throughout the war.

Britain, France, and Germany, the three European powers which had dominated the world scene prior to September 1939, emerged from the war much reduced in international status. From henceforth, the world's military spectrum was to be dominated by the U.S.A. and the U.S.S.R., the two new superpowers.

PACIFIC OCEAN

INDIAN OCEAN

ATLANTIC OCEAN

PACIFIC OCEAN

AUSTRALIA

ANTARCTICA

ASIA

AFRICA

EUROPE

NORTH AMERICA

SOUTH AMERICA

Index of Place Names

Supplementary Index

Index of People